Muslims
and
Christians

FACE *to* FACE

Other books on Islamic Studies published by Oneworld:

City of Wrong: A Friday in Jerusalem, M. Kamel Hussein (trans. Kenneth Cragg), ISBN 1-85168-072-1

Companion to the Qur'án, William Montgomery Watt, ISBN 1-85168-036-5

Defenders of Reason in Islam: Mu'tazilism from Medieval School to Modern Symbol, Richard C. Martin and Mark R. Woodward, ISBN 1-85168-147-7

The Event of the Qur'án: Islam in its Scripture, Kenneth Cragg, ISBN 1-85168-067-5

The Faith and Practice of Al-Ghazálí, William Montgomery Watt, ISBN 1-85168-062-4

Islam and the West, Norman Daniel, ISBN 1-85168-129-9

Jesus in the Qur'án, Geoffrey Parrinder, ISBN 1-85168-094-2

Muhammad: A Short Biography, Martin Forward, ISBN 1-85168-131-0

Muslim Devotions: A Study of Prayer-Manuals in Common Use, Constance E. Padwick, ISBN 1-85168-115-9

On Being a Muslim: Finding the Religious Path in the Modern World, Farid Esack, ISBN 1-85168-146-9

The Qur'án and its Exegesis: Selected Texts with Classical and Modern Muslim Interpretations, Helmut Gätje, ISBN 1-85168-118-3

Qur'án, Liberation and Pluralism, Farid Esack, ISBN 1-85168-121-3

Rabi'a: The Life and Work of Rabi'a and Other Women Mystics in Islam, Margaret Smith, ISBN 1-85168-085-3

Rúmi: Poet and Mystic, Reynold A. Nicholson, ISBN 1-85168-096-9

A Short History of Islam, William Montgomery Watt, ISBN 1-85168-109-4

A Short Introduction to Islamic Philosophy, Theology and Mysticism, Majid Fakhry, ISBN 1-85168-134-5

Voices of Islam, John Bowker, ISBN 1-85168-095-0

Muslims
and
Christians
FACE *to* FACE

Kate Zebiri

ONEWORLD
OXFORD

MUSLIMS AND CHRISTIANS FACE TO FACE

Oneworld Publications
(Sales and Editorial)
185 Banbury Road
Oxford OX2 7AR
England
http://www.oneworld-publications.com

Oneworld Publications
(US Marketing Office)
160 N. Washington St.
4th floor, Boston
MA 02114
USA

ISBN 1–85168–133–7

Cover design by Peter Maguire
Printed and bound by WSOY, Finland

To those who struggle with their religious and cultural identity
in an increasingly complex world

CONTENTS

PREFACE AND ACKNOWLEDGEMENTS

I am very grateful to the Nuffield Foundation and the Spalding Trust, whose generous financial support helped make the research for this book possible; to the School of Oriental and African Studies who gave me a reduced teaching load in 1994–5; and to the editors at Oneworld for their unfailing co-operation and efficiency.

I would like to thank all those friends, students and colleagues who kindly asked after the progress of my research, read and commented on parts of the typescript, lent me books or made helpful suggestions on various matters. Special thanks to Humphrey Fisher, whose wonderfully detailed comments drew my attention to (among other things) my undisciplined use of pronouns. I would like to express my heartfelt thanks to Jonathan Birt, not just for research assistance but also for enlightening conversations and valuable help with sources; and to Kate Daniels, who patiently undertook the unenviable task of looking after the bibliographical and other tiresome details. None of the above bears any responsibility for any of the ideas expressed in this book.

Qur'anic quotations are adapted from Marmaduke Pickthall's *The Glorious Koran* and Yusuf Ali's *The Holy Qur'ān: Text Translation and Commentary*.

Transliterations follow the system laid out in *The International Journal of Middle East Studies*; diacritics have been omitted from familiar words and names such as Muhammad, Qur'an and Hadith.

All dates are CE unless otherwise stated.

LIST OF ABBREVIATIONS

AJISS	*American Journal of Islamic Social Sciences*
BHMISS	*Bulletin of the Henry Martyn Institute of Islamic Studies*
CMS	Church Missionary Society
CSIC	Centre for the Study of Islam and Christian–Muslim Relations
DFI	Dialogue with People of Living Faiths and Ideologies
EI²	*Encyclopaedia of Islam. 2nd ed. Leiden: Brill, 1960–*
GRIC	Groupe de Recherches Islamo-Chrétien
IBMR	*International Bulletin of Missionary Research*
ICMR	*Islam and Christian–Muslim Relations*
IDEO	Institut Dominicain d'Etudes Orientales
IQ	*Islamic Quarterly*
IRM	*International Review of Mission*
ISCH	*Islamochristiana*
JIMMA	*Journal of the Institute of Muslim Minority Affairs*
MIDEO	*Mélanges de l'Institut Dominicain d'Etudes Orientales*
MW	*Muslim World*
MWBR	*Muslim World Book Review*
PCID	Pontifical Council for Interreligious Dialogue
PISAI	Pontificio Istituto di Studi Arabi e d'Islamistica
WCC	World Council of Churches

INTRODUCTION

Muslims living in the West have recently coined the term 'Islamophobia'. It gives a name to what is perceived to be a multi-faceted phenomenon, most immediately visible in negative images of Islam portrayed in the Western media, but having far-reaching historical roots stretching in an unbroken chain from the Crusades through the Inquisition to imperialism and Zionism. Some Western political observers have fuelled such ideas by suggesting that with the demise of the Soviet Union, international Islamism is now the most ominous political threat.[1] The Western discourse of a violent and threatening Islam is inverted in a growing discourse of victimization on the part of Muslims, who see in international political events ongoing evidence of an inveterate Western hostility to Islam. In a much-quoted remark, British Muslim Shabbir Akhtar suggested that Muslims would be the next to go to the gas chambers.[2] Muslims continue to evince a profound distrust of the Western study of Islam, which may be indiscriminately branded as 'orientalism'.[3]

Some are beginning to draw attention to the parallel phenomenon of 'occidentalism'. A prominent British Muslim and anthropologist, Akbar Ahmed, writes that 'an examination of what contemporary orientals think of the occident would reveal images as distorted and dishonest as in the worst forms of orientalism'.[3] The West is stigmatized in Islamist discourse as the unacceptable other: morally bankrupt, predatory and unscrupulous; symbolically voiceless, because what it says is not to be believed. In this discourse, Christianity is still inextricably linked with the West and with imperialism, even though the centre of gravity of contemporary Christianity has now shifted away from the West, and the relationship between Western governments and Christianity is generally a tenu-

1

ous one. In fact it is Muslim rather than Western governments who are now more likely to be found sponsoring activities aimed at religious propagation. Christianity may not be so awesome an adversary as 'the West', but it may nevertheless, on a selective reading of history and current events, be characterized in exactly the same way that some orientalists and journalists have irresponsibly characterized Islam: as a religion of fanaticism, intolerance and violence. It seems that the communications revolution has not necessarily made for more effective communication, and that the information explosion has made it possible for diverse peoples to know more *about* each other selectively, without knowing each other.

There is a fast-growing literature on what may be termed 'Muslim–Christian studies'.[4] To date, more has been written on Christian or Western perceptions of Islam than on Muslim perceptions of Christianity.[5] In this study, I have chosen to juxtapose Muslim and Christian perceptions of each other, in part out of an idealistic desire to make it as difficult as possible for either Muslims or Christians to recoil at the other's distorted or inaccurate perceptions while remaining complacent about their own. While it would be unrealistic to claim to be able to remove the barriers to communication, one can aspire to name and describe some of them, and perhaps make it easier for people possessing disparate worldviews to speak a common language.

On an academic level, the approach adopted here may contribute to the study of comparative religion. In view of the difficulty of finding an adequate typology or basis on which to compare religions that does not privilege one over another, it might be useful to approach the comparison through the mutual perceptions of religious believers, allowing each group in turn to set the terms of the debate according to the priorities and categories that arise to some extent from their own religious identity. It is also possible that the simultaneous observation of Muslim views of Christianity and Christian views of Islam will throw into relief certain underlying dynamics which would otherwise remain hidden. In the many interweaving threads of polemic, counter-polemic or selective affirmation one can discern echoes and reflections.

This study essentially consists of an analytical survey of selected bodies of literature; it looks at Muslim writings on Christianity and Christian writings on Islam in the contemporary period. In order to retain some kind of parallelism for comparative purposes, in both cases the material was divided into popular and scholarly, thus producing four main chapters. This was a heuristic device and not intended to imply any strict equivalence between the Muslim and Christian material on either level. The desire to find some kind of counterpart to Muslim popular literature led me to Christian missionary or evangelistic works on Islam as the nearest equivalent, but there was nevertheless a considerable difference in ethos and aims between the two. As with any classification, the lines between one category and the next are not clear-cut, and there is some overlap between them. Kenneth Cragg, one of the most accomplished Christian Islamicists, may be described as both missionary and evangelical; on the Muslim side, even some of the most sophisticated scholarly expositions occasionally gravitate towards polemics.

The literature studied is largely confined to the post-World War II period, which has witnessed momentous changes in social and political life. The emergence of the mass media, improved communications and large-scale migration have brought members of different religious communities into contact with each other on a greater scale than ever before. With the decline of imperialism, Christians have had to rethink assumptions about Western superiority and the relationship between religion and culture, particularly since the Church in the Third World is in many cases more dynamic and thriving than that in the West. This has contributed to important new developments in Christian thought, not least in the theology of religions and missiology. For most Muslims, on the other hand, post-independence euphoria has been replaced by disillusionment in the face of continuing economic dependency and political repression, contributing to a reassertion of Islamic religious identity. At the same time, changing patterns of literacy and education, and migration to the West, have produced Muslims who are able and willing to contribute to the Western academic tradition, so that after centuries of living in relative isolation from each other, Christians and Muslims participate once again in the same intellectual culture.

The Muslim material which is analysed here is that which is published or distributed in the West. In fact, there is a relatively high degree of continuity between works on Christianity in indigenous Muslim languages and those in European languages, and both are influenced directly or indirectly by certain seminal works such as that of the medieval polemicist and historian of religions Ibn Ḥazm (d. 1064) or of the Indian scholar Maulana Rahmat Allah Kairanawi (d. 1891).[6] However, authors who are familiar with European languages have access to a wider range of literary and scholarly resources on Christianity; the bibliographies and footnotes of their books bear witness to an extensive use of Western sources. Where possible, works written by Muslims actually resident in the West have been consulted, but others, most notably those originating from the Indian subcontinent, have also been included on the basis that they are a formative influence on the attitudes of Muslims in the West. Among European languages, English in particular is growing in importance as an 'Islamic language'. Some of the most innovative and influential material by Islamic activists and thinkers is being published in English, and is accessible not only to Muslims living in Europe and North America but to large numbers of educated Muslims living in South-East Asia, the Indian subcontinent, and parts of Africa. Certain prominent Muslim organizations which have a high publishing profile, such as the Jama'at-i-Islami and the International Institute of Islamic Thought, are either based in the West or active there.[7]

The literature surveyed is highly diverse, differing with regard to both academic quality and intended function; in each case the self-definition and intended audience are factors to be taken into account. It is not necessarily appropriate, for example, to employ the same criteria when evaluating missionary or polemical material on the one hand, and scholarly works on the other. Also, there is considerable variation in the authors' relationships to their respective religious communities, some holding positions of religious leadership while others are less representative or even marginal. In most cases one is dealing with living authors, who may well undergo an evolution of thought during their lifetimes, and whose ideas are not unrelated to their existential situations; I have therefore endeavoured where appropriate to complement textual analysis with consideration of extra-textual factors, and have tried not to misrepresent any author by citing an isolated, uncharacteristic opinion or one taken out of context.

In assessing relations between members of different communities it is important to consider the relations of power that obtain between them. The encounter between Western Christians and Third-World or recently westernized Muslims is an uneven one, but there is a paucity of material on Islam written by Christians living in Muslim countries, for whom centuries of minority status have engendered a defensive mentality. The often delicate state of intercommunal relations has an inhibiting effect on academic or quasi-academic study of Islam on the part of Christians there, and interfaith initiatives, when they occur, tend to be low-key.

In contrast to the medieval period, when Muslim scholars were often more sophisticated and informed in the study of religions than their Christian counterparts, it is now, generally speaking, Christians who, as participants in the Western academic tradition, are more qualified in this field and more likely to have assimilated the insights of recent developments in the study of religions. One contemporary Muslim scholar comments that 'Christianity is benefiting from a historical position which at present the other religions cannot attain: it expresses itself, it acts, it develops in societies which have attained a level of democratization, of the conquest and diffusion of knowledge, material wealth, scientific and technological possibilities the equivalent of which is still far out of reach of the rest of the world.'[8] Until relatively recently Christians dominated the Western study of Islam, while there is no corresponding expertise in Christianity on the Muslim side; on the popular level, however, a different situation obtains: the average Western Christian is likely to be no better informed about Islam than is the average Westerner.

Among religions, the interrelationship between Christianity and Islam is of particular interest. Accounting for approximately half of the world's population between them, both are missionary religions with mutually exclusive claims to universality and finality, and this inherent conflict of interests is compounded by a long history which has often been fraught with conflict and antagonism. Even the common ground which they share as participants in the Abrahamic monotheistic tradition has frequently been a cause of discord rather than harmony. For Muslims, this element of continuity is integral to their self-definition, while for Christians the opposite is true: it is difficult to accord validity to Islam without in some sense undermining the finality and the ultimacy of the revelation they believe they have received in Christ.

The question of chronology is vital in assessing Muslim and Christian attitudes towards each other. Islam represents a particular challenge to Christians, not only because it is the only major post-Christian religion, but also because it possesses its own internal logic to account for Christianity; it purports to be the culmination of the Judaeo-Christian tradition and therefore in effect to supersede it. In the Qur'an, Jesus is seen as one of a succession of prophets who are entrusted with essentially the same message, the final and perfected version of which was brought by Muhammad. Responding to Muslim complaints about the Christians' failure to acknowledge Muhammad as a prophet, the French Islamicist Fr. Jacques Jomier suggests that the Muslim recognition of Jesus 'does not cost them anything', since his function in the Qur'an is to support Muhammad; however, a corresponding recognition of Muhammad by Christians would 'go against everything they are told by the weightiest religious documents in their possession'.[9] A parallel is sometimes drawn with the Jewish failure to recognize Jesus, or with Muslims' refusal to recognize any posterior claims to prophethood such as that made by

Qadiyanis on behalf of Ghulam Ahmad. In each case, the later religion is in a position to accord a certain (usually unwelcome) recognition to the former, which cannot easily be reciprocated.

The fact that Muslims find in the Qur'an a definitive account of central Christian beliefs, as well as prescriptions for behaviour towards Christians, means that the Qur'an is the most authoritative source for a Muslim understanding of Christianity, and takes priority over other sources. This tends to act as a deterrent to empirical study, so that judgements about Christianity are often based on the Qur'an rather than on a practical knowledge of 'lived' Christianity. It also helps explain why Muslims show little interest in aspects of the Bible or Christianity which have no particular positive or negative bearing on Islam, for example the careers of the non-Qur'anic prophets and the central institutions and concepts of the Old Testament such as priesthood and sacrifice. Since Muslims believe that the original revelation brought by Jesus was essentially the same as the message brought by Muhammad, the divergence between the latter and Christianity as understood by most Christians, with its central tenets of Incarnation and atonement, mean that, as one modern Muslim writer puts it, 'for Muslims, Christianity is a historical reality based on a metaphysical fiction'.[10]

A similar dynamic is at work in the Muslim view of Christian scripture. On the basis of several Qur'anic passages which imply that Jews and Christians forgot, altered or suppressed parts of their own scriptures, Muslim scholars elaborated the doctrine of *taḥrīf* (scriptural alteration or corruption).[11] While the Qur'anic passages containing this word may be understood as referring to either misinterpretation or textual corruption of former scriptures, with the progression of time the latter interpretation was increasingly favoured, and is virtually unchallenged today;[12] some see this development as due in part to worsening relations between Muslims and Christians, but there is also an inner logic to it in that it accounts for the doctrinal and other discrepancies between the Bible and the Qur'an. The doctrine of *taḥrīf* does not preclude the authentication of selected verses which can be interpreted as predicting the coming of Muhammad or as supporting Muslim beliefs such as the non-divinity of Jesus, but it does mean that most Muslims feel little need to take the biblical text as a whole seriously, or to engage with the beliefs contained in it, as opposed to rejecting them on *a priori* grounds.

In contrast to the Muslim view of Christianity, in the absence of any clear scriptural mandate there has never been, and in the nature of things never could be, a unified or official Christian attitude towards

Islam. Prior to the twentieth century, Christian attitudes to Islam were by and large negative and inimical. William Muir, the nineteenth-century colonial administrator and supporter of missions, no doubt expressed the feeling of many when he described Islam as 'the only undisguised and formidable antagonist of Christianity'.[13] However, in recent decades there has been a tangible change of attitude on the official and academic levels, although it would be difficult to gauge how far this has affected ordinary Christians on a grass-roots level. Increased openness to other faiths has to a great extent been a natural outcome of the Christian ecumenical movement, and for the last three decades or so both the Vatican and the World Council of Churches have been actively promoting interfaith dialogue. Paradoxically, the lack of specific scriptural restraints accounts in part for both the greater virulence of Christian anti-Islamic polemic in the medieval period, and the greater flexibility and openness in the contemporary period.

Christians and Muslims have probably been equally prone to considering the other's religion to be a truncated or distorted version of their own, although for different reasons. For Muslims, such a view is intrinsic in that the true, original Christianity is considered not to have differed in essence from Islam, and any departure from that essence is necessarily an aberration. Christians, on the other hand, see some of the 'reflected glory' of their own religion in the Qur'an, containing as it does many of the biblical stories and an honoured place for Jesus; yet they are liable to find the Qur'anic Jesus 'sadly attenuated'.[14] Both Muslims and Christians may be tempted to conclude, and generally have concluded during the course of history, that the other's faith adds nothing to their own; for Muslims, any additions are by definition distortions, and for Christians, Islam appears as a retrogression to the Jewish model of law and prophecy, the line of Hebrew prophets having already reached fulfilment in Christ. Nevertheless, in the contemporary period some scholars on both sides have made attempts at a positive appreciation of the other, even at times acknowledging its distinctive 'religious genius'.

Almost all the works cited in this study contain an element of implicit or explicit comparison between Islam and Christianity from a variety of perspectives. By way of providing a point of anchorage, it seems pertinent to mention some caveats on the comparative venture itself and to present a cautious and, it is to be hoped, uncontroversial overview of some of the more important contrasts between the two religions.

As world religions, both Islam and Christianity, and especially the latter, accommodate a high degree of religious and cultural heterogeneity, and a spectrum of theological views. Points of contention between members of one faith and another often reflect areas of contention within the traditions themselves, and there are likely to be areas of overlap between those who are marginal in each community: unitarian Christians may in some respects be closer to Muslims than to other Christians, while the obverse might be true of Muslims who stress God's immanence over His transcendence. However, the majority of committed adherents to both traditions retain a consciousness of an essential core upon which is based a real sense of unity; one might venture to suggest that in the case of Islam, this would be the ideal Sharī'a, including the basic pillars of belief and praxis, and in the case of Christianity, the rather narrower ground of the perceived centrality of the 'Christ-event'.

Another consideration is that it is highly questionable whether different faiths are commensurable; there is no agreed definition of 'religion', and some believe that to use the term at all is an unhelpful reification.[15] Although the same themes, symbols and terms occur in different religious traditions, their meaning and function is likely to differ according to their relation to the whole; one cannot assume that the same is meant by 'faith' or 'salvation' when used by Christians and Muslims. Rather than giving different answers to the same questions, the religions may more accurately be viewed as asking different questions.

Some scholars of religion have attempted to identify certain characteristic emphases in the respective faiths in such a way that most Muslims and most Christians would concur. Marshall Hodgson sees suffering and evil as prominent themes in Christianity, in contrast to Islam which 'has shied away from the poignant, from the passionate and the paradoxical in life'.[16] Islam is a religion of 'sober moderation',[17] inspiring a strong sense of responsibility and human dignity. While Christianity is characterized by 'personal responsiveness to redemptive love in a corrupted world', Islam emphasizes 'personal responsibility for the moral ordering of the natural world'.[18] Charles Adams brings out the underlying ethos of each religion in such a way as to reveal, notwithstanding obvious similarities, 'two religious entities of quite different outlines, characters, and structures'.[19] He does this by observing their answers to three fundamental questions: What is the human problem? By what means is the problem solved? To what desired state does the solution lead? He finds that the Christian answers consist of the nexus of sin–redemption–salvation (or living in a state of grace), while the corresponding Muslim nexus is ignorance–guidance–success (in this world and the next).

While for Christians theology is the foremost religious science, Muslims tend to highlight praxis rather than doctrine and give priority to jurisprudence. Observers comment on Islam's relative doctrinal simplicity and vigour. Islam stresses God's transcendence over His immanence, and conceives of man's relationship to Him as that of an obedient servant rather than a beloved but sometimes wayward child. While Muslims take pride in the realism, moderation and attainability of the ethical prescriptions of their religion, Christians find enshrined in the New Testament, particularly in the Sermon on the Mount, an ethical ideal to which they should aspire but which they can never fully realize this side of eternity. While in Islam good morality is a prerequisite of salvation, in Christianity 'morality flows out of, not into, salvation'.[20]

The relationship between religion and state is an area which has been particularly productive of misunderstandings on both sides, with charges abounding of repressive theocracy on the one hand, and abdication of political responsibility on the other. Generally speaking, Muslims envisage as an ideal a closer identification between the two, and are more optimistic about the possibility of righteous government upholding the rule of God as embodied in the Sharī'a. They consider themselves members of an *umma* (religious community) which transcends geographical boundaries but which is nevertheless closely identified with society as a whole. For Christians, God's reign is expressed in the eschatological concept of the 'Kingdom of God' which exists in the hearts of believers and which will only be fully inaugurated at the end of time. They consider themselves members of a universal Church which is 'in but not of' the world, acting on it and redeeming it. In relation to the political order, the role of faith is often seen as exercising a corrective influence rather than directly informing it, and temporal government is seen as a necessarily flawed human institution; for society as for the individual, the ideal is more nearly attainable in Islam.

The themes of revelation and prophecy form one of the most important areas of potential misunderstanding, since the same words are used in Islam and Christianity to mean different things. The Qur'anic terms *waḥy* and *tanzīl*, which may both be translated as 'revelation', have been fairly narrowly defined by Muslims in accordance with Qur'anic usage.[21] Both terms convey the idea of the externality of the revelation to the prophet; *tanzīl* refers to the 'sending down' of the message from the heavenly to the earthly realm, with the implication that no change occurs *en route*, while *waḥy* refers to the process whereby God's word is conveyed verbatim to His chosen messengers. Their role is simply to hear and faithfully to convey the message; as far as the actual revelatory process is concerned, they are essentially passive channels of communication between God and other humans. In this respect all prophets were the same, although only the revelation given to Muhammad has been preserved intact for posterity.

Christian views of revelation are at once more nuanced and more varied, although it is not possible to do justice to that variety here. Revelation is seen as God's disclosure of His character no less than His will, and these are conveyed through His actions as well as His words. Revelation has a strong relational element; Christians emphasize that it conveys not just propositional truth but also personal knowledge of God, as opposed to knowledge about Him. In the Bible, Christians see the drama of redemption and salvation being played out over the course of many centuries, reaching its culmination in the coming of Christ. There is therefore a sense of gradual unfolding of revelation, and the model of prophecy is evolutionary rather than repetitive. The process of inspiration, by which God's Word is translated into scripture, is usually seen as a divine–human collaboration; the characters, idiosyncracies and life stories of the individual prophets are inextricably bound up with the message they bring.

Different views of scriptural inerrancy arise in part from the different models of revelation in Islam and Christianity. Seyyed Hossein Nasr speaks for almost all Muslims when he says that 'no Muslim would accept any other view than that the Qur'an came verbatim from heaven'.[22] The transmission, collection and preservation of the Qur'an are seen as guaranteed by God. While there is a Qur'anic basis for this belief (75:17), it may also be seen as the logical consequence of the verbatim model of revelation; to call into question the authenticity of any part of it would undermine the view of the Qur'an as God's Word in a literal and absolute sense.

For Christians, the human element in both transmission and recension has generally been taken for granted. Scripture has usually been held to be 'authoritative rather than inerrant', and it was only at certain times and places that the 'dictation' model of prophecy and the idea of the infallibility or inerrancy of the scripture *per se* was subscribed to.[23] Moreover, different levels and definitions of inerrancy have been invoked; it may be seen, for example, as residing in the propositional truth of biblical statements, in its salvific doctrinal content, or in the achievement of its intended purpose. For Christians, the role of the Holy Spirit, both in the original process of inspiration and in the individual believer's reading of scripture, has generally been at least as important as the exact preservation of every word in the process of scriptural recension.

Scriptural exegesis also depends to some extent on the revelational and prophetic model. Allegorical interpretation was common among Christians right from the earliest period, and was in fact necessitated by the Christian incorporation of the Hebrew Bible, many parts of which were seen as foreshadowing Jesus. In contrast to the relative univocality of the Qur'an, the diversity of genres, authors and historical and social circumstances of the different Books of the Bible led to the elaboration of relatively sophisticated hermeneutical tools and methods.

Since the rise of higher biblical criticism in the wake of the Enlightenment, even evangelical Christians have grown accustomed to submitting the sources of their own faith to critical scrutiny. In the nineteenth century the most prominent Western Islamicists began to apply methods evolved in biblical scholarship to the Qur'an – a procedure that was largely unacceptable to Muslims. For various reasons, and not just due to social and political constraints, textual criticism as applied to the Bible has not been applied by Muslims to the Qur'an; the non-existence of pre-'Uthmanic manuscripts and the fact that the Qur'an is not seen as having any earthly 'sources' are two highly relevant considerations. Modernists usually confine themselves to applying new hermeneutical methods to the text. It is sometimes assumed by Christians and others that it is only a matter of time before Muslims apply the methods of biblical criticism to the Qur'an, but it should be clear from the above that in several important respects the Muslims' view of the Qur'an does not correspond with the Christians' view of the Bible. Rather than viewing the Qur'an as parallel to the Bible, many scholars have suggested that a more appropriate parallel is between the place of the Qur'an in Islam as eternal and uncreated,[24] and the place of Christ in Christianity; both provide a point of contact between the transcendent and the immanent.

Finally, some remarks on the implications of observing or studying one religious tradition from the perspective of another are in order. It is generally agreed in the sociology of knowledge that there is no disinterested standpoint, and that even in the scientific venture the researcher is always part of the equation; seemingly neutral 'facts' are channelled through human experience and therefore interpreted or culturally conditioned. In response to this there has grown up within the study of religions a cluster of ideas and principles referred to as the phenomenology of religion. An important concept is the desirablity of abstaining from value-judgements when commenting on religious phenomena. However, there is also a recognition of the inevitability and even desirability of an element of subjectivism – the active engagement of the personal qualities of the researcher, including his or her religious identity (insofar as this is a consciously and critically held position), may be seen as preferable to an attitude of cold detachment or illusory claims to objectivity.[25] Another important principle in phenomenology is that priority should be given to what the believer says about his or her own religious tradition. However, the assumption that the adherents of a given tradition are uniquely qualified to understand and interpret it is problematic in view of the diversity within each tradition, and some suggest that personal attributes such as a capacity for empathy might be a more significant factor than formal religious allegiance.[26] Furthermore, the enterprise of comparative religion is predicated on the assumption that it *is* possible for understanding to transcend religious boundaries. Charles Adams suggests an intermediate position, drawing attention to the need to combine a sensitivity to the feelings of others with the need to be true to one's own best insights, holding the two factors in tension.[27]

There has been considerable cross-fertilization between Christian theology and the study of religions, and many Christians have absorbed some of the insights of the phenomenology of religion. The following sentiment expressed by a Christian scholar is not an isolated example: 'Christians who come to the Qur'an responsibly and respectfully must acknowledge that this scripture belongs first and foremost to the Muslim Community. And they should be mindful of the dynamic and powerful relationship that exists between text and community which results in a distinctively Islamic perspective of what the text means.'[28] Another says more pointedly that 'rather than accepting and enjoying the position of guests who, grateful for the opportunity to cross at least the threshold of the house of Islam, enter primarily to become acquainted and to understand, some non-Muslim historians of religions behave as if they have been called by the Muslims as counselors and advisers to restructure and redirect that household of faith which they themselves have decided not to join'.[29]

Not all scholars would concur with the above sentiment. There are some who discern within the contemporary Western study of Islam in general and Christian study of Islam in particular, an element of unshriven guilt with regard to past excesses and failings. The French Islamicist Maxime Rodinson, a professed atheist, comments that 'the anti-colonialist left, whether Christian or not, often goes so far as to sanctify Islam . . . thereby going from one extreme to the other', and expresses his regret that 'any exposition of Islam and its characteristics by means of the normal mechanisms of human history' is liable to be branded as medievalistic or imperialistic.[30]

Taking into account the self-understanding of Muslims and Christians, Norman Daniel in his important study of Western images of Islam concludes that in Islam and Christianity 'there are irreducible differences between non-negotiable doctrines . . . The Christian creeds and the Qur'an are simply incompatible and there is no possibility of reconciling the content of the two faiths, each of which is exclusive, as long as they retain their identities.'[31] Most Muslims and Christians are likely to agree, and to resist attempts at syncretism or absorption of one by the other. While the recent move towards more irenical attitudes may be regarded as an improvement on past polemicism and more conducive to cordial interfaith relations, the attempt to bring harmony where dissonance has prevailed may be prone to its own distortions. The rejectionism of the past may be replaced by an acceptance which fails to acknowledge difference in the 'other', which in turn becomes a more subtle form of 'cultural imperialism'.

Notes

1. See especially S. Huntington, 'Islam and the Clash of Civilizations' (*Foreign Affairs*, 72, Summer 1993). Not all Muslims deplore this; there is a triumphalist discourse which takes pride in Western fear of Islamic unity and welcomes the elevation of Islam to an international force to be reckoned with.
2. Cited in Asad, *Genealogies of Religion*, p. 305.
3. A. Ahmed, *Postmodernism and Islam*, p. 178.
4. See Bijlefeld, 'Christian–Muslim Studies', pp. 13–14.
5. For perceptions of Islam, among the more important are Bennett, *Victorian Images of Islam*; Daniel, *Islam and the West*; Hourani, *Islam in European Thought*; M. Rodinson, *Europe and the Mystique of Islam* (Seattle: University of Washington Press, 1987); E. Said, *Orientalism*, 2nd ed. (Harmondsworth: Penguin, 1991); Southern, *Western Views of Islam in the Middle Ages*. Since Muslim discussion of Christianity tends to revolve around issues of Qur'anic exegesis, many of the most relevant studies are in this area; see McAuliffe, *Qur'ānic Christians*; Robinson, *Christ in Islam and Christianity*. On Muslim perceptions of Christianity with particular reference to Egypt, see Goddard, *Muslim Perceptions of Christianity*, and on Muslim perceptions of the West generally, see, e.g., N. Rahimieh, *Oriental Responses to the West* (Leiden: Brill, 1990).
6. Ibn Ḥazm, *Al-Fiṣal fi'l-Milal wa'l-Ahwā' wa'l-Niṣal*, 2 vols. (Cairo: Al-Maṭba'at al-Adabiyya, 1899); Kairanawi's main work has been translated into English: Maulana M. Rahmatullah Kairanvi, *Izhar-ul-Haq*, 4 vols. (London: Ta-Ha Publishers, 1989).
7. The Jama'at is a Pakistani movement founded by Abul Ala Mawdudi in 1941, and the International Institute, founded in 1981, has its headquarters in Washington, DC.

8. Arkoun, 'Is Islam Threatened by Christianity?', p. 56. The same points are made at greater length by other Muslim scholars: see, e.g., Talbi, 'Islam and Dialogue: Some Reflections on a Current Topic', pp. 4–6, and Ayoub, 'Roots of Muslim–Christian Conflict', p. 42.
9. Jomier, *How to Understand Islam*, pp. 140–1.
10. 'Ata ur-Rahim, *Jesus, Prophet of Islam*, p. 3 (from the introduction by Shaykh 'Abd al-Qadir al-Sufi).
11. This verb occurs in several places in the Qur'an: 2:75, 4:46, 5:13, and 5:41. For references to other verbs used with a similar meaning in the Qur'an, see Groupe de Recherches Islamo-Chrétien, *The Challenge of the Scriptures*, p. 78; for a fuller treatment of the subject, see J. Gaudeul and R. Caspar, 'Textes de la Tradition musulmane concernant le tahrif (falsification) des Écritures' (*ISCH*, 6, 1980).
12. Several eminent Muslim scholars, including al-Ṭabarī, al-Ghazālī, al-Rāzī, Ibn Kathīr and Ibn Khaldūn, upheld the integrity of the biblical text in the medieval period, as have Sayyid Ahmad Khan and Muhammad 'Abduh in the modern period.
13. Cited in Hourani, *Islam in European Thought*, p. 19.
14. Cragg, *The Call of the Minaret*, p. 261.
15. W. C. Smith expounded this thesis in his *The Meaning and End of Religion*, where he suggested 'faith' and 'cumulative tradition' as more useful categories.
16. Hodgson, 'A Comparison of Islam and Christianity as Framework for Religious Life', pp. 53, 56.
17. Ibid., p. 56.
18. Hodgson, *The Venture of Islam*, vol. 2, p. 337.
19. Adams, 'Islam and Christianity: The Opposition of Similarities', p. 287.
20. Smith, *Islam in Modern History*, p. 21.
21. See T. Izutsu, *God and Man in the Koran: Semantics of the Koranic Weltanschauung* (Tokyo: Keio Institute of Cultural and Linguistic Studies, 1964), chapter 7, for a detailed analysis of the use of these terms in the Qur'an.
22. Nasr, 'Response to Hans Küng's Paper on Christian–Muslim Dialogue', p. 98.
23. See Goddard, 'Each Other's Scripture', esp. p. 18.
24. This is the traditionally accepted view and still the majority, though not unanimous, opinion.
25. An account of the historical development of the phenomenology of religion is given in Sharpe, *Comparative Religion*.
26. J. Wach in Kitagawa, *The Comparative Study of Religions*, pp. 10–14; Hodgson suggests that 'it is often far easier for congenial temperaments to understand each other across the lines of religious or cultural tradition than it is for contrasting temperaments to make sense of each other's faith even when they follow the same cult and offer the same creed' (*The Venture of Islam*, vol. 1, p. 28).
27. Adams, 'The History of Religions and the Study of Islam', p. 189.
28. F. P. Ford, 'The Qur'ān as Sacred Scripture', p. 161.
29. Bijlefeld, 'A Prophet and More than a Prophet?', p. 5.
30. Rodinson, 'The Western Image and Western Studies of Islam', p. 59.
31. Daniel, *Islam and the West*, pp. 335–6.

one

FACTORS INFLUENCING MUSLIM–CHRISTIAN RELATIONS

Muslim and Christian perceptions of each other are coloured by many factors, and this chapter aims to describe some of the more influential ones affecting both groups. Since the Qur'an is central in determining Muslim attitudes, it is important to know what the Qur'an has to say about Christians and Christianity, and the way in which the Qur'anic material has been interpreted. While there is no biblical equivalent, there will be some discussion of Christian theological attitudes to other religions later on in the chapter. A brief overview of the history of Muslim–Christian relations will throw light on the way in which communally preserved memories of historical events or encounters continue to affect attitudes in the present. The relationship between Christian missions and imperialism is of particular interest in view of the strong influence this has had on Muslim attitudes to Christianity in the modern period. The ecumenical and interfaith movements, by contrast, have primarily affected Christian attitudes, although small numbers of Muslims have also participated in them; a brief look at Christian and Muslim views on dialogue will illustrate some of the differing preconceptions and expectations on each side, and should go some way towards explaining the communication gap which is so often observable in Muslim–Christian encounter.

The Qur'anic Paradigm

Islam has been described as the 'most entity-like' of religions.[1] Dating back to the earliest period, the concept of 'religion' was a highly reified one for Muslims, and the Qur'an itself has, among scriptures, a uniquely developed awareness of religious plurality, at one point even appearing to offer a rationale for the existence of competing religions: 'For each We have appointed a divine law and a traced-out way. Had God willed He could have made you one community. But [He wished] to try you by that which He has given you; so vie with one another in good works' (5:48). In so far as one can trace within the Qur'an the progressive consolidation of Islamic religious identity, it is inextricably linked with the religious identity of others, notably Jews and Christians.[2] Muslims find a ready-made apologetic and polemic in the Qur'an, as it reflects the Muslims' fluctuating relations with polytheists, Jews and Christians.

The relationship between the Qur'an and its environment is undeniably important in seeking to understand particular verses, though it raises some sensitive issues. Muslims have not welcomed the great interest shown by orientalist scholarship in environmental, particularly Jewish and Christian, 'influences' on the Qur'an, which have usually carried the implication that the Qur'an is of human rather than divine origin.[3] However, Islamic scholarship has always implicitly acknowledged the relationship, and one of the exegetical sciences, namely the 'occasions of revelation' (*asbāb al-nuzūl*), was devoted to discovering the particular circumstances in which a verse was revealed in order to clarify its precise import. This was one means by which potentially conflicting statements could be reconciled. The fact that the revelations came in response to, and therefore reflect, particular circumstances does not necessarily detract from the belief in the Qur'an's eternal validity or even its pre-existence; Muslims believe, for example, that 'like everything else, the vicissitudes of Muhammad's relations with Christians were foreordained and that the revelations were therefore given to him on the appropriate occasions'.[4] It could also be argued that in order to be intelligible to its contemporary audience, the Qur'an had perforce to take into account their situation, including their level of knowledge and understanding. While such considerations provide a means for modernist Muslims to reinterpret the Qur'an in accordance with changed conditions, few Muslims would wish to pursue this line of enquiry too far, since it appears to view the Qur'an on a par with other literature as historically conditioned, and to detract from the idea of its universal validity and absolute inerrancy.

Most Western scholars regard the Qur'anic material on Christianity as reflecting or responding to the heterodox forms and divided state of

Christianity in contemporary Arabia and the surrounding areas.[5] The main forms of Christianity with which the Arabs of Muhammad's time would have come into contact were Nestorianism, which was dominant in South Arabia and the Lakhmid buffer state affiliated to the Sassanid Empire, and Monophysitism, which prevailed in the Ghassanid northern buffer state affiliated to the Byzantine Empire. Outside the peninsula, Christianity was represented by the Nestorians of Persia and Iraq, the Jacobites of Syria, the Copts of Egypt, and the Armenians of the eastern Anatolian highlands. The differences in Christology between the Byzantines, the Monophysites (Copts, Jacobites and Armenians) and the Nestorians were largely differences in emphasis between the historical (or human) and the cosmic (or divine) dimensions of Christ. These differences, exacerbated by cultural and linguistic differences, were the ostensible cause of persecutions and accusations of heresy, but doctrinal conflict often became the arena for political rivalries.

Although the information for central Arabia is relatively sparse, it seems that apart from a very few Christian Arab tribes there were only scattered groups and individuals, probably of Nestorian or Monophysite persuasion, some of whom would have taken refuge from Byzantine persecution. Some have speculated on the existence of groups of Jewish Christians, including Ebionites and Elkaisites, or Manichean or Gnostic elements, but this has been on the basis of internal Qur'anic evidence which may be seen as reflecting doctrines held by these groups (e.g. the denial of the crucifixion and the humanity of Jesus) rather than on any external evidence.[6]

The Christian doctrines explicitly refuted in the Qur'an are therefore not necessarily those of mainstream orthodox Christianity. Just as Jews are criticized for taking 'Uzayr (i.e. Ezra) to be a son of God (9:30),[7] despite the fact that this can only have been true, if at all, of a limited and heretical section of Judaism, so some have argued that it is tritheism rather than the Trinity *per se* which is criticized in the Qur'an, and that the sonship of Jesus is conceived in physical, rather than spiritual or metaphorical terms. To see the Qur'an as reflecting and rejecting temporary and aberrant beliefs in Judaism or Christianity is not necessarily to attribute error to it, although some Western scholars do not hesitate to speak of its 'mistaken' or 'inadequate' perception of Christianity.[8] Viewed on its own terms, the Qur'an does not claim to provide a scientific description or definition of other religions, but it does seek to address issues of immediate concern, including the refutation of erroneous beliefs.

The Qur'an does not lay claim to doctrinal originality but sees itself as confirming a succession of previous revelations vouchsafed to former messengers (e.g. 2:40, 89, 91), including many of those regarded as patriarchs or kings, as well as those regarded as prophets, in the Judaeo-Christian tradition. Approximately a quarter of the Qur'an is devoted to telling the stories of past prophets, many of which are found in the Bible. The Qur'anic narratives do not usually give any indication of chronology, and contain very little historical or environmental detail; they are characterized by brevity, allusion and ellipsis. The Qur'an therefore presupposes to some extent a basic knowledge of biblical stories in its hearers, but its distinctive narrative style, with a didactic or homiletic emphasis, as well as significant differences in the details of the stories, constitutes a form of originality which belies a direct dependence on the biblical material.[9] The Qur'an also has a distinctive prophetology, with its cyclical view of the history of revelation. Each prophet brings essentially the same message – the rejection of idolatry and the call to worship the one true God – and each perseveres in the face of strong opposition; divine retribution is visited on those who refuse to heed the message, usually in their earthly life as well as in the Hereafter.[10] The strong sense of continuity and identification between Muhammad and the former prophets, who delivered the same message and suffered the same opposition, enhances the value of these stories which serve to console Muhammad, encourage his followers and warn his opponents.

The message, then, although perhaps differing in details (for example the progressive relaxation, first by Jesus and then by Muhammad, of the strict food laws imposed on the Jews – 3:50; 6:145–6), remains the same in essence. The terms *islām* and *muslim* are sometimes used in their original, non-reified sense of 'submission' or 'one who submits' (i.e. to God); Abraham is thus described as 'neither a Jew nor a Christian, but an upright *muslim*' (3:67), and the disciples of Jesus also proclaim themselves '*muslims*' (3:52). The Qur'an may therefore provide a mandate both for an evolutionary view of religions, with Islam as the culmination of all previous revelations, and for viewing Islam as the primordial religion, the blueprint to which all other religions conformed in their original state before becoming corrupted and distorted.[11]

The Qur'anic material on Christians and Christianity[12] is characterized by a certain ambivalence, in that it contains both critical or confrontational and laudatory or irenic references. For an optimum understanding of the Qur'an it is therefore important to observe both the circumstances of revelation, where possible, and subsequent interpretation which is likely to have partially preserved the understanding of those whom it originally addressed. Taking into account the chronological order of the revelations, some have detected a progressive hardening of attitudes towards Christians as well as other non-Muslims.[13] In subsequent Qur'anic interpretation the effect of this would have been compounded by the hermeneutical and legislative device of *naskh* (abrogation), whereby in case of apparent contradiction later revelations were deemed by the classical scholars to have abrogated earlier ones. While several auspicious contacts with Christians are attributed to the earlier part of Muhammad's prophetic career, such as Waraqah ibn Nawfal's confirmation of his prophetic vocation and the Abyssinian Negus' granting of refuge to the Muslims who left Mecca to escape persecution, in the later Medinan period there was military conflict with both Jews and the Byzantine Christians.

Along with Jews and Sabaeans, Christians are included in the Qur'anic category of 'People of the Book' (*ahl al-kitāb*), who enjoy something of a privileged status in view of the fact that they possess their own revealed scriptures and worship the true God. Although some passages imply that Christians and Jews have altered or misinterpreted parts of their scriptures, some verses seem to accord a degree of legitimacy to extant Christian scriptures: 'Let the people of the Gospel judge by that which God has revealed therein. Whoever does not judge by that which God has revealed, they are the iniquitous' (5:47). One passage favourably compares Christians with Jews, who are said to be 'the most implacable of mankind in enmity toward those who believe'; Christians are described, by contrast, as 'the nearest in affection' to Muslims, 'because there are among them priests and monks, and because they are not proud' (5:82). The following verse, believed by some to be a reference to the Negus of Abyssinia, describes how their eyes overflow with tears when they listen to the Qur'anic revelation, in recognition of the truth. In another verse God says that 'We placed in the hearts of those who followed him [i.e. Jesus] compassion and mercy' (57:27), although it goes on to disparage the practice of monasticism (in contrast to the commendation cited above) as a man-made rather than divinely ordained institution.

On the other hand, Christians (usually along with Jews) are criticized in the Qur'an for their failure to follow their religion properly, corruption, suppression or misinterpretation of their scriptures, exclusivism, complacency, sectarianism, and, not least, their desire to lead Muslims astray and failure to acknowledge Muhammad's prophethood.[14] Some verses advise disassociation from them, warning Muslims not to take Jews or Christians as friends or allies (5:51, 3:61), while others advocate either verbal or military confrontation in particular circumstances (e.g. 9:29). The harshest strictures, however, are reserved for the doctrinal aberrations of Christians, notably the divinity and sonship of Jesus, and the Trinity (or tritheism, depending on one's interpretation). In some cases it is stated that these doctrines are tantamount to *kufr* (unbelief) or *shirk* (associating partners with God), thus blurring the distinction between Christians and pagans (e.g. 4:171, 5:17, 72–3).

The Qur'anic perception of Jesus differs markedly from that of the New Testament, and has generated much study (and some creative interpretation) on the part of Christians.[15] Little is said about the content of Jesus' teaching, although he is described as confirming the scriptures which came before him and making lawful some of that which Jews had been forbidden (3:50), warning his followers against idolatry on pain of hell-fire (5:72), and promising paradise to those who are killed when fighting 'in the way of God' (9:111). In addition he foretold the coming of Muhammad (61:6, 7:157), and performed the *ṣalāt* (ritual prayer) and *zakāt* (almsgiving) (19:31). His mortality is insisted upon – one passage describes him as 'none other than a messenger', and points out that other messengers have passed away before him, and that he and his mother 'used to eat food' (5:75), while in others he is described as a 'servant ('*abd*) of God' (e.g. 19:30, 4:172).

Although he is commonly referred to as 'son of Mary', Jesus is given various honorific titles and is in some respects distinguished from other prophets. The virgin birth is confirmed (3:47), and he is described as the Messiah, as God's word, and 'a spirit from Him' (4:171, 3:45). In his mission he was strengthened by the 'holy spirit' (e.g. 2:87) and granted several miracles, including speaking as a baby, healing the sick, bringing the dead to life, and breathing life into a clay bird (3:49, 5:110). Although some of the foregoing may seem to lend themselves to a Christian understanding of Jesus, the Qur'an itself tends to forestall such interpretations. In the performance of miracles Jesus resembled Moses, and it is stressed that they were performed only 'by God's leave', and the miraculous creation of Jesus with no human father is compared to the creation of Adam who had neither father nor mother (3:59). Although the Qur'an does not elaborate on the terms 'Messiah' or 'word of God', the latter phrase has been explained by Qur'anic interpreters as arising from the fact that Jesus came into being through God's verbal command (cf. 3:59), and the former is interpreted in various ways, usually related to the Hebrew sense of 'anointed'.[16] The same verse which describes Jesus as God's 'word' and a 'spirit from Him' insists that he is 'only a messenger' and denies his sonship (4:171).

The verses concerning the end of Jesus' earthly life are open to more than one interpretation. The majority Muslim understanding of the key passage (4:156–8) is that he was not crucified, but a substitute was killed in his place; Jesus was taken up to God without suffering death (cf. 3:55). Some verses (e.g. 43:61, 4:159) can be interpreted as indicating an eschatological role for Jesus, and the majority Muslim view, based on Hadiths as well as the Qur'an, is that he remains alive with God and will return to earth at the end of the world. At that time, he will be associated in some way with the awaited Mahdi, if he is not the Mahdi himself.[17]

While some verses (especially 2:62, 5:69), taken at face value, indicate that the People of the Book will attain salvation or success in the Hereafter, others appear to make a distinction between good and bad People of the Book, opening up the possibility that their treatment or eternal destiny could be accordingly varied. According to one verse, 'some of them are believers, but most of them are iniquitous', while an adjacent verse has a slightly different emphasis: 'They are not all alike. Of the People of the Book there is an upright community who recite the verses of God . . . enjoin right conduct and forbid indecency, and vie with one another in good works . . . Of the good they do, they will not lose the reward' (3:110, 113–5). There is some ambiguity concerning the necessity of their conversion to Islam; verses expressing a desire for this vary from the wistful to the threatening (e.g. 3:110, 4:47). One verse which has traditionally been understood in an exclusivist way: 'Whoever desires a religion [or way of life] other than Islam, it will not be accepted of him, and in the Hereafter he will be among the losers' (3:85), can be differently interpreted if *islām* is taken in the general sense of submission to God.

One can interpret the varying attitudes prescribed by the Qur'an either in terms of two alternative paradigms – a 'pattern of affirmation' and a 'pattern of confrontation',[18] one or other of which may be prioritized by Muslims according to circumstances, or in terms of the aforementioned distinction between good and bad People of the Book. The latter has been the path followed by the majority of Qur'anic commentators both classical and modern. According to this view, the 'true' Christians praised in the Qur'an are those whose beliefs about Jesus coincided with Muslim beliefs, and who either accepted Muhammad's message or would have done so had they heard about him.[19] On this understanding, the promise of salvation applies only to a small minority of actual Christians.

Although the Sunna often clarifies and elaborates on the Qur'anic teachings, it contains relatively little in the way of definitive guidance on the treatment of, or appropriate attitude towards, Christians. A few Hadiths explicitly state that those Christians (or Jews) who hear Muhammad's message and fail to affirm it will go to hell.[20] In others, Muhammad is portrayed as urging his followers to distinguish themselves in physical appearance or religious observance from the People of the Book, while yet others appear to have an apologetic function, depicting the lower rank of Jews and Christians in relation to Muslims in the final judgement.[21]

Qur'anic commentators and jurists in the classical period, perhaps partly influenced by polemical exchanges, came increasingly to consider Christians as polytheists or unbelievers, choosing to uphold the more austere interpretations of the Qur'an and the Sunna.[22] While such attitudes have survived into the modern period, there is now a broader spectrum of interpretation and a greater tendency to acknowledge the respect due to the People of the Book and the possibility of their salvation, without enquiring too closely into their theology. While the influence of modern ideals of humanitarianism and religious pluralism may have played a part in this, there is also strong Qur'anic support for such opinions.

The Historical Legacy

Muslim–Christian relations in history have been characterized by both discord and harmony. An overview of political history suggests that the former has been dominant, although the more finely tuned instruments of the social historian and the biographer would no doubt uncover some more auspicious Muslim–Christian encounters. Only the briefest of outlines highlighting events or elements with lasting repercussions can be accommodated here, and the reader is referred to other sources for a fuller picture.[23]

The Byzantine Empire was the main political embodiment of Christianity at the time of the Arab Muslim conquests. With the conversion of the Emperor Constantine in the fourth century, the situation of Christianity in the late Roman world had undergone a transformation; from being the faith of a persecuted minority it became an established religion and an integral part of the social and political order, inaugurating the phenomenon of 'Christendom' as a territorial entity. Byzantium became in its turn a persecutor of heretical or dissenting beliefs; the substantive theological issues at stake concerned the nature of Christ, but differences were aggravated by the fact that the doctrinal formulations of the ecumenical councils of the fourth and fifth centuries were expressed in Greek philosophical categories and were therefore uncongenial to Christians who were not familiar with this tradition. The Muslim conquerors encountered a divided Christendom, and some Christians, particularly the Copts in Egypt, had reason to prefer their new masters to their Byzantine oppressors.

The situation of Christians under Muslim rule varied; although various discriminatory measures were applied at different times and places, actual persecution was rare and in this respect Muslim societies compared favourably with other medieval polities.[24] There was necessarily some continuity in the administrations of the conquered territories, and Christians and other non-Muslims with valuable skills sometimes occupied important positions, often as physicians or administrators. From the eighth century Christians, especially Nestorians, actively participated in the burgeoning Islamic civilization, and were among those who undertook translations of the Greek, Persian and Indian heritages. However, Christians in general suffered a gradual decline in status over the following centuries; large-scale conversion to Islam resulted in an attrition of the Church, which in the case of North Africa was almost complete, and Muslim–Christian relations deteriorated in the aftermath of the Crusades and the Mongol invasion.

The Islamic polities posed a serious military threat to Christendom down to the eighteenth century, when the balance of power between the Ottoman Empire and Europe swung in favour of the latter. Muslim political unity had begun to fragment much earlier, however, and Europe had effected some limited reconquests on the margins of the Islamic Empire, for example in Sicily and later Spain, where the Inquisition provided perhaps the most extreme example of religious persecution in European history up to that time. The challenge posed by Islam was not only perceived in military terms; Europeans' defensiveness and hostility was exacerbated by an awareness of their own cultural and civilizational inferiority.

The Crusades have had an impact on mutual perceptions of Muslims and Christians which has been disproportionate to their direct political effect. They were undertaken from a complex combination of motives, both religious and temporal: rivalries between competing commercial interests and between the emerging nation-states of Europe; the Pope's desire to reunite Christendom under his authority following the East–West schism of 1054; a response to the initial Muslim conquests and to the coming of the Seljuqs, and a desire to regain control of the 'holy places' of Palestine; and, the ostensible reason, to secure the passage of pilgrims to Jerusalem. Ill-conceived and poorly orchestrated, once unleashed the Crusades gained a momentum of their own, and the excesses, in which both religious zeal and worldly ambition played their part, have been well documented.[25] Militarily speaking, the Crusades represented only a marginal threat to Muslims, for whom they seemed like yet another barbarian raid on the borders of the Islamic world, with no particular religious significance. There was no resulting intensification of anti-Christian polemic, and the word 'Crusade' does not appear in contemporary Muslim writings at all.[26] Nevertheless, there is a legacy of resentment and bitterness among those (Jews and Eastern Christians as well as Muslims) who suffered from the indiscriminate ravages of the Crusaders. Initially, the memory of the Crusades was preserved in the Western mind, and their effect was to perpetuate negative Western Christian attitudes to Islam. However, the Crusades now loom larger in the consciousness of Muslims, for whom they can be seen in retrospect as a precursor to colonialism. While Muslims often view the Crusades as a symbol of inveterate Christian hatred of Islam, contemporary Christians almost unanimously abjure them as a betrayal of the true spirit of Christianity.

While there has been a strong element of continuity in Muslim attitudes to Christianity over the centuries, due in part to the pervasive influence of the Qur'anic teachings which were outlined on pp. 15–22, there has been considerable evolution in Christian perceptions of Islam. John of Damascus (d. 749), an official in the Umayyad court who knew both Arabic and Greek, is regarded as the first Christian to have made a serious attempt to study and understand Islam.[27] As was generally true of the writings of Christians living under Muslim rule, his was a work of Christian apologetic rather than anti-Muslim polemic, concentrating on those areas of Christian belief which were attacked by Muslims. In contrast to most Western Christian writers well into late medieval times, he had some accurate knowledge of Islamic teachings. Conceiving of Islam as a Christian heresy, he acknowledged some common ground between them but took issue on certain doctrinal differences, and refuted the prophethood of Muhammad on Christian grounds. John of Damascus' work has been described as 'calm and charitable in tone',[28] but he laid the groundwork for future disputation and interreligious polemic which was not always so moderately expressed. He wrote at a time when Christians still enjoyed cultural superiority; the situation changed in the ninth century, when Muslims, in the forefront of whom were the Mu'tazila, the first school of scholastic theologians in Islam, acquired the intellectual tools of the Greek philosophical tradition and were able to equal and often surpass Christian sophistication.

Byzantine Christian writings on Islam were more polemical than those of Arab Christians; for them, the Muslims represented a military threat, but, not being under actual Muslim rule, they were freer to express open hostility.[29] Some of the themes of Byzantine polemic were later carried over into Western Christian views of Islam. Muhammad was sometimes seen as a figure inspired by Satan or even identified as the Antichrist; among other things, it was said that he encouraged sexual promiscuity and suffered from epileptic fits, that Muslims were idolaters, and that the Qur'an was a jumbled collection of materials from biblical and non-biblical sources.

European Latin Christendom apparently remained in a state of near ignorance about Islam down to the twelfth century, when the first glimmerings of knowledge came, mainly via Muslim Spain. It was from about this time that the Arabic versions of Greek philosophers, especially Aristotle and the Neoplatonists, as well as the original works of Muslim philosophers such as Ibn Sina (d. AH 428/1037) and Ibn Rushd (d. AH 595/1198) began to be translated into Latin. This inaugurated a significant phase of fruitful academic communication between Muslims and Europeans; as well as providing an opportunity for some positive appreciation of the Islamic heritage, it contributed to an intellectual awakening in Europe which culminated in the Enlightenment. In spite of certain remarkable scholarly initiatives in the twelfth century, notably the translation into Latin and study of the Qur'an and other texts under the auspices of Peter the Venerable of Cluny (d. 1156), ignorance, sometimes wilful, continued to be widespread for centuries to come. In the absence of accurate information, Western images of Islam during this period were highly imaginative and contained elements of pure invention. Some fabrications, such as the legend that Muhammad trained a dove to peck grain from his ear while pretending to receive revelations from it, or that the trance-like state in which he received revelations was attributable to epilepsy, were designed to portray him as an impostor or a false prophet; others, for example the assertion that he was a drunkard and an idolator, or was himself worshipped by Muslims, were diametrically opposed to the facts. Other accounts depicted Muhammad as a magician or a renegade cardinal who, failing to obtain promotion to the papacy, absconded to Arabia to found a rival religion. A quote from the twelfth-century scholar Guibert de Nogent succinctly illustrates the attitude underlying some of these stories: 'it is safe to speak evil of one whose malignity exceeds whatever ill can be spoken'.[30]

It would be facile to attribute such anti-Muslim polemic to sheer degeneracy on the one hand, or simple ignorance on the other. One can assume that such ideas appealed because they fulfilled certain needs on the part of those who subscribed to them. Negative and stereotypical images of Islam provided an antithesis to Europeans' own self-image, thus serving to bolster their own identity in the face of the perceived external threat; on a more popular level, they satisfied the demand for imaginative stimulation. It was a polemic intended for internal consumption, and Muslims were mostly unaware of its existence until modern times. Muslims were not the only targets of such attacks, and there existed parallel and sometimes worse polemic against other groups or constructed enemies, while hostility towards Muslims was sometimes relieved by guarded admiration and even romanticization of Muslim chivalry in battle, or religious fervour.[31]

From Renaissance times one can chart the beginning of the new humanism, which was able to view Islam in a more detached way; individual scholars, including some who were religiously motivated, such as Nicholas of Cusa and John of Segovia,[32] were increasingly concerned to base their studies on reliable sources. The establishment of chairs of Arab studies from the seventeenth century and specialist orientalist societies from the eighteenth marked the beginning of organized academic study of Islam in the West, which, if it did not eliminate prejudice, at least promoted the dissemination of more accurate information.

Another development, dating approximately from the time of the Reformation, was the use of Islam as a theme in internal Christian polemic, both Protestants and Catholics drawing parallels or even unfavourable comparisons between their opponents and Islam. Catholics, for example, portrayed Islam with its iconoclasm and lack of religious hierarchy as a forerunner to the Reformation. By a similar process, in

Enlightenment thought Islam could be enlisted by deists or humanists in the cause of discrediting Christianity – either as a model of the excesses of religion in general, as with Voltaire or Gibbon, or by being upheld in contrast to Christianity as the religion of nature, simplicity and rationalism, as with Rousseau. Islam also began to be admired for its own sake by some, who held that such a vigorous and enduring movement represented an outstanding human achievement.

The nineteenth century witnessed an explosion in the gathering and classification of information in all spheres of knowledge, not least in the study of religions. Then as at other times, Christians partook of the prevailing worldviews of their societies, and one can trace parallels between secular and Christian thought. Secular historians and philosophers did not generally rank Islam's contribution to civilization very highly, seeing its main role as the passive one of preserving the Greek heritage.[33] The racialist theory espoused by Renan and others, who contrasted the rigid Semitic spirit with the dynamic Aryan one, was analagous to the view that contrasted the progressive nature of Western civilization (attributed to the influence of Christianity) with the stagnant nature of societies inspired by Islam, which was seen as incapable of developing or reforming itself.

While some of the medieval views persisted, inevitably the availability of more reliable information influenced attitudes to Islam. Muhammad's sincerity, for example, was increasingly recognized.[34] There was some polarization among Christians; while the attitudes of liberals towards Islam and other faiths were undergoing a transformation, many conservatives continued to see Islam as a religion spread by the sword which encouraged fatalism, sensual indulgence and moral laxity, with a corresponding view of Muhammad as a deceiver and a man of worldly ambition, particularly in the Medinan period.[35] From the early twentieth century, however, more conciliatory attitudes began to emerge, even among missionaries to Muslims such as Temple Gairdner and Lewis Bevan Jones.

The question arises as to how far historical European attitudes can be characterized as Christian. There is no simple answer to this; in so far as European society generally could be described as 'Christian', any hostility towards Islam would be likely to be expressed in Christian idiom. In some cases religious motives led Christians to dissent from prevailing attitudes of intolerance or to oppose military aggression, while in others, religious or apocalyptic ideas engendered a deep pessimism and animosity towards Islam.[36] It would be fair to say that the need to account for Islam in an overall framework of salvation history, whether as a Christian or Jewish heresy, a man-made or satanic religion, a scourge from God on a decadent and corrupt Christianity or a portent of the Apocalypse, was religiously motivated. In medieval as in modern times, Christians of strong conviction were more likely than others to perceive Islam as a threat or a rival. Whatever may have been the effect of the ethical teachings of the New Testament on the attitudes of individual Christians towards others, Western Christian theologians of the pre-modern period had neither the existential security nor perhaps the intellectual tools to formulate more positive theological views of non-Christian religions *per se*, although there were some who believed that non-Christians might attain salvation.

While the historical evolution of Christian perceptions of Islam has been relatively well documented, the study of corresponding Muslim perceptions has received less attention.[37] This may be partly due to the relative inaccessibility of the Muslim material, which is dispersed in different genres.[38] Since Europe has historically been the Islamic world's most inveterate military adversary, and since it has been perceived by Muslims in primarily religious terms, references to Christians in Muslim writings have usually been hostile. In the light of Europe's military and civilizational inferiority, which endured for several centuries, references to Europe or Christendom in Muslim writings were often disdainful.[39] In Persian and Turkish as well as Arabic, Christians have commonly been referred to as *kāfirūn* (infidels), while in Ottoman usage in particular it was customary to add curses or insults to the names of Europeans.[40]

As has already been mentioned, Muslim attitudes have been based to a great extent on unchanging theological considerations; while there is obviously some latitude for Muslims in deciding which elements of their religious teachings to emphasize, and socio-political factors are bound to have some effect on this, there has been rather less variation than in Christian writings. There have, however, been some tangible changes in the modern period. It would probably be true to say that colonialism and the missionary movement have had a greater impact on Muslim attitudes towards Christianity than any previous historical phenomena.

Missions and Imperialism

Islam and Christianity are both avowedly missionary faiths. Many Muslims would agree that 'Islam . . . aims at bringing its message to all corners of the earth. It hopes that one day the whole of humanity will be one Muslim community, the "Umma"'; Muslims living in the West often express the hope that the West will one day be won over to Islam through peaceful persuasion, i.e. *da'wah* ('invitation' to Islam).[41] Although in the past Christian missionary activity has been more highly organized, structured and financed than Islamic *da'wah*, Muslims are now increasingly adopting the methods and strategies which have been evolved in the Christian context.[42] The twentieth century has witnessed the formation of transnational Islamic organizations incorporating *da'wah* as one of their aims, such as the Muslim World League, the World Islamic Call Society, and the Islamic Council of Europe.[43] More recently there has been a substantial growth of Muslim non-governmental organizations which are involved in aid and development work while simultaneously undertaking *da'wah* activities, such as the provision of Islamic literature and education.[44] While in the past *da'wah* has most often been directed at lax or heterodox Muslims, it now increasingly targets non-Muslims, especially in the Western context.

Despite these growing similarities between mission and *da'wah*, Christian missionary activity continues to attract condemnation, with Muslims sometimes calling for a moratorium on the activities of missionaries in Muslim lands.[45] Whether or not it is conceded in principle that missionary activity is legitimate for Christians as for Muslims, indictments of Christian mission often take the form of objections concerning practical or ethical issues such as methodology or political involvement. The most frequent allegations concern 'ulterior motives' of Christian aid and development work and material inducements to convert.[46] The paradoxical situation whereby Muslim objections to Christian mission are more vehement than Christian objections to Islamic *da'wah*, despite the fact that the conversion rate from Christianity to Islam is almost certainly considerably higher than the reverse (for which there are no available statistics), is to be explained at least in part by the fact that the very idea of conversion of Muslims to another religion is anathema. Some modernists have argued against the traditional death penalty for apostasy on the grounds that the Qur'an only specifies other-worldly punishment, but many Muslims continue to regard conversion from Islam as treasonable.[47]

Be that as it may, the Muslim discourse on Christian missions almost invariably refers to the historical relationship with imperialism, which is felt to be ongoing. Although actual Western political hegemony may have declined, missionaries are charged with being agents of secularization and with continuing to serve the interests of Western governments. A British Muslim intellectual asserts that 'most Christian missionaries exhibit the major characteristics of liberal secularism – imperialistic tendencies, dehumanization, domination and meaninglessness'.[48] Indeed, Christian missionary activity is frequently characterized in Muslim discourse in precisely the same terms as colonialism: as oppressive, exploitative, unscrupulous as to methodology, ruthless, arrogant, immoral, and destructive of indigenous cultures. The assertion that in the name of mission 'Christians have carried out, and continue to carry out, programmes of brutal extermination of members of "pagan" faiths as well as adherents of traditional world views' is not exceptional.[49]

As with the Crusades, the perceived history often takes priority over discovering what was actually the case. The fact of the interrelationship between colonialism and Christian missions has become deeply embedded in the consciousness of most Muslims,[50] and, as in Marxist discourse, has come to form part of the anti-Western rhetoric. The debate on the degree of collusion between missions and imperialism has become ideologically charged in the era of anti-colonial reaction, and often fails to take into account the haphazard nature of both colonial expansion and missionary activity.

The modern missionary movement dates back to the foundation of missionary societies and institutions beginning in the eighteenth century; the following century witnessed a spectacular growth of Protestant missions, in particular. Western imperialist expansion into far-flung corners of the world made possible the propagation of the Christian message on an unprecedented scale, and has resulted in a Christian presence in virtually all areas of the world. By and large, missionaries not only acquiesced in the imperialist venture but saw it as a good thing, both because it would be in the interests of the colonized, and because of the providential opportunity which it afforded to bring the gospel to the 'unreached'. The belief that the progress which had been achieved in the West was largely due to the influence of Christianity encouraged the view that other societies would follow the same path, and attain the same prosperity, once the gospel had been disseminated among them. The exporting of Western culture and patterns of commerce could therefore be seen as complementary, if ultimately subordinate, to the diffusion of the Christian message.

In the field, the relationship between colonial administrators and missionaries, like colonial policy itself, varied greatly, and many factors dictated against a straightforwardly symbiotic relationship between them.

The missionaries in a given country were always of diverse national backgrounds; colonialist administrators sometimes discouraged or prohibited missionary activity for fear of inciting religious unrest; and the idealism and humanitarianism of many missionaries sometimes brought them into conflict with colonial administrators when the latters' policies were perceived to be unjust or exploitative.[51] In the minds of missionaries, the colonialist venture was essentially a means to a professedly higher end, and their motives were religious rather than political. They saw their role as temporary, and there was general agreement on the desirability of cultivating indigenous leadership, even if this did not become the rule in practice until the second half of the twentieth century.

One of the more controversial areas of discussion is the impact of missions on indigenous cultures. Like traders, travellers and colonizers, missionaries were agents of cultural change. The processes of education and literacy which they helped to promote inevitably opened countries up to external influences, for better or worse. It would be a caricature of the indigenous cultures, however, to imply that they were static prior to the missionaries' arrival, and it has been suggested that to characterize them as passive recipients of foreign influence is to underestimate their resilience. In the African context, there is evidence that local cultures demonstrated a capacity for creative adaptation in the face of both Muslim and Christian expansion into their lands.[52]

As men and women of their time, missionaries generally shared the prevailing assumptions of Western cultural superiority, a view that seemed to be corroborated by impressive scientific and scholarly advances; although there were notable exceptions, their attitudes towards local cultures were often negative or paternalistic. Cultures were not seen as religiously neutral, and many elements appeared to conflict with Christian ethics, especially when these were interpreted in the light of Victorian values. In practice, however, missionaries' actual experience and contact with colonized peoples modified their attitudes, and many were prepared to distinguish between the 'innocent usages of mankind' and customs seen as actually contravening the teachings of the gospel.[53]

One modern scholar of missions has drawn attention to an element of missionary activity which had the effect of affirming and promoting indigenous cultures, namely the translation of the Bible into local vernaculars.[54] Given the close relationship between language and culture, this involved a degree of cultural adaptation on the part of the translators, and the accompanying compilation of grammars and dictionaries helped to preserve local languages which were in some cases under threat from the lingua franca of the region. Paradoxically, the translation process not only helped to imbue converts with a sense of national or ethnic pride, thereby contributing to national independence movements and precipitating the end of colonial rule, but also gave them the tools with which to challenge the foreign missionaries' authority on specific matters.[55]

Now that the link between Christianity and Western civilization has become more tenuous, Western Christians find it easier to take a critical view of the latter.[56] In retrospect, it is not difficult for contemporary Christians to draw a distinction which was presumably not easy to make at the time: 'the error of nineteenth-century missionaries . . . was to mistake the contingent values of one particular philosophical tradition – the Enlightenment – for the eternal values which the Christian counter-culture must seek to express'.[57] Christians view the age of missions and colonialism as a historical phase which has now passed, to give way to an era in which indigenous Church leadership and cultural diversity are taken for granted, and in which Third-World Christianity is itself an active contributor to both the missionary enterprise and the theological tradition. For Muslims, however, the page is not so easily turned, and the memory of past subjugation is constantly renewed by the manifestions of neo-colonialism in the present.

Muslim–Christian Dialogue

The Christian ecumenical movement arose in part from the missionary movement. The first three international missionary conferences in Edinburgh (1910), Jerusalem (1928) and Tambaram (1938), provided a forum both for theological reflection on the significance of other faiths and for a new emphasis on intra-Christian unity and collaboration. The World Council of Churches, founded at Amsterdam in 1948, now comprises over 300 members, including most Protestant and Orthodox denominations, with Catholic and Uniate Churches having observer status. Due to the great variety of trends and views represented in the WCC it has not usually been able to issue unified and authoritative statements in the manner of the Vatican; nevertheless, its formation represented a significant step in the direction of Christian co-operation and unity.

It was not surprising that the new spirit of openness among Christians should eventually carry over into Christian attitudes towards those of other religions, giving rise to the interfaith movement which has in recent decades found expression in organized dialogue. The Vatican set up its Secretariat for Non-Christian Religions (now the Pontifical Council for Interreligious Dialogue or PCID) in 1964, with the aims of promoting the study of other religious traditions and sponsoring interfaith dialogue.[58] The Commission for World Mission and Evangelism of the World Council of Churches established a sub-unit on Dialogue with People of Living Faiths and Ideologies (DFI) in 1971, with both practical and theoretical aims: to promote good relations with members of other faiths and to reflect on the theological basis of relations between Christians and non-Christians.[59] Both have been active in organizing interfaith meetings at various levels and on a variety of themes since about 1970, and they have sometimes co-operated to this end.[60]

The dialogue movement has been preceded and accompanied by much thinking about the relationship of Christianity to other religions. Prior to the modern age this has sometimes been expressed in the dictum: 'no salvation outside the Church' (*extra ecclesiam nulla salus*), a formula originally used against schismatic Christians. This view was often upheld by theologians and church leaders concerned to strengthen Christian identity and establish the boundaries of the Christian community. Although some thinkers have upheld a distinction between general revelation, available to all (e.g. through nature or reason), and special revelation, located in the particularity of scripture and the events it portrays, and although the operation of God's grace was not generally seen as being confined to the Church, such ideas were rarely translated into positive attitudes towards other religions (indeed, pre-modern Christians scarcely thought in terms of a plurality of 'religions'). Nevertheless, there have always been thinkers, such as Justyn Martyr (d. *c*.165) and Thomas Aquinas (d. 1274), who have acknowledged that wisdom and truth may be found in non-Christian systems of thought. Among other things, the intellectual evolution of Western thought since the Enlightenment and the actual encounter with non-Christians have combined to provoke new departures and greater sophistication in Christian thinking about other religions in the contemporary period.[61]

Many Christian theologians have found it useful to speak in terms of three broad theological positions vis-à-vis other faiths: exclusivism, inclusivism and pluralism. These represent a continuum rather than three distinct positions, and there is considerable variety within each category. Exclusivism is closest to the traditional view. It stresses the particularity of the gospel as God's definitive revelation, and tends to emphasize the discontinuity between Christianity and other faiths. However, an extreme exclusivist position which holds that there is no possibility of salvation apart from membership of the Christian Church is now relatively rare among theologians. There are different types of exclusivism; some exclusivists are primarily concerned with issues of truth rather than soteriology, and there is a respectable tradition of refraining from pronouncing on the salvation of non-Christians.[62] Inclusivism retains the idea of salvation being effected through Christ, ontologically speaking, but asserts that this can happen implicitly, through the structures of people's own religions, particularly in the case of those who have not heard the gospel. It tends to stress the continuity between Christianity and other religions, and view them as being fulfilled or finding their completion in the gospel. The pluralist position commonly sees all religions as on a par, being imperfect human attempts to seek after God and all equally likely to lead to salvation.[63] Pluralism has been growing in popularity but is still only held by a minority of Christian intellectuals, while inclusivism of one form or another is becoming increasingly prevalent within the World Council of Churches and represents the official position of the Catholic Church since the Second Vatican Council (Vatican II).

The documents which issued from Vatican II (1962–5) represented a significant change in official Catholic attitudes towards other faiths. To some extent Vatican II was an acknowledgement of ideas that were already current among some members of the Church, especially those in close contact with members of other faiths. The most sustained passage concerning Muslims is contained in *Nostra Aetate* (Declaration on the Relationship of the Church to Non-Christian Religions). Since the wording is rather delicately balanced, it is worth reproducing in full rather than paraphrasing:

> Upon the Muslims too, the Church looks with esteem. They adore one God, living and enduring, merciful and all-powerful, Maker of Heaven and earth, Speaker to men. They strive to submit wholeheartedly even to His inscrutable decrees, just as did Abraham, with whom the Islamic faith is pleased to associate itself. Though they do not acknowledge Jesus as God, they revere Him as a prophet. They also honour Mary, His virgin mother; at times they call on her, too, with devotion. In addition they await the day of judgment when God will give each man his due after raising him up. Consequently, they prize the moral life, and give worship to God especially through prayer, almsgiving, and fasting.

Although in the course of the centuries many quarrels and hostilities have arisen between Christians and Muslims, this most sacred Synod urges all to forget the past and to strive sincerely for mutual understanding. On behalf of all mankind, let them make common cause of safeguarding and fostering social justice, moral values, peace, and freedom.[64]

Elsewhere it is stated that 'the plan of salvation also includes those who acknowledge the Creator. In the first place among these are the Moslems, who, professing to hold the faith of Abraham, along with us adore the one and merciful God',[65] while another passage claims that 'the Catholic Church rejects nothing which is true and holy in these [non-Christian] religions'.[66] In the light of other statements contained in Vatican II, however, it is clear that the positive appreciation of elements of other religions was not understood as negating either the final and definitive nature of God's revelation in Christ or the need to communicate the gospel to non-Christians.[67]

Some Catholics, as well as some Muslims, have regretted that no mention (and therefore no explicit affirmation) was made either of Muhammad or the Qur'an. The relevant passages usually seek to relate to Muslims rather than Islam, and cautiously refrain from formulating an explicit theological position; this in any case would not have been feasible given the difficulties which were already experienced in arriving at an agreed final draft.[68] Muslim reaction to Vatican II has been predictably mixed; while some have welcomed it as a marked improvement on previous attitudes, others have been disappointed that it does not adopt a pluralist theological position. Some also perceive a certain paternalism in its wording.[69] Whatever its limitations, however, the least one can say is that the Council has been instrumental in encouraging a more positive and respectful attitude towards those of other faiths. The PCID's *Guidelines for Dialogue between Christians and Muslims*, written by Maurice Borrmans (1990, originally published in French in 1981), provides a good example of the outworking in detail of the transformation in Catholic attitudes towards Islam.

For their part, Muslims have been slow to initiate and participate in organized dialogue. It is only very recently that a few established organizations have began to consider dialogue as part of their brief, and the few Muslim initiatives have tended to be on the official governmental level, for example in Libya, Tunisia and Jordan.[70] The problem of representation is not easy to resolve on the Muslim side; governments do not necessarily have strong Islamic credibility, the '*ulamā*' (Muslim religious scholars) are not always willing to participate, and when they do they are often either representing their governments or constrained by government views.[71] Most of those who have participated as individuals have been from the liberal end of the Islamic spectrum, often resident in the West or having spent time there.

There are many reasons for Muslims' hesitancy with regard to dialogue. The dialogue movement has on the whole been a Western Christian initiative, and Muslims express a sense of being invited guests, of not having set the agenda, and of feeling they have little to gain.[72] The belief that Christian missions were an adjunct of colonialism feeds a mistrust of Christian motives, and dialogue is feared to be a covert form of evangelism; the awareness that Christians have figured prominently among 'orientalists' (pejoratively understood), fuels suspicions that Christians are incapable of viewing Islam dispassionately. No less importantly, Muslims are deterred by what they see as Western-perpetrated global injustice, especially the Israeli–Palestinian conflict. Muslim inhibitions therefore appear to arise more from historical and political rather than intrinsically religious factors, and some Muslims argue that dialogue is not only acceptable but imperative in Islam.[73] Nevertheless, even when they are willing to engage in dialogue, Muslims tend to have different priorities to Christians. They often feel there is little to gain from debating theological issues (which may be seen as divisive),[74] and tend to be more concerned with the economic and political problems of their co-religionists in the developing world.

There is no agreed definition of dialogue; it functions as an umbrella term covering many different kinds of activity. Organizationally, dialogue can take place at various levels, ranging from the governmental to the grass-roots. Theorists have enumerated several different types and aims of dialogue.[75] Categories which are usually mentioned in these typologies (although the nomenclature varies) include the 'dialogue of life', which is the spontaneous dialogue which takes place wherever religious communities live in proximity to one another;[76] 'discursive dialogue', which essentially consists of an exchange of information and operates on the level of debate and intellectual enquiry, and which may be seen as a prerequisite for other types of dialogue; the 'dialogue of needs', which focuses on areas of practical co-operation such as social justice and ecological issues; and 'spiritual dialogue', which may include shared prayer and contemplation, and devotional reading of each other's scriptures and spiritual classics. What one hopes to achieve through dialogue will be related to one's theological presuppositions and existential situation; while some envisage a shared spiritual adventure, others may feel that the most important aim is to reduce political conflict. Many testify that it can be a means of understanding one's own faith better as one sees oneself in the mirror of 'the critical eyes of the other'.[77]

It is generally agreed that dialogue requires an attitude of openness, mutual respect and a willingness to listen to the other. It is sometimes further assumed that participants need to modify their beliefs in order to engage in meaningful dialogue with others. The best known instance of this is the view of pluralists John Hick, Alan Race and others that Christians need to move from a Christocentric to a theocentric position (this becomes further diluted to a 'realitycentred' position when non-theistic religions are involved).[78] Others, however, argue that to require the abandonment of the central tenets of a religion as a prerequisite to participation would act as a deterrent, and feel that the aim of dialogue is to see and understand the 'other' as they really are, rather than to arrive at theological agreement or reduce the different religions to a lowest common denominator.[79] There will therefore be a tension in which 'conviction and openness are held in balance'.[80] It is sometimes pointed out that openness implies a degree of risk and vulnerability, and that if one is not changed in the process, no true encounter will have taken place.[81] Some therefore argue that 'conversion' in the general sense of a change of heart, as opposed to the specific sense of a change in religious allegiance (although the latter cannot be ruled out), is an essential part of the dialogue process if it is truly reciprocal.[82]

The thorny issue of the relationship between dialogue and mission has exercised many minds. Christians and Muslims at either extreme of the theological spectrum – pluralist or conservative/exclusivist – are likely to see dialogue as antithetical to mission or *da'wah*, believing that one compromises the other. The most representative statements on the Christian side, both Catholic and Protestant, have not seen a contradiction between the two, although conversion is not seen as the primary aim of dialogue.[83] Dialogue and mission (frequently the less assertive term 'witness' is preferred) are both seen as essential religious duties, neither obviating the need for the other. Many would add that the two cannot be separated–dialogue, to the extent that it involves referring to one's own beliefs, inevitably includes an element of 'witness', while mission in the broadest sense, which covers a wide range of phenomena from institutionalized proselytization to 'presence theology',[84] and which may not involve verbal evangelism at all, must necessarily encompass the dialogue process. It may even be explicitly held that to invite another to one's faith in the context of dialogue is not a question of 'spiritual or institutional imperialism', but represents 'the highest compliment that one man can pay another', and concerns 'the right of man to change'.[85] Muslims have not produced an equivalent literature on the relationship between *da'wah* and dialogue, but it seems that they are increasingly coming to view dialogue as a part of *da'wah*.[86]

In some respects, the position of mainstream Muslims is comparable to that of conservative evangelical Christians, who initially at least expressed strong reservations about dialogue, fearing that it would lead to religious syncretism and compromising the essentials of faith.[87] Some have since become more open to the idea of dialogue, sometimes on the understanding that it should include in some form an invitation to the gospel.[88] Muslims concerned with *da'wah* and evangelical Christians are likely to give priority to 'discursive dialogue'; at the very least this may serve to eradicate distortions and misunderstandings and thereby eliminate obstacles to conversion. Some feel that the aim of dialogue is 'the removal of all barriers between men for a free intercourse of ideas where the categorical imperative is to let the sounder claim to the truth win'.[89] Dialogue may also be a means of becoming better acquainted with what the 'other' actually believes in order to facilitate the communication of the message to them in an appropriate form.[90]

The theoretical issues raised by dialogue are of relevance to the ways in which Muslims and Christians relate to and perceive one another. Some of the different attitudes, aims and assumptions which have been reviewed will reappear in the writings of authors discussed, many of whom have been active participants in organized dialogue.

Notes

1. Smith, *The Meaning and End of Religion*, p. 79.
2. Rahman, 'A Muslim Response', p. 69.
3. See Kronholm, 'Dependence and Prophetic Originality in the Koran', pp. 52–60, for a useful survey of scholarship in this area.
4. Robinson, *Christ in Islam and Christianity*, p. 33.
5. For a detailed study of these forms of Christianity, see A. S. Trimingham, *Christianity Among the Arabs in Pre-Islamic Times* (London: Longman, 1979). Useful summaries are given in K. Cragg, *The Arab Christian: A History in the Middle East* (London: Mowbray, 1992), chapter 2; Robinson, *Christ in Islam and Christianity*, chapter 3; and Watt, *Muslim–Christian Encounters*, chapter 1.

6. Robinson, *Christ in Islam and Christianity*, pp. 21–2.
7. See Lazarus-Yafeh, *Intertwined Worlds*, chapter 3: 'Ezra-'Uzayr: The Metamorphosis of a Polemical Motif'.
8. Watt states forthrightly that 'it is clear that for a modern person the Qur'anic perception of Christianity is seriously inadequate and at some points erroneous', and adds, 'it is important, however, that the Christian of today should not take this as a reason for denying that Muhammad was inspired by God' (*Muslim–Christian Encounters*, p. 24).
9. See on this point Fueck, 'The Originality of the Arabian Prophet'; Kronholm, 'Dependence and Prophetic Originality in the Koran'; Waldman, 'New Approaches to "Biblical" Materials in the Qur'an'.
10. Brinner, 'Prophets and Prophecy in the Islamic and Jewish Traditions', p. 68.
11. This view is reinforced by a well-known Hadith to the effect that 'every child is born with a true faith of Islam (*'ala al-fiṭrah*) but his parents convert him to Judaism, Christianity or Magianism' (al-Bukhārī, *Ṣaḥīḥ al-Bukhārī*, vol. 2, p. 247, no. 441).
12. Useful overviews of this material are given by Watt, *Muslim–Christian Encounters*, chapter 2, and Sherif, *A Guide to the Contents of the Qur'an*, pp. 130–7.
13. Robinson lists Qur'anic verses on Christianity in order of Nöldeke's chronology, and concludes that there is an identifiable evolution in attitudes (*Christ in Islam and Christianity*, pp. 27–33). He stresses the need for caution, however, since there is no uniform agreement on the exact chronological order of the revelations.
14. See, e.g., 2:75; 2:109; 2:111; 4:171; 5:14; 5:18; 5:81.
15. See, e.g., Cragg, *Jesus and the Muslim*; J. Michaud, *Jésus selon le Coran* (Neuchatel: Editions Delachaux et Niestlé, 1960); Parrinder, *Jesus in the Qur'ān*; H. Raisenen, *Das koranische Jesusbild. Ein Beitrag zur Theologie des Korans* (Helsinki: Missiologian ja Ecumeniikan, 1971), and 'The Portrait of Jesus in the Qur'an: Reflections of a Biblical Scholar' (*MW*, 70, 1980); Robinson, *Christ in Islam and Christianity*, and 'Jesus and Mary in the Qur'an: Some Neglected Affinities', (*Religion*, 20, 1990). For a succinct account of Jesus in the Qur'an see ''Isā', *EI²*.
16. Parrinder lists some variant interpretations in *Jesus in the Qur'ān*, pp. 31–2.
17. See 'al-Mahdī', *EI²*.
18. Kerr, 'The Problem of Christianity in Muslim Perspective', p. 154.
19. See McAuliffe, *Qur'ānic Christians*, pp. 286–90.
20. Wijoyo, 'The Christians as Religious Community', p. 88.
21. For Hadiths which urge the distinctions, see Muslim, *Ṣaḥīḥ Muslim*, vol. 3, p. 965, no. 4366, and al-Bukhārī, *Ṣaḥīḥ al-Bukhārī*, vol. 1, p. 334–5, no. 578. For the latter type of Hadith, see *Ṣaḥīḥ Muslim*, vol. 2, p. 406, no. 1862, and *Ṣaḥīḥ al-Bukhārī*, vol. 4, p. 441, no. 665.
22. Wijoyo, 'The Christians as Religious Community', pp. 95ff.
23. See, e.g., Daniel, *Islam and the West*, and *Islam, Europe and Empire* (Edinburgh: Edinburgh University Press, 1966); Hourani, *Europe and the Middle East*, and *Islam in European Thought*; Rodinson, 'The Western Image and Western Studies of Islam'; Southern, *Western Views of Islam*; Sweetman, *Islam*

and Christian Theology; Watt, *Muslim–Christian Encounters*. See also 'Bibliographie du dialogue islamo-chrétien' in issues of *Islamochristiana* from 1975 onwards.

24. See 'Dhimma', *EI²*.
25. For a one-volume treatment see H. E. Mayer, *The Crusades*, trans. J. Gillingham (Oxford: Oxford University Press, 1988).
26. Lewis, *The Muslim Discovery of Europe*, p. 22; Charfi, 'Polémiques islamo-chrétiennes à l'époque mediévale', p. 272.
27. See D. Sahas, *John of Damascus on Islam: The 'Heresy of the Ishmaelites'* (Leiden: Brill, 1972).
28. Daniel, *Islam and the West*, p. 15.
29. See A. Khoury, *Les Théologiens byzantins et l'islam, textes et auteurs (VIIIᵉ–XIIIᵉ siècle)*, 2nd ed. (Louvain and Paris: Editions Nauwelaerts, 1969), and *Polémique byzantine contre l'islam (VIIIᵉ–XIIIᵉ siècle)* (Leiden: Brill, 1972).
30. Southern, *Western Views of Islam*, p. 31.
31. Joseph, 'Islam: Its Representation in the West', pp. 82–3.
32. On these two, see Southern, *Western Views of Islam*, pp. 86–94.
33. For examples, see Hourani, 'Islam and the Philosophers of History', in *Europe and the Middle East*.
34. See, in general, P. Almond, *Heretic and Hero: Muhammad and the Victorians* (Wiesbaden: Harrassowitz, 1989), and in particular Thomas Carlyle's treatment of Muhammad in *On Heroes and Hero-Worship* (London: Chapman and Hall, 1841).
35. In the former category, one could mention F. D. Maurice and C. Forster, and in the latter, W. Muir and W. St Clair Tisdall. Bennett includes these in his *Victorian Images of Islam*, which analyses the writings of six nineteenth-century Christian thinkers who are characterized as either 'conciliatory' or 'confrontational'.
36. Examples of the former include St Francis of Assisi (d. 1226) and Ramon Lull (d. 1316), while the latter tendency is exemplified by the Cordoba Martyrs of Spain in the ninth century, and Martin Luther and other German Protestants preoccupied with the Ottoman Turkish expansion in the sixteenth: see Southern, *Western Views of Islam*, pp. 19ff., 104–7.
37. For studies of individual Muslim polemicists, see the bibliographies in *Islamochristiana*. Brief surveys of Muslim polemical writings on Christianity can be found in Lazarus-Yafeh, *Intertwined Worlds*, esp. chapters 2 and 6, and Waardenburg, 'World Religions as Seen in the Light of Islam'. More detailed studies are Anawati, 'Polémique, apologie et dialogue islamo-chrétiens'; Charfi, *Al-Fikr al-Islāmī fī'l-Radd 'ala al-Naṣārā ila Nihāyat al-Qarn al-Rābi'*, and M. Steinschneider, *Polemische und apologetische Literatur in arabischer Sprache* (Hildesheim: Olms, 1966, repr. from 1877).
38. Waardenburg lists the most relevant ones in 'Types of Judgment in Islam about Other Religions', p. 138.
39. Lewis, *Cultures in Conflict*, p. 13.
40. Lewis, *The Muslim Discovery of Europe*, pp. 172–4.
41. Badawi, *Islam in Britain*, p. 26. See also al-Faruqi, 'Islamic Ideals in North America', p. 269, and Murad, *Da'wah among Non-Muslims in the West*, p. 8.

42. See generally Poston, *Islamic Da'wah in the West*, and *The Oxford Encyclopaedia of the Modern Islamic World*, ed. J. Esposito, s.v. 'Da'wah'.

43. See Siddiqui, 'Muslims' Concern in Dialogue', pp. 148ff., and S. von Sicard, 'Contemporary Islam and its World Mission' (*Missiology*, 4, 1976).

44. Siddiqui, 'Muslims' Concern in Dialogue', p. 177.

45. See, e.g., Askari, 'Christian Mission to Islam', p. 328; al-Faruqi, 'Islam and Christianity', pp. 6–7; von Denffer, *Some Reflections on Dialogue*, p. 16.

46. See 'Statement of the Conference on "Christian Mission and Islamic Da'wah"' in *Christian Mission and Islamic Da'wah*, ed. E. Castro et al., pp. 100–1, and Sardar, 'The Ethical Connection', p. 61.

47. See, e.g., al-Faruqi, *Islam*, p. 68.

48. Sardar, 'The Ethical Connection', p. 61.

49. Ibid., p. 58. See also Rasjidi and Barwani, 'Christian Mission in the Muslim World', and the series of case studies on Christian mission to Muslims published by the Islamic Foundation in Leicester.

50. See Ayoub, 'Roots of Muslim–Christian Conflict', pp. 34ff. for examples.

51. Stanley, *The Bible and the Flag*, p. 70.

52. Sanneh, 'Christian Experience of Islamic Da'wah', p. 54. See also T. Ranger's contributions to *Religion, Development and African Identity*, ed. Petersen, esp. pp. 42, 153.

53. Stanley, *The Bible and the Flag*, pp. 158–60.

54. See L. Sanneh, *Translating the Message: The Missionary Impact on Culture* (Maryknoll, NY: Orbis, 1989), and 'Christian Missions and the Western Guilt Complex'.

55. Sanneh, 'Christian Missions', p. 332.

56. See, e.g., the writings of Lesslie Newbigin, especially *Foolishness to the Greeks: The Gospel and Western Culture* (Geneva: WCC, 1986), and *The Gospel in a Pluralist Society* (Grand Rapids: Eerdmans, 1989).

57. Stanley, *The Bible and the Flag*, p. 173.

58. Two important journals on Muslim–Christian relations, the annual *Islamochristiana* and the monthly *Encounter – Documents for Muslim–Christian Understanding*, are published by the Pontifical Institute for Arabic and Islamic Studies (PISAI) in Rome.

59. Mulder, 'Developments in Dialogue with Muslims', p. 155.

60. Chronological listings of Christian–Muslim meetings organized by these two bodies and other groups are contained in M. Borrmans, *Guidelines for Dialogue between Christians and Muslims (Pontifical Council for Interreligious Dialogue)*, trans. R. Marston Speight (New York: Paulist Press, 1990), and Siddiqui, 'Muslims' Concern in Dialogue', pp. 187–96. *Christians Meeting Muslims: WCC Papers on 10 Years of Christian–Muslim Dialogue* (Geneva: WCC, 1977), and S. Brown, *Meeting in Faith: Twenty Years of Christian–Muslim Conversations Sponsored by the World Council of Churches* (Geneva: WCC, 1989), contain some of the key texts issuing from the WCC-sponsored colloquia. For a general overview, see C. Kimball, 'Muslim–Christian Dialogue', in *The Oxford Encyclopaedia of the Modern Islamic World*, ed. J. Esposito.

61. For surveys of recent thinking see G. D'Costa, *Theology and Religious*

Pluralism: The Challenge of Other Religions (Oxford: Blackwell, 1986); Knitter, *No Other Name?*; A. Race, *Christians and Religious Pluralism: Patterns in the Christian Theology of Religions* (Maryknoll, NY: Orbis, 1983).

62. Both Karl Barth (d. 1968) and Hendrik Kraemer (d. 1965), the two most eminent exclusivist theologians of this century, believed in the possibility of salvation for non-Christians.

63. Collected essays arguing for a pluralist position are contained in J. Hick and P. Knitter (eds), *The Myth of Christian Uniqueness: Toward a Pluralistic Theology of Religions* (London: SCM Press, 1987).

64. Abbott (ed.), *The Documents of Vatican II*, p. 663.

65. Ibid., p. 35.

66. Ibid., p. 662.

67. Yates, *Christian Mission in the Twentieth Century*, pp. 167ff.

68. Robinson, 'Massignon, Vatican II and Islam as an Abrahamic Religion', pp. 194–5.

69. See, e.g., al-Faruqi, 'Islam and Christianity', p. 29.

70. Siddiqui outlines the position on dialogue of the World Muslim Congress, the Muslim World League (both with headquarters in Mecca), the World Islamic Call Society of Libya, and the Al Albait Foundation of Jordan.

71. See M. Borrmans, 'The Muslim–Christian Dialogue of the Last Ten Years', p. 35; and Siddiqui, 'Muslims' Concern in Dialogue', pp. 59, 175.

72. One of Siddiqui's interviewees sees dialogue as 'an extension of a whole Western Christian domination' ('Muslims' Concern in Dialogue', p. 59).

73. See, e.g., Abedin, 'Dawa and Dialogue'; Askari, 'The Dialogical Relationship between Christianity and Islam', p. 42; Ghrab, 'Islam and Christianity', p. 42.

74. See Abedin, 'Dawa and Dialogue', pp. 54–5; al-Faruqi, *Christian Ethics*, p. 3; Talbi, 'Islam and Dialogue'.

75. Useful typologies of dialogue are included in D. Eck, 'What do we mean by Dialogue?' (*Current Dialogue*, 11, 1986); E. Sharpe, 'The Goals of Inter-Religious Dialogue', in *Truth and Dialogue: The Relationship between World Religions*, ed. J. Hick (London: Sheldon, 1975); and the 1984 publication of the Vatican's Secretariat for Non-Christian Religions on mission and dialogue: *The Attitude of the Church Toward the Followers of Other Religions: Reflections and Orientations on Dialogue and Mission*.

76. This is commonly regarded as the most important type of dialogue: see, e.g., the WCC's *Guidelines on Dialogue*, p. 19, and Borrmans, 'The Muslim–Christian Dialogue of the Last Ten Years', p. 16.

77. D'Costa (ed.), *Christian Uniqueness Reconsidered*, p. xix, citing Jürgen Moltmann.

78. See J. Hick, *An Interpretation of Religion* (London: Macmillan, 1989) for the shift to a 'realitycentred' position.

79. Lochhead, *The Dialogical Imperative*, pp. 90ff.; World Council of Churches, *Guidelines on Dialogue*, p. 13.

80. World Council of Churches, *Guidelines on Dialogue*, p. 16.

81. Moltmann, 'Christianity and the World Religions', p. 194.

82. Knitter, *No Other Name?*, pp. 211–2.

83. See World Council of Churches, *Guidelines on Dialogue*, pp. 11 and 16, and van

Lin, 'Mission and Dialogue', p. 171. Post-conciliar Catholic texts which deal with this issue are analysed in R. Fitzmaurice, 'The Roman Catholic Church and Interreligious Dialogue: Implications for Christian–Muslim Relations' (*ICMR*, 3, 1992), and in L. Pruvost, 'From Tolerance to Spiritual Emulation' (*ISCH*, 6, 1980).

84. This idea was pioneered by Charles de Foucauld (d. 1916), who spent the last sixteen years of his life living as one of the Touareg in Algeria, and whose vocation has been described as 'one of being present among people with a presence willed and intended as a witness to the love of Christ' (M. Warren, in the preface to K. Cragg's *Sandals at the Mosque*, p. 12).

85. Drummond, 'Toward A Theological Understanding of Islam', pp. 200–1.

86. Siddiqui, 'Muslims' Concern in Dialogue', pp. 76–7. See also von Denffer, *Some Reflections on Dialogue*, p. 18.

87. See A. Glasser, 'A Paradigm Shift? Evangelicals and Interreligious Dialogue' (*Missiology*, 9, 1981).

88. A clear expression of this is found in the words of David Hesselgrave: 'Any form of dialogue that compromises the uniqueness of the Christian gospel and the necessity that the adherents of other faiths repent and believe it should be rejected and supplanted by forms of dialogue that enjoin conversion to Christ' ('Evangelicals and Interreligious Dialogue', p. 126). On the Muslim side, Khurram Murad expresses a similar view more prosaically: 'there is no point in entering into dialogue unless it is *Da'wah*' (Siddiqui, 'Muslims' Concern in Dialogue', p. 76).

89. Al-Faruqi, 'Islam and Christianity', p. 9. John Stott, a prominent Anglican evangelical, similarly envisages an important aim of dialogue to be 'that the truth should emerge', as in the Platonic tradition ('Dialogue, Encounter, Even Confrontation', p. 171).

90. As Stott puts it, 'dialogue puts evangelism into an authentically human context' (ibid., p. 170). See also Brewster, 'Dialogue: Relevancy to Evangelism', p. 516.

two

MUSLIM POPULAR
LITERATURE ON
CHRISTIANITY

M uslim popular literature here roughly designates that which is easily available in Muslim outlets in the West and widely circulated; a relatively high proportion of literate Muslims will be exposed to at least some of it, and to that extent it merits the epithet 'popular'. This material fulfils a primarily apologetic function and is not always considered or intended to be a contribution to *da'wah per se*; its function and readership, therefore, does not correspond particularly closely to that of Christian missionary literature on Islam, which is described in chapter 3.

In a survey of Muslim polemic during the Abbasid period (i.e. the eighth to thirteenth centuries), the Tunisian scholar Abdelmajid Charfi identifies several functions of this material in relation to the situation then pertaining. In the early Abbasid period when the Muslims still constituted a ruling minority there was a need to demonstrate the superiority of Islam vis-à-vis the non-Muslim majority and to assert the originality of Islam in order to prevent its dilution by already existing religions (especially Christianity). Other possible motives which would have operated at different times and places were the need to integrate new converts and counteract their continuing Christian susceptibilities; jealousy of highly qualified Christians whose skills were needed in the new administration; and the need to justify discriminatory measures against non-Muslims.[1] Then, as now, the polemic was primarily addressed to fellow Muslims rather than Christians. The situation of Muslims may have greatly changed since the early centuries of Islam, but anti-Christian polemic continues to have a *raison d'être* and an appeal.

While there is a relatively high degree of continuity with the medieval polemic with regard to some of the themes, such as the role of St Paul and the identification of alleged errors and contradictions in the Bible, the function of such material has been subject to some evolution. Given the close identification in Muslim writings between Christianity and the West, a primary factor must be the still-fresh memory of the colonial experience, compounded by the continuing economic and political dominance of Western countries. In these circumstances, some dignity at least can be preserved by the claim to moral and religious superiority. In a situation where there has been a real risk of being absorbed into a more powerful 'other' (which finds an echo in the danger of assimilation among Muslims who emigrate to the West) the polemic serves to reinforce the lines of demarcation between self and 'other'. A small but growing proportion of this literature, particularly in the Western context, also aims to convert Christians to Islam. A further reason for the continuing validity of religious disputation is the model provided by the Qur'an itself, which engages Christians (as well as pagans and Jews) in argument over their beliefs. Muslim participants in public debates with Christians sometimes invoke the following verse at the beginning or end of the proceedings: 'If anyone disputes with you concerning him [i.e. Jesus] after the knowledge which has come to you, say: "Let us gather together our sons and your sons, our women and your women, ourselves and yourselves, and pray and invoke the curse of God on those who lie"' (3:61).[2]

For the most part this literature is an intra-Muslim phenomenon. A good illustration of the divide between Muslim and non-Muslim literature is the so-called Gospel of Barnabas (not to be confused with the apocryphal Epistle of Barnabas). In its present form it originated as an Italian manuscript discovered in Amsterdam in the eighteenth century; it appears to date back to the sixteenth century and to have no prior textual tradition.[3] Since being translated into Arabic early this century, it has been widely acclaimed by Muslims as a more authentic record of Jesus' life than is offered by the four canonical Gospels. Purporting to be an original eye-witness account of Jesus' life, it portrays Jesus in accordance with Qur'anic teachings: he aspires only to the status of prophethood and denies being the Son of God, gives specific prophecies of Muhammad and acts as his forerunner. In accordance with a common interpretation of Qur'an 4:157, Judas is made miraculously to take on Jesus' likeness and is crucified in his place. The account draws extensively on the four

Gospels and demonstrates considerable familiarity with both the Old and New Testaments, and it contains several features which suggest a medieval context.[4] It contradicts the Qur'an in a few particulars, for example referring to Muhammad rather than Jesus as the Messiah, and stating that Mary gave birth to Jesus without pain. While Western (especially Christian) scholars, in the face of Muslims' continuing acceptance of the Gospel at face value, have been at pains to demonstrate that it is a forgery, neither its appeal nor its circulation have diminished. Although one or two Muslims have, in academic articles, dismissed the Gospel of Barnabas as a counterfeit,[5] the vast majority who express an opinion about it assume it to be genuine.[6] The issue demonstrates that the function of such literature is of overriding importance, fulfilling as it does certain needs which take priority over academic considerations.

When speaking of contemporary Muslim attitudes towards Christianity, it is scarcely possible to avoid reference to Ahmed Deedat (b. 1918). The extensive popularity and influence of his works are unquestionable, and for this reason it seems appropriate to attempt some description of his activities and publications, even though they are undeniably inauspicious for Muslim–Christian relations. Deedat is a South African of Gujurati origin who has achieved near-celebrity status among many Muslims for his rebuttals of Christianity. He received no formal religious training and his academic knowledge of Christianity appears to be quite limited. His lecture tours have taken him to Europe, the United States, and many Muslim countries, some of which have broadcast his debates on national television networks. His pamphlets are often distributed free of charge, and these, as well as video and audio tapes of his lectures and debates, are widely available in Muslim bookshops and have been translated into several languages. In 1986 he received international recognition when Saudi Arabia awarded him the prestigious Feisal award for services to Islam. Christians who have participated in debates with Deedat include the Americans Jimmy Swaggart and Josh McDowell, and Anis Shorrosh, a Palestinian Christian. Both the original audiences and the consumers of the resulting products have been predominantly Muslim.

Deedat states that he began his activities in response to charges made against Islam by Christian missionaries, and he urges Muslims to launch a counter-offensive by actively pursuing *da'wah* to non-Muslims. One pamphlet concludes with the remark that his efforts would have been worthwhile 'if even one sincere disciple of Jesus . . . were to be led to the truth and be removed from fabrications and falsehood'.[7] The lampooning of missionaries occupies a prominent place in Deedat's publications. Missionary or 'born again' Christians are regularly referred to as 'Bible-thumpers', 'hot-gospellers', 'cultists', and 'crusaders'. Their main characteristics are aggressiveness on the one hand, and duplicity on the other. He refers to the 'menace', 'tyranny' and 'ruthless attacks' of 'these slinking missionaries',[8] and writes that 'in the current crusade, the Christian world has launched their "scud" (The Holy Bible) in two thousand different languages'. The translation of the Bible into Arabic dialects is described as a 'Christian onslaught'[9] and Christians deploying mission ships in Indonesia are said to 'invite the native for refreshment and entertainment on board the ship and subtly initiate them into their blasphemy'.[10]

Deedat's flamboyant rhetorical style seems as much designed to entertain as to edify; he employs ridicule and sarcasm, and not infrequently raises laughter from the Muslim section of his audience. He also utilizes crude language and images which seem designed to shock. His arguments against the divinity of Jesus, for example, tend to focus on bodily functions, including the more intimate ones, and he implies that Christians believe that Jesus was the product of a physical act of procreation between God and Mary.[11]

Deedat acknowledges that he has been strongly influenced by Rahmatullah's *Izhar ul-Haqq*, and he draws on it extensively when impugning the biblical text. The *Izhar* is a seminal work for modern Muslim refutations of Christianity; it is a product of the Muslim–Christian debates in nineteenth-century India and more specifically a response to the German missionary Carl Pfander's *The Balance of Truth*.[12] In his pamphlet *Is the Bible God's Word?*, Deedat expounds the errors, contradictions and 'multiple versions' (which include variant translations) of the Bible, and goes so far as to recommend that the Bible should be censored on the grounds that it constitutes pornographic literature (p. 49). After relating some of the less savoury incidents which occur in the Old Testament, he claims a causal connection between the 'rapes and murders, incests and beastialities [*sic*]' of the Bible with the contemporary moral and social decay in Western nations (p. 47). He comments that 'you will come across perverted people who will gorge this filth', and adds that 'such filth certainly has no place in any "Book of God"'.[13]

It is a sobering thought that Deedat gains more exposure than any of the writers cited in this chapter, although strictly speaking the quality of his work, which after all hardly aspires to go beyond the level of rhetoric and apologetic, is poor even by the standards of religious polemic. It is on the basis of both quality and genre (as with Christian missionary literature, tracts were not incorporated) that his works have not been included in the material used below, although one does sometimes find some of his points or anecdotes reproduced in other works.

This chapter draws on sources which were available in Muslim bookshops in the West. The results of tentative enquiries suggest that there is a high degree of continuity between the sources circulated in different parts of Europe and America. In fact, of the eighteen main works reviewed, ten were published in the Indian subcontinent, five in North America, and three in the United Kingdom. The only material which was deliberately excluded was books of particularly poor quality or which made no useful contribution, in that they said nothing which had not already been said more effectively in other sources. The approach was empirical, with the topics treated arising more or less organically from the material studied, but emphasis has been laid on those elements which represent new departures with respect to the classical period. Hence a substantial portion of this chapter is devoted to the relationship between Christianity and modern Western civilization and the characterization of contemporary Christians, whereas there is little specifically on doctrine.[14]

Several of the authors are Western converts to Islam. Maurice Bucaille is a French neurosurgeon, Maryam Jameelah an American Jewish convert who emigrated to Pakistan, while Abdalhaqq Bewley and Ahmad Thomson are members of the Darqawi Sufi order based in Norwich, England. Ruqaiyyah Waris Maqsood, an English convert from Christianity, is something of an exception in this chapter for three reasons: she has some training in Christian theology; her style is non-polemical; and her publisher is the Christian SCM Press – the only non-Muslim publisher of all works cited in this chapter. It is debatable whether her work could be considered 'popular' in the same sense as the others, and in some ways it could more appropriately have been included in the chapter on Muslim intellectuals. In fact, her book falls into an intermediate category, since it is not strictly speaking an academic work, and has been included in this chapter because of its greater thematic continuity with the topics which arise here.

The majority of the rest originate from, and mostly still live in, the Indian subcontinent. The exception is Adeleke Ajijola, a Nigerian lawyer who was educated in missionary schools in Nigeria and graduated from King's College, London. Ahmad Azhar was also educated in a Christian school, in Pakistan, and spent four years in London working for the Pakistan High Commission. Among the more learned in the Islamic sense are Muhammad Ansari, who graduated from Aligarh, Kauser Niazi, an Imam who held various posts in Bhutto's government, and Muhammad Taqi Usmani, a Muslim jurist who has served as a judge on the Shariat Appellate Bench of the Supreme Court of Pakistan. His book originally formed the introduction to an edition of Rahmatullah's *Izhar ul-Haqq*, which he himself edited and translated into Urdu. Muhammad 'Ata ur-Rahim was a colonel in the Pakistani army and has spent some time in England; he clearly has a connection with the Darqawi Sufi order since the introduction to his book is contributed by its leader, Shaykh 'Abd al-Qadir al-Sufi, and the author also acknowledges the help of Thomson and Bewley. Ulfat Aziz-us-Samad teaches English in the University of Peshawar, while Professor Mahmud Barelvi is a Pakistani who has lived and worked in the Middle East and Africa, as an educationalist and as Director of External Affairs for the Islamic Congress in Cairo. Dr Abdul Hamid Qadri appears to have a connection with the Da'wah Academy of the International Islamic University of Islamabad, while Akbarally Meherally is an ex-Ismaili who was educated in Bombay and now lives in Canada. Ahmed Shafaat, another resident of Canada, is a lecturer in Maths and Business Statistics. He is of Pakistani origin and has spent time in Saudi Arabia and in England, at the Islamic Foundation in Leicester. Virtually no information is available on Professor Jaliluddin Ahmed and Dr M. H. Durrani, except that the latter temporarily converted to Christianity and the places of publication of their books indicate a connection with Pakistan and India respectively.

It emerges that these authors are mostly professionals with little or no formal training in Christianity; most have acquired what knowledge they have through private reading. This indicates a relatively low level of institutionalization for this type of religious apologetic. The fact that six writers (Ajijola, Azhar, Barelvi, Durrani, Niazi and Ansari) make explicit mention of the fact that they are responding to Christian polemic or missionary activity indicates the degree to which the Muslim polemic continues to be a reactive phenomenon, as was the early modern literature such as *Izhar ul-Haqq*.

Page references given in the text refer to the following titles of the authors cited: J. Ahmed, *Christianity: Its Appeal, Reaction and Failure*

(1994); Ajijola, *Myth of the Cross* (1979); Ansari, *Islam and Christianity in the Modern World* (1965); 'Ata ur-Rahim, *Jesus, Prophet of Islam* (1991, first published 1977); Azhar, *Christianity in History* (1991, first published *c*.1968); Aziz-us-Samad, *A Comparative Study of Christianity and Islam* (1986, first published 1971); Barelvi, *Islam and World Religions* (1983, first published 1965);[15] Bewley, *The Key to the Future* (1992); Bucaille, *The Bible, the Qur'an and Science: The Holy Scriptures Examined in the Light of Modern Knowledge* (1978); Durrani, *The Qur'anic Facts about Jesus* (1992); Jameelah, *Islam Versus Ahl al-Kitab: Past and Present* (1989, first published 1978); Maqsood, *The Separated Ones: Jesus, the Pharisees and Islam* (1991); Meherally, *Understanding the Bible through Koranic Messages* (1989); Niazi, *Mirror of Trinity* (1991, first published 1975); Qadri, *Dimensions of Christianity* (1989); Shafaat, *Islam, Christianity and the State of Israel as Fulfillment of Old Testament Prophecy* (1989); Thomson, *Blood on the Cross: Islam in Spain in the Light of Christian Persecution through the Ages* (1989); Usmani, *What is Christianity?* (1987). Full details of these titles are given in the Select Bibliography.

The Bible: Text and Interpretation

All the authors in this chapter who write on the subject believe that the actual text of the Bible, and not just its interpretation, was corrupted in the process of its compilation. Equally, however, all appeal to verses from the Bible to support their views, either on the basis that some authentic passages have survived, or because some verses can be reinterpreted rather than rejected, or simply in order to put forward a hypothetical argument which is based on premises that one's opponents can't reject.

The collection of the New Testament is generally presented as an arbitrary process. The following quotation from 'Ata ur-Rahim represents views that are fairly widely held: 'In 325 A.D., the famous Council of Nicea was held. The doctrine of the Trinity was declared to be the official doctrine of the Pauline Church, and one of the consequences of this decision was that out of the three hundred or so Gospels extant at that time, four were chosen as the official Gospels of the Church. The remaining Gospels, including the Gospel of Barnabas, were ordered to be destroyed completely' (p. 40). No reference is given for the alleged destruction. Azhar is more explicit in seeing the New Testament as the outcome of a power struggle between heretical Christians (i.e. the followers of Paul) and the true Christians: 'Wherever the original record did not conform to the doctrines dear to the new (Gentile) cause espoused by neo-enthusiasts like Paul . . . such record was first condemned, then carefully destroyed and finally nonchalantly declared as "lost"' (p. 30).

The process of the collection of the Bible is seen as categorically different from that of the Qur'an, with no parallels acknowledged. The role of the oral tradition, for example, seen as positive in the case of the Qur'an and, usually, the Hadith, is used only as an argument for unreliability in the case of the Bible.[16] Similarly, the role of the criterion of apostolicity as applied in canonical selection has strong echoes in the idea of the *isnād* (chain of narrators), but the only writer even to mention apostolicity is Barelvi, who alone concedes that the canon of the New Testament was more or less agreed upon by the end of the second century (p. 183). On the other hand, one or two writers do draw parallels between the collection or authenticity of the Hadith and that of the Bible. According to Bucaille, 'the collection of hadiths are to Muhammad what the Gospels are to Jesus . . . their authors were not eyewitnesses'; he draws a clear-cut distinction between these and the Qur'an, which is unique in being free from contradictions (pp. 125, 251). Maqsood complains that few Muslims have taken the trouble to inform themselves on the subject of Christian form criticism, and that most of them 'do not even bother to study the Christian Bible on the grounds that it is all legendary material and not reliable', despite the fact that 'the same arguments can be made regarding the Hadith', which Muslims sometimes elevate almost to the same level as the Qur'an (p. 178).

Although *taḥrīf* has usually been taken to apply to alterations made to the biblical text before Islam, the process of distortion is sometimes believed to be ongoing. Different translations are sometimes assumed to be significantly different 'versions' of the text.[17] While Christians consider that continuing research into early manuscripts or the discovery of new ones gives rise to an ever more accurate scripture, for many Muslims any slight alterations to the text which may result, for example, from the discovery that a given verse is not in the earliest manuscripts, is scandalous; they find no Islamic equivalent for this, and habitually contrast this situation with that of the Qur'anic text which was fixed at an early period. Ajijola states that 'the instances of the verses which have now been removed can be multiplied to any number', and wonders 'how the words of God can be removed or amended at the whim of the Church Leaders?' (p. 102). He alleges that several verses or phrases were deleted from the biblical text, not due to manuscript evidence but in response to difficulties Christians encountered in controversy with Muslims in the nineteenth century (pp. 107–10). One example given is the omission of the phrase where Jesus speaks of the necessity of both prayer and fasting to drive out certain kinds of demons (Matt. 17:21); Ajijola attributes this omission to the fact that a belief in the efficacy of fasting would support the idea of salvation by works rather than faith.

Several authors refer to the Dead Sea Scrolls. Qadri asserts that their discovery has 'rendered many "sacred and trusted" chapters of the Bible liable to drastic revision, as a result of which many Christian dogmas, so devoutly adhered to in the past, are likely to fall to the ground' (p. 40). 'Ata ur-Rahim claims that portions of the Dead Sea Scrolls have been withheld from publication because they contradict 'the post-Nicene manuscripts' (p. 196). The interpretation of the actual significance of the Scrolls tends to be via selected Western writers; Meherally follows F. E. Peters in the opinion that the Scrolls show Jesus' movement to be 'a fairly ordinary type of Jewish reform' (pp. 86–7), while Ajijola quotes Stendhal's opinion that the ramifications of the Scrolls mean that Christianity should be 'understood as an episode of human history rather than propagated as dogma and divine revelation' (p. 101). Shafaat makes use of the Scrolls to support the view that Muhammad was predicted in the Christian scriptures (pp. 23–7), while 'Ata ur-Rahim and Thomson use them in support of the theory that Jesus was an Essene.[18]

Not unexpectedly, the biblical text and its compilation are viewed according to Islamic rather than Christian categories. A view of revelation which sees the human as excluding the Divine, and vice versa, is an obvious case in point. Barelvi asserts of the Bible that 'instead of being a book written by God in heaven, it is a literary collection containing history, law, biography, hymns, oratory, proverbs, visions, dreams, epigrams, and even erotic love stories' (p. 3), on the assumption that it could not be both simultaneously, while Jameelah describes the Gospels as 'apocryphal biographies written *about* Jesus in a language utterly foreign to him' (p. 200). While it is generally accepted in Christian scholarship, and is indeed a basic assumption of form criticism, that the Gospel writers had differing backgrounds and wrote for different audiences, or that the New Testament writings reflect the concerns of the early Christian community, for Muslims such considerations are likely to be seen as invalidating the scriptures. Aziz-us-Samad, for example, maintains that the Gospels were 'composed to propagate the special teachings of the different schools and their authors showed no hesitation in tampering with the . . . material regarding the life and teaching of Jesus Christ to bring them in line with the views of their schools' (p. 10), while Bucaille says more plainly that 'the evangelists make Jesus say whatever suits their own personal outlook' (p. 66).

Much Muslim biblical interpretation is on a fairly basic and unsophisticated level. The two areas of greatest continuity with the medieval period are the citation of alleged errors and contradictions in the Bible and the identification of verses which predict Muhammad. In view of the Qur'anic assertion that the former scriptures and Jesus himself foretold the coming of Muhammad (7:157, 61:6), there is a widespread if not unanimous belief that the extant Bible contains verses predicting Muhammad's mission. Lists of such verses are usually no different from those that were drawn up in the medieval period; they are often the same verses that Christians have understood as referring to Jesus.[19]

The most elaborate and original treatment of this subject is given by Shafaat. In his *Islam, Christianity and the State of Israel as Fulfillment of Old Testament Prophecy*, he deals with it in the larger context of messianism and biblical prophecy as a whole. A major concern of his work is to refute the idea that the present State of Israel represents a fulfilment of biblical prophecy, and to this end he emphasizes the tentative and often non-literal nature of Old Testament prophecy (pp. 77–8). However, the author himself also sees world events in apocalyptic terms, believing, for example, that the sufferings of the Jews in the modern age have been directly attributable to their nationalistic exclusivism (pp. 66–7) and that Israel is 'probably doomed to destruction' (according to the author's understanding of certain Hadiths) unless the Jews turn to Islam (pp. 72–3). He advances the thesis that John the Baptist, Jesus and Muhammad form a 'messianic trinity' which was foretold or alluded to in the scriptures of all three Abrahamic religions (p. 19). The author explains that despite the Qur'an's use of the title 'the Messiah' for Jesus, 'it does not define the sense of the title . . . nor does it tell the story of Jesus in a way that would allow us to recognize Jesus as the Messiah in any established sense of the title' (p. 22). Shafaat prefers the view that Jesus was just 'one of the agents of the fulfillment of messianic prophecies' (p. 21). In relation to the Old Testament passages that have been understood as speaking of the suffering of a future messianic figure, the author affirms that 'the road to achievement of noble goals . . . passes through suffering . . . not due to any fault of the sufferer's but due to the sinfulness of others' (p. 90). He claims that these passages apply less to Jesus than to Muhammad, who endured 'the most terrible kinds of suffering for a long period of 13 years' (p. 85); in particular 'the story of Muhammad's life parallels that of the suffering servant of Is[aiah] 53, if due allowance is made for the dramatic and poetic element in the song' (p. 90). The aforementioned arguments, as well as the author's broad definition of messianism as the fulfilment of universal religious or materialistic hopes, enable him to contend that Muhammad has a messianic role which equals or surpasses that of Jesus, in contrast to mainstream Muslim belief.

The treatment of contradictions and errors does not seem to have evolved noticeably since the medieval period; alleged contradictions are sometimes based on a very superficial reading of the text. Qadri's list of these, for example, includes 'alternate promises (Mt. vi: 33; xix: 29) and denial (Mt. x: 34–35) of temporal blessings'.[20] Bucaille feels that the contradictions contained in the Gospels are such that 'there can be no doubt that a complete reading of the Gospels is likely to disturb Christians profoundly' (p. 44), and repeatedly alleges that problematic areas are glossed over in publications for mass consumption (pp. 2, 9, 45, 49, etc.). He has a more holistic approach to the text than most, and makes selective use of modern scholarly research in areas such as the chronology of Jesus' last days and the resurrection appearances, although, like others, he considers the fact that one Gospel mentions a particular circumstance whereas another does not, to constitute a contradiction (pp. 94–108).

Another common feature is the selection of particular texts which support one's case, while ignoring other texts which may contradict it or declaring them to be later interpolations. One fairly common example of this is the reproduction of verses from the Gospels which emphasize Jesus' humanity or portray him as subservient to God, without referring to other verses which intimate a unique status for Jesus.[21] However, there is an occasional attempt to reinterpret such passages in order to harmonize them with Jesus' humanity. Usmani reproduces Gospel passages which refer to Jesus as saving people from their sins, giving his life as a 'ransom for many', and pouring out his blood for the forgiveness of sins. He interprets these to mean that 'Jesus is willing, in order to save people from misguidance and to give them the means of causing their previous sins to be forgiven, to even sacrifice his life' (pp. 48–9). The Gospel of John, commonly regarded by Muslims as the least reliable of the Gospels because of its doctrinal content, as well at its probable later date, is nevertheless appealed to by many both for texts which emphasize Jesus' humanity and for those which are seen as predicting the coming of Muhammad.[22] At times, the meaning of verses is distorted or even reversed by being taken out of context. One example of this occurs in no less than three separate sources; Paul's saying: 'For if the truth of God hath more abounded through my lie unto His Glory; why yet am I also judged a sinner?' (Rom. 3:7–8), is taken to be a cynical ends-justifies-means argument and an admission of dishonesty on Paul's part, even though the verse in question is immediately followed by Paul's condemnation of such reasoning.[23]

By contrast with such atomistic treatments of the text, the two most sustained and sophisticated examples of biblical interpretation, interestingly, are offered by converts: Bucaille and Maqsood. Bucaille's *The Bible, The Qur'an and Science* represents an attempt to demonstrate that while the Qur'an does not contain 'a single statement that [is] assailable from a modern scientific point of view', the Bible contains 'statements totally out of keeping with the cast-iron facts of modern science' (p. viii). He feels that Christian interpreters of the Bible have avoided 'a frank and thorough comparison with scientific ideas', since 'they realize that this would lead people to contest notions about the truth of Judeo-Christian Scriptures, which have so far remained undisputed' (p. 20). His work is of particular interest in that it looks at the Bible and the Qur'an in parallel, thus raising questions of comparative methodology.

Bucaille declares his intention to exclude 'religious problems' such as the virgin birth and God's appearance to Moses, since these are mysteries that have no scientific explanation (p. viii). He feels that 'a belief in divine miracles and in science is quite compatible: one is on a divine scale, the other on a human one' (p. 82). However, he does not attempt to provide any objective criteria for deciding what is to be treated as miracle, in which God suspends the ordinary laws of nature, and what is to be tested against the criteria of modern scientific knowledge. His approach seems to allow for the possibility of religious considerations superseding scientific ones when he states that the Qur'an 'does not aim at explaining certain laws governing the Universe . . . it has an absolutely basic religious objective' (p. 121).

In Bucaille's view, there are three main problem areas in the Old Testament: the stages of the creation of the universe, the date of the earth's creation and of man's appearance on it, and the description of the Flood. The latter is taken (with some textual justification) to be universal in the Bible but not in the Qur'an, with the result that the Bible, but not the Qur'an, is seen as contradicting archaeological evidence (pp. 215–7). The alleged date of the Creation according to Christians (and Jews) is based on the genealogical material contained in the Bible and is in harmony with calculations of the Orthodox Jewish calendar, according to which the earth is now some fifty-seven centuries old (pp. 29ff). Bucaille does not address the fact that very few Christians actually believe this, nor does he discuss Christian understandings of the genealogies, any attempt to harmonize them with modern knowledge being considered 'cunning dialectics' (p. 32).

When one observes Bucaille's treatment of the biblical text alongside his treatment of similar features in the Qur'anic text, it becomes clear that he applies rather different criteria to each. With regard to the Creation story, Bucaille describes the Genesis account as 'a masterpiece of inaccuracy from a scientific point of view' (p. 22), one example of this inaccuracy being the fact that the creation of light and the succession of night and day are mentioned before the creation of the sun. Bucaille takes the accounts literally and makes no reference to literary style or poetic language; in fact, he explicitly rejects 'the excuse that the Biblical authors were expressing ideas in accordance with the social factors of a different culture or mentality' (p. 37). However, he harmonizes an alleged contradiction in the Qur'anic text wherein one passage (41:9–12) which describes the Creation appears to add up to eight days rather than six and does not relate the events in their correct scientific order, by suggesting that it may be 'a simple reference to events juxtaposed without any intention of bringing in the notion of the one following the other' (p. 137); the same reasoning could presumably be used to harmonize the Genesis accounts. Bucaille states that 'the idea that successive phases of the Creation . . . could have been compressed into the space of one week is one that cannot be defended from a scientific point of view' (p. 27). At first sight this is surprising, since the Qur'an also states that the creation took 'six days'. Bucaille's explanation for this is that while the word 'day' is to be understood metaphorically as 'period' in the Qur'an, in the Bible it is to be understood literally as twenty-four hours. In this connection he mentions a Qur'anic verse which speaks of 'a day whereof the measure is a thousand years of your reckoning' (32:5), but omits to mention an almost identical biblical verse

(2 Pet. 3:8); nor does he refer to the fact that the same Semitic word for 'day' is used in the Qur'anic Arabic and the original biblical Hebrew.

More fundamentally, Bucaille claims that 'passages in the Qur'an, especially those relating to scientific data, are badly translated and interpreted', and that the older commentators 'could not possibly have understood the real sense of the word or phrase which has only become clear in the present day thanks to scientific knowledge'. In the light of this, he feels it is necessary to undertake new translations and interpretations. Without explaining why, he adds that 'these problems of translation are not present for the texts of the Judeo-Christian Revelation: the case described here is absolutely unique to the Qur'an' (pp. 118–9). With reference to passages of the Qur'an that are expressed in poetic rather than scientific language, such as the one which speaks of God 'raising the canopy' of the heavens, 'spreading out' the earth and 'fixing firmly' the mountains (79:27–33), Bucaille states that this is 'expressed in a language suited to farmers or nomads on the Arabian Peninsula'.[24] Citing a verse which speaks of God 'stripping the night of the day', Bucaille explains that it 'simply provides an image' (p. 163); the Qur'an, unlike the Bible, is thus permitted to be couched in descriptive or poetic rather than scientific language. Bucaille's method clearly allows a great deal of freedom in eisegesis (reading things *into* the text), as opposed to exegesis (drawing things *out of* the text), a technique which has met with resistance from Muslim religious scholars in the past, and which has generally been more characteristic of Christian than Muslim scriptural interpretation.

Bucaille's is therefore an interesting but not impartial attempt to demonstrate that Islam is more in keeping with modern science than is Christianity.[25] It is nevertheless noteworthy as being an extremely popular book, which has been translated into many languages, both Islamic and European, and which, of all Muslim writings on Christianity in European languages, is probably second only to Deedat's pamphlets in terms of breadth of circulation. This is no doubt due to the fact that it combines a demonstration of the superiority of Islam over Christianity with the 'scientific' exegesis of the Qur'an, an increasingly popular form of apologetic, as witnessed by the proliferation of publications which enumerate the scientific elements in the Qur'an as proof of its miraculous nature (*i'jāz*).

Maqsood's *The Separated Ones: Jesus, the Pharisees and Islam* is refreshingly non-polemical in style, although her approach assumes that the Gospels do not constitute an altogether faithful representation of

Jesus' ministry. Her book is not so much an original contribution to biblical interpretation as a synthesis of the findings of certain scholars. Maqsood draws on recognized and relatively recent sources in her chosen area, namely the identification of continuity between the teaching of Jesus and that of the Pharisees.[26] This continuity stands in tension with the negative attitude towards the Pharisees in certain passages of the Gospels, and Maqsood concludes, as do some of her sources, that these were invented or elaborated on by the Gospel writers for their own purposes.

What is of interest here is the Islamic dimension the author brings to her work. She regrets that 'Pharisaism' has become a pejorative term, 'and has cast a virtually ineradicable slur upon those believers who were "muslim", submitted in every aspect of their lives . . . to the will of God' (p. 172). The God-consciousness which Maqsood sees as being epitomized in the concept of 'the Hedge', supplementary rules intended as a safety-net to ensure that the Pharisees didn't fall into error, is likened to the Muslim concept of *taqwā*, or piety (p. 6), and she points out that 'the Pharisees and later the Muslims considered that the whole of human life ought to be capable of holiness, not just one's activities at certain times and in certain places. Nothing in human life was considered too trivial to be beneath the divine concern [*sic*]' (p. 77).

Maqsood perceives a strong element of continuity between the Islamic and the Jewish understanding of religious law, and defends both against any charges of dry legalism, commenting that the Pharisees, 'like the Muslims of today, certainly did not regard the *Halachoth* [the Jewish law] as a burden but as a joy' (p. 60). She further comments that 'like the Muslim *ulemah* [religious scholars] exercising *ijma* [consensus] and *ijtihad* [juristic reasoning], the Pharisees saw it as their key role to save the religious life of those who submitted to God from stagnation, from "bull-headed" blind obedience to an archaic set of commands' (p. 39). Maqsood feels that Muslims and Pharisees have more in common with each other than with Christians, for the religious law 'was a system in which humans had dignity and honour, in which they could work out their redemption for themselves, by the sweat of their own brows, or the loving care of their own hands, and the warmth of their own hearts', in contrast to 'trinitarian Christian theology, which taught that no matter how good a person managed to be, the cards were still stacked against them because of the "original sin" of Adam' (pp. 60–1). However, another dimension of Pharisaism identified by Maqsood is closer to Christianity even in its trinitarian form: 'believers had to become like children before their Father, not appealing to any rights or merits, but simply willing to love, and to be given a gift in return' (p. 62). She emphasizes such things as the concern with the spirit and not just the letter of the Law, and the love of debate among Pharisees, and sees the teachings of Jesus in general and the Sermon on the Mount in particular as demonstrating 'a very powerful Pharisaic influence' (p. 146).

Maqsood is unusual among Muslims in expressing sympathy for the Pharisees; most Muslims believe that the rationale for the sending of the Christian revelation was at least in part to counteract or modify Jewish legalism, as exemplified by the Pharisees. Apart from the assumption that Christians were wrong to abandon the religious law, surprisingly few Muslims explore the possibility of a *rapprochement* with Judaism in order to highlight the deviation of Christianity;[27] this may be because the Qur'an on the whole speaks more favourably of Christians than of Jews. Maqsood's view also tends to diminish Jesus' actual prophetic contribution even in the Islamic sense, since he becomes rather less distinctive vis-à-vis other religious figures of his day.

The Jesus of the Gospels and the Jesus of the Qur'an

Many Muslim writers draw a distinction between the real Jesus, as portrayed in the Qur'an, and the Jesus of the New Testament, the latter being accepted only to a limited degree. Azhar claims that, in the past, Christian missionaries have been free to insult Muhammad, secure in the knowledge that Muslims could not retaliate because for them Jesus was a revered Prophet; he suggests that viewing 'the Jesus of the Christian Gospels and the Isa of the Quran' as absolutely distinct from each other frees Muslims from a 'pseudo-Islamic respect for the Christian Jesus'.[28] Often a complete discontinuity is envisaged between Jesus on the one hand and Christianity on the other; Qadri says that 'it is generally, though wrongly, claimed that Christianity sprang from the teachings of Jesus', while 'Ata ur-Rahim holds that 'present-day Christianity is a "mask" on the face of Jesus . . . the Muslim believes in the Jesus of history and refuses to accept the "mask"'(p. 1).

In the light of the distinction between the Christian and the Islamic Jesus, whether or not it is made explicitly, the Jesus of the Gospels may be spoken of disparagingly. Ajijola expounds on the evidence for the 'sins of Jesus' in the Gospels. These include the fact that he was baptized by John, when John's baptism was 'for the forgiveness of sins'; the fact that he offered wine to people; and, something which is mentioned by several authors, the fact that he treated his mother 'with contempt' on two occasions (p. 40). Since these are widely cited by Muslim authors, they are worth reproducing; one was at the wedding in Cana when Jesus' mother approached him to help out with the shortage of wine, and received from him the reply: 'Woman, what have you to do with me?' (John 2:4), while the other was an occasion when his mother and brothers were waiting to speak to him, and he asked: 'Who is my mother, and who are my brothers? . . . Whoever does the will of my father in heaven is my brother and sister and mother' (Matt. 12:48–50).[29] Pointing out that such conduct does not even qualify as ordinarily decent behaviour, since 'respect for mothers is a common virtue even among primitive communities', Ajijola concludes that in giving credence to such incidents 'Christians do not hold Jesus in half the reverence in which they hold the fabricated Gospels' (p. 123). Azhar feels that the two incidents show that according to Jesus, 'woman and family are things to be shunned' (p. 114), while Aziz-us-Samad draws even more far-reaching conclusions: 'There is nothing in the reported sayings of Jesus which might serve as an incentive to raise the status of women. His whole attitude towards the female sex was one of distrust, as is clear from his treatment of his own mother. The polemic against the family in the Gospels is a matter that has not received the attention that it deserves' (pp. 148–9).

According to Durrani, 'Jesus committed acts of violence as well as deceit'. The example given for the former is the driving of the money changers from the Temple, while the latter are said to include Jesus' telling the Jews that he would raise the Temple in three days (when in fact he was referring to his own body), and giving his disciples the impression that the final judgement would come before they died (pp. 12–13). Jesus' prayer in Gethsemane to have the cup of suffering taken away and his uttering the words: 'My God, my God, why have you forsaken me?' from the Cross are seen by some as unworthy of a prophet, and as falling short even 'from the point of view of ordinary human virtues'.[30]

One or two writers venture outside the Qur'anic witness in their search for the historical Jesus, sometimes in ways which sit uneasily with the Islamic view. Azhar, for example, on the subject of alleged miracles performed by Jesus, which he rejects, mentions with apparent approval how Renan 'dilates upon Jesus's ignorance of the positive science of the day and shows him as a man confusing the mundane with the miraculous' (p. 60). He also cites Renan's description of the 'extreme frustration and morbidity of Jesus's last days', and suggests that there might be some truth in the theory that Jesus was an Essene who had to suppress his love for Mary Magdalene because of the vow of celibacy (p. 106). Easier to reconcile with the view of Jesus as an Islamic prophet is Maqsood's tentative suggestion that he may have been a Pharisee (p. 7).

'Ata ur-Rahim offers the most detailed reconstruction of the life of Jesus, almost wholly inspired by the Dead Sea Scrolls. The preface states that 'in this book an attempt is made, perhaps for the first time, to study the sacred life of Jesus, using all available sources' (p. 1); the latter include not just the scriptures and the Dead Sea Scrolls, but also 'modern research', the Qur'an and Hadith, and the Gospel of Barnabas, which 'covers Jesus's life more extensively than the other Gospels' (p. 17). 'Ata ur-Rahim speculates that Jesus was sent to the Essenes to be brought up, and subsequently became one of them – an ascetic, sworn to celibacy. This formation resulted in not only a gnostic but also a militant element to his teaching, since the author claims that the Essenes considered it a sin to recognize Roman rule and that the Jewish militants known as the Zealots were in fact a subdivision of the Essenes (pp. 22, 24). When he grew to adulthood, Jesus joined fellow-Essene John the Baptist's 'movement', and inherited the leadership on the latter's death (p. 29). Claiming that the entire Jewish resistance movement against the Romans centred on Jesus (p. 32), 'Ata ur-Rahim cites alleged historical sources to the effect that 'Jesus was the leader of a band of highway robbers numbering nine-hundred men', or that he had between 2,000 and 4,000 armed followers (the latter belief derived from 'a medieval Hebrew copy of a lost version of a work by Josephus' [p. 33]). He also describes various military conflicts in which Jesus was directly or indirectly involved (p. 34), and presents the 'cleansing of the Temple' as a military takeover, albeit an ultimately unsuccessful one. Jesus' aim in all this was not the acquisition of worldly power *per se*, but 'solely to establish worship of the Creator in the manner in which the Creator had ordained'; to this end, 'he and his followers were prepared to fight anyone who tried to prevent them from living as their Lord wished them to' (p. 34). Jesus is portrayed as an astute, if not calculating, leader: 'with foresight and prudence, he began to prepare and organise the Jews' (p. 32); he was a 'freedom fighter' who at the last 'went underground', and 'made good his escape' when Judas Iscariot was mistakenly arrested, and subsequently crucified, in his place.[31]

One or two Muslim authors use not just the Gospel of Barnabas but also Islamic sources for the life of Jesus. 'Ata ur-Rahim's work includes a chapter on 'Jesus in Hadith and Muslim Traditions'; according to the author, the latter 'were originally gathered together by the earlier followers of Jesus, especially those who spread to Arabia and North Africa', many of whose descendents and followers subsequently embraced Islam (p. 221). These Traditions can now be found in Tha'labi's 'Stories of the Prophets' (*Qiṣaṣ al-Anbiyā'*) and al-Ghazālī's 'Revival of the Religious Sciences' (*Iḥyā' 'Ulūm al-Dīn*), and they give a 'clear and unanimous picture of the ascetic prophet who prepared the way for the final Messenger' (p. 222). As in many Sufi sources, the examples which are given tend to portray Jesus as a wise teacher, often expressing himself in aphorisms, such as: 'The world consists of three days: yesterday which has passed, from which you have nothing in your hand; tomorrow of which you do not know whether you will reach it or not; and today in which you are, so avail yourself of it' (p. 223). Niazi refers to Ibn Ishaq for Jesus' genealogy via Imran, allegedly Mary's father (p. 4), and lists four persons whom Jesus brought to life, two of whom are only mentioned in a Muslim source (p. 28).

Most of the authors feel that Jesus' message was not intended to be universal, and several refer to Jesus' apparent reluctance to minister to the Canaanite woman whose daughter was demon-possessed (Matt. 15:21–28, Mark 7:24–30) and consider the famous Great Commission where Jesus exhorts his followers to make disciples of all nations (Matt. 28:19) to be a later interpolation. However, by comparison with the polemical writings of the past, a growing number of Muslims seem to be acknowledging the legitimacy of a broader role for Christianity. A few seem to be influenced by the consideration that to share what was, after all, a genuine revelation and to that extent 'good news' with all, rather than restricting it to the Jews, might be the more virtuous choice. 'Ata ur-Rahim, who portrays Barnabas as an exemplary disciple who preserved the true teachings of Jesus, holds that he did at first feel that the message should be brought to any who could benefit from it, but subsequently realized, on his travels with Paul, 'the futility of trying to spread a guidance that had only been intended for the Jews, among the Gentiles' (p. 66). Qadri is ambiguous, firstly positing that according to the Gospels, Jesus was sent only to the house of Israel, but then criticizing such exclusivism as a 'discriminational bar' which would be 'quite illogical and absurd, because such an attitude is really unbecoming of God'.[32] Maqsood presents Jesus as a Jewish reformer, yet believes that the revelation received by Hebrew prophets was wrongly confined to the Jews, thus implying that Jesus' message was also intended to be universal (p. 3). Shafaat sees the inclusion of the Gentiles as a positive development in Christianity, but feels that the Christians did not succeed in wholly eradicating Jewish particularism (p. 30). Crucial to the question of the universality or particularity of Jesus' mission is the Council of Jerusalem, as described in Acts 15, and related developments. At the Council, even disciples who are usually viewed favourably by Muslims, such as James and Barnabas, agree in principle that the message is to be shared with non-Jews. Usmani is the only one to consider the matter of the Council (pp. 58–61), and he does this primarily in order to discuss the status of the Jewish Law, but in the process he implicitly acknowledges the validity of broadening the dispensation to include the Gentiles.

When Jesus is compared with Muhammad, there is a tendency to minimize the differences between the two. Niazi expresses the common view that in trying to identify what constitutes the original teachings of Jesus, 'it is not difficult for a Muslim to decide this in the presence of the Qur'an', and that 'everyone who is not prejudiced can see that the fundamental tenets of Christ closely correspond with the basic beliefs of Islam' (pp. 19, 22–3). The essential elements of Jesus' message are summed up by one writer as being the Oneness of God, the fact that he sends revelation through the Prophets, and the Day of Judgement; another comments that 'Islam is the true religion of Jesus'.[33] Such a view tends to dilute the religious significance of Jesus as an individual; Bewley implies that Muslims could have nothing to learn from the Christian Jesus in that 'the life of Muhammad compares in every respect with that of Jesus – in compassion, in patience, in courage, in generosity, in concern for others, in simplicity of life, in intensity of worship – and is even in a certain sense more remarkable in that Muhammad lived a full human life as husband and father, trader and soldier, political leader and spiritual guide' (p. 3). Only Maqsood really portrays the character and teachings of Jesus as distinctive, commenting for example that 'there was an urgent, all-or-nothing quality to much that he said', and 'a strong eschatalogical element to his thoughts' (p. 78).

Alongside the usual Islamization of Jesus, one occasionally finds Muhammad portrayed in terms which resemble the Christian portrayal of

Jesus. Aziz-us-Samad, sometimes citing Western authors, presents Muhammad in unusually meek and mild terms: he 'never even lifted his finger against anyone . . . freely forgave all his enemies . . . was the greatest friend of the poor and the downtrodden' (p. 49); he was 'pure-hearted and beloved . . . of sweet and gentle disposition . . . sensitive to human suffering in every form', and 'tender and womanly' (pp. 50–1); he also had 'infinite love for his followers and had suffered to the utmost for them and for the truth' (p. 63).

Some assert the superiority of the historical record for Muhammad's life, contrasting Muhammad as a 'thoroughly historical character' with Jesus, whose life is 'shrouded in mystery'.[34] Aziz-us-Samad feels that the search for the historical Jesus is a hopeless quest (p. 33), although she does feel that there is indisputable historical evidence that Jesus actually existed and takes the trouble to refute individual theories which have been put forward to suggest otherwise (chapter 2). The outcome of this, according to 'Ata ur-Rahim, is that 'the physical aspect of what Jesus brought, his code of behaviour, is today irrecoverably lost' (p. 199), and Christians have been left without any definite guidance on how to live their daily lives: 'There is no record of how Jesus walked, how he stood, how he kept himself clean, how he went to sleep, how he woke up, how he greeted people', etc. This leaves a vacuum, because 'extracting a moral principle from the Gospels and trying to live by it is not the same as acting in a certain manner because it is known that Jesus acted that way in that situation. One course of action is the fruit of deductive knowledge, the other course of action is by revealed knowledge' (p. 200).

Ajijola feels that Muhammad 'transcends all the other Prophets in his moral example' and that Jesus did not reach the same spiritual heights as Muhammad, even though he 'cannot believe that Jesus was as devoid of good morals as the Gospels make him out to be' (pp. 121–2). Niazi argues in response to missionary attempts to demonstrate Jesus' superiority on the basis of his superior miracles that 'it is bad taste to compare one Prophet with another'; however, he does in fact go on to assert the superiority of Muhammad on various counts and to allege that he performed greater miracles than Jesus did (pp. 31, 36).

Several writers draw a contrast between Muhammad's success and Jesus' relative failure. Niazi comments that Jesus' miracles failed to have the desired effect, since 'no one believed in him except twelve disciples', and even one of those betrayed him (p. 35), while according to Qadri, because of the small number of followers whom Jesus was able to attract during his brief ministry, his message was 'killed in its cradle and was buried forever' (p. 73). Aziz-us-Samad concurs that 'Jesus was faced with failure throughout his life', that even his family disbelieved in him and his own mother 'doubted his sanity and wanted to take him away and keep him in confinement' (presumably a reference to Mark 3:21), and contrasts this with the case of Muhammad: 'those who knew him most intimately were the strongest in their faith in him' (pp. 61–2). Like other Muslims, she is unimpressed by the disciples, one of whom betrayed Jesus, another of whom disowned him, and all of whom deserted him in his hour of need;[35] one is aware of an implicit contrast with the Companions of the Prophet. In a tabular comparison between Jesus and Muhammad, Durrani points out that Muhammad 'wrought a mighty revolution and made the Arabs master of the then civilized world', whereas Jesus 'could not free his people from the yoke of the Romans' (p. 39).

Such ideas suggest that it was not just in intrinsic merit, but also in circumstance and timing, that Muhammad's superiority consisted. Aziz-us-Samad maintains that 'Jesus did not get the opportunity to become a perfect model for men in all walks of life as the Prophet Muhammad did. We have no doubt that if Jesus had got the chance he would have behaved exactly as the Prophet Muhammad did' (p. 56). Since he did not marry he could not become the ideal husband and father; since he didn't achieve victory over his enemies he 'had no occasion to show real forbearance and forgiveness'; and since he didn't attain power he couldn't provide a model of 'a benevolent and just ruler and judge' (pp. 56–7). Furthermore, he didn't live long enough (the author does not say how or when he died) to put his teachings into practice (pp. 64–5); Aziz-us-Samad feels that the Old Testament 'advocates massacre, condones polygamy, [and] accepts slavery', and observes that Jesus 'apparently had no time to do away with these evils' (p. 148).

There is little appreciation of aspects of Jesus' life which have no direct bearing on Islamic concerns. One might have expected the parables to appeal to those from non-Western cultures in which the art of storytelling is still very much alive, but in fact there is scarcely any reference to them, apart from a feeling articulated by one or two that they represent unnecessary circumlocution.[36] Maqsood is unusual in affirming aspects of Jesus' ministry which are usually neglected or rejected by others; these include Jesus' washing of the disciples' feet (John 13), seen as a sign of humility and service (p. 49), and his forgiveness of the adulterous woman (John 8), where he is seen as having acted with dignity and compassion.[37] Only Shafaat refers to the distinctive eschatological dimension of Jesus' teaching; he is aware that 'a few of his sayings suggest paradoxically the presence, through him, of a suprahistorical age within the historical age', but finds this creates a tension between this world and the next which 'produces almost total confusion', leaving Jesus' role in both 'painfully unclear'. This is in contrast to the Qur'an's 'clear and consistent picture of the future of man' (pp. 36-7).

Attitudes to the Sermon on the Mount (Matt. 5–7) provide a good illustration of the varying extent to which the Jesus of the Gospels is accepted. Azhar objects the most vehemently to the Sermon, and comments that it is 'flaunted by one and all Christians . . . as the best and most spiritual teaching ever offered to man by any teacher of humanity'; in view of its widespread acceptance despite its obvious inadequacies, he actually doubts 'if anybody much has had time to examine this Sermon closely or in detail' (p. 141). In his view it is not only 'pathetic and escapist' (p. 85) but also reactionary; originally intended to appease the Roman overlords, it makes a virtue out of suffering and oppression and prevents action in this world by offering consolation in the next. The idea of 'turning the other cheek' is seen as representing an 'utter lack of guts'; Azhar asks: 'If somebody looks askance at one's wife . . . should one offer him one's daughter also?' (p. 155). The idea of praying in secret is seen as a failure to set a good example and spread a good habit, and praying for daily bread is regarded as unspiritual (pp. 150–1). Aside from being 'meek and spineless', the Sermon on the Mount is also unrealistic and impracticable, and this has given rise to torture and killing throughout the history of Christendom (pp. 152–4). Azhar explains this by referring to a psychological law: 'Suppress an instinct completely, and you have laid sure foundations for the opposite instinct' (p. 155).

A few writers consider that the teachings of the Sermon form a genuine, or even central, part of Jesus' message.[38] Maqsood feels that the Sermon contains 'beautiful teachings', with which any 'submitted person' would be in accord (p. 161); she also refers to the Lord's Prayer as a 'sublime piece of teaching', similar in content to the opening Sura of the Qur'an, the Fatiha (p. 169). Only occasionally does she point out dissimilarities with Islamic teachings. She contrasts the fact, for example, that the Sermon seems to consider evil thoughts on a par with evil actions with the distinction upheld in Islam, which does not penalize evil thoughts and wherein 'one could actually earn credit if one had evil thoughts, if the outcome was that the person overcame the temptations contemplated' (p. 153). Interestingly, it is two of the three females among the authors, Aziz-us-Samad and Maqsood, who feel able to affirm the teaching of loving or praying for one's enemies,[39] even though Aziz-us-Samad feels that 'turning the other cheek' is somewhat unrealistic and not intended as a universally valid teaching (p. 135).

How and Why Christian Doctrine Became Corrupted

There is general agreement among the authors under discussion that the central doctrines of Christianity, namely the Trinity, Incarnation and redemption, formed no part of Jesus' original teachings, and that 'Christians since St. Paul's time have forgotten the message and instead taken to worshipping the Messenger'.[40] For Pauline Christianity, 'the life and teaching of Jesus while he was alive was no longer important', and there was a shift of emphasis from the human 'Jesus' to the cosmic 'Christ'.[41] Muslims are naturally led to try and identify the reasons for the perceived changes, as well as the means by which they were introduced.

The most common hypothesis is that Christianity was exposed to, or rather overwhelmed by, external influences in the early period. The weakness of the early Christians, who needed to conciliate others either in order to survive or in order to grow, is often considered a major factor in facilitating this influence: 'To please the Jews they retained the hue of Monotheism, but in order to stave off the objections of other pagan cults, they incorporated pagan trinities'.[42] Qadri, who treats this topic the most fully, maintains that 'every salient episode in the career of Jesus (as represented in the Gospels) corresponds to some episode in the myth of a god or a demi-god of the sun-worship cults. The fact is that the overwhelming onslaught of paganism penetrated every nerve and sinew of Christianity and dyed it in pagan colours. What we find in Christianity now is not the teaching of Jesus . . . but is an admixture of Greco-Roman and Egypto-Persian heathen ideas' (p. 49). Of the mystery religions, Mithraism is often singled out as having the most striking similarities to Christianity. Qadri suggests that Christianity 'was caught up between two powerful foes. Mithraism was as formidable an enemy as Judaism. This struggle for survival was quite critical . . . The personality of Jesus succumbed to the figure of Mithra, whose myth ran quite parallel to the episodes of the life of Jesus' (p. 64). Even Buddhism and Hinduism are felt to have been obvious precursors of Christianity, and Qadri states that the Buddhist and Hindu 'trinities' are identical with the Christian trinity.[43]

For the period immediately following Jesus' life, many writers seek to emphasize any divisions between Paul and the other disciples. According to Aziz-us-Samad, Paul 'despised and shunned the original disciples of Jesus' (p. 18), and 'there were bitter controversies and charges and counter-charges between Paul and his associates on the one hand and the Jerusalem community of the followers of Jesus on the other', although she observes that only 'faint echoes of these controversies can still be heard in the New Testament' (p. 115). Usmani asserts that after Paul began introducing changes to original beliefs, 'the disciples separated themselves from him completely' (p. 55). Those who remained in Jerusalem, with James at their head, are generally seen as having preserved the true teachings of Jesus until they were forced to flee in 70 CE, when 'the original faith of Jesus received a stunning blow from which it could not fully recover'.[44]

Those who refer to the Gospel of Barnabas as an authentic source for the life of Jesus often consider Barnabas to be a key figure among those who remained loyal to Jesus' original teachings. The occasion where Paul and Barnabas part company owing to a disagreement as to whether John Mark should accompany them on their missionary journey (Acts 15: 39–40) provides an opportunity to speculate that there were also doctrinal disagreements between the two.[45] 'Ata ur-Rahim elevates the status of Barnabas to the extent of having been a 'constant companion' of Jesus and even a strong influence on his thinking: 'the meeting of Jesus and Barnabas meant the fusing together of all that was best in the gnostic teaching of the Essenes and the orthodox Judaism of the Temple' (pp. 51–2). He holds that after Jesus' death 'Barnabas and his followers continued to preach and practise the Christianity they had learned from Jesus himself . . . From among them came saints and scholars respected by every sect of Christianity'. These 'followers of Jesus and Barnabas' formed small communities, particularly in Asia and North Africa, which 'retained the lifestyle of Jesus' (pp. 72–3).

This division between Paul and his followers on the one hand and James, Barnabas and other disciples on the other, is often extended in history to postulate a bipartite division throughout the early centuries of Christianity. The opponents of Paul are variously termed the 'followers of

Jesus', the Judaeo-Christians or the Nazarenes; they remained staunchly monotheistic and retained the Jewish law. Thomson holds that 'terms such as "the early Christians" and "the early Church" . . . have traditionally been used to disguise the fact that there was not one body, but two: a body of people called the Nazarenes who believed in Jesus and followed Jesus, as well as the body of people called the Christians who believed in Christ and followed Paul' (p. 18). The time-scale as to precisely when the Pauline faction became dominant varies. Bucaille maintains that at the time when the New Testament began to be written down, 'the two rival communities were engaged in a fierce struggle, with the Judeo-Christians still retaining the upper hand', but believes that the situation was reversed with the fall of Jerusalem in 70 CE (p. 52). According to Usmani, however, the two sides were fairly evenly matched for the first three centuries, but 'when . . . Christianity was declared the official state religion of the Byzantine empire, the protectors and supporters of Paul dominated the government of that day. And they not only attempted to exterminate the opponents of Paul but also to destroy all the material on which the opponents of Paul could base their arguments' (p. 71). Others extend this division through the whole of Christian history. Thomson's book, *Blood on the Cross*, purports to be 'an analysis of the interaction between the Unitarian and Trinitarian Christians' and upholds the view that 'the Trinitarian Christians . . . have always, as the historical record so clearly demonstrates, waged war both ideologically and physically on whoever affirmed the Unitarian view' (Preface). 'Ata ur-Rahim similarly asserts that 'the thread of unitarianism within Christianity has never been broken, and the movement has in fact grown in strength, surviving the continual and brutal persecution of the established Churches in the past and their indifference today' (p. 13); his list of unitarian Christians in history incorporates the more important among the early Church Fathers, including Origen, Irenaeus and even Tertullian, known for his formulations of the Trinity (p. 77).

On the subject of Paul's role in the formation of Christianity, most are more or less agreed that Christianity in its present state constitutes a 'super-structure of dogma' based on 'the whimsical musings of a self-proclaimed and self-styled apostle of Jesus'.[46] Thomson allows that Paul's influence was largely a case of 'misguided zeal' and that 'it is possible that Paul sincerely and ardently believed in his actions' (p. 7), but almost all others see him as deliberately distorting the teachings of Jesus rather than being sincere but misguided.[47] Some suggest that he was motivated by hatred, whether of 'Jewish traditions and law', or of the Jews themselves and even the Romans.[48] Here, Muslims are able to draw on the strand of biblical scholarship which observes Paul's role in the formation and elaboration of Christian doctrine. Usually the most extreme possible view of this is chosen, and Paul is held responsible for the invention of not only the essential Christian tenets and doctrines but also the basic events in the life of Jesus as portrayed in the Gospels.

According to Azhar, Paul 'allowed his zeal to outrun his veracity', and his 'rich and virile imagination . . . created the concepts of Trinity, sonship of God, Redemption, Resurrection and Miracles' (p. 69), thus outdoing the pagan religions and causing Christianity to prevail. In addition to the above, it is sometimes either said or implied that the Eucharist, original sin and even the Crucifixion were creations of Paul.[49] Some of these require Paul to have interpolated the relevant sections into the Gospels, or even to have written the Gospels himself; Ajijola believes them to be 'the sole work of Saint Paul and not Jesus'.[50] Others prefer to de-emphasize Paul's role in support of the idea that the Bible contains no reference to certain Christian doctrines; Thomson maintains that 'Paul never actually preached the divinity of Jesus nor the doctrine of the Trinity', although he prepared the way for them.[51]

That Paul was able to wield such influence is variously explained; Azhar comments with regard to Paul's ability to 'do away with the law altogether' that he 'has obviously already become so powerful that he can say anything' (p. 149), although he does not elaborate on the nature of this power. Ajijola, on the other hand, attributes Paul's ability to introduce innovations 'completely at variance with the original teachings of Jesus' to the fact that he came from 'an affluent and respectable family' and to the 'sheer force of his personality' (pp. 68–9). The true disciples of Jesus, by contrast, because of their simplicity and illiteracy, are said to have been 'utterly helpless before the onslaught of the fiery speeches and arguments of Paul and his companions' (p. 71).

In the modern as in the medieval Muslim writings on Christianity, one of the most serious or consequential errors committed by Paul is considered to be the 'abrogation' of the law, an issue which is related to the universalization of the message which was discussed in the previous section. However, the sequence of events starting with the famous vision or dream of Peter and the subsequent spontaneous conversion of Gentiles, apparently with God's blessing (Acts 10) and culminating in the Council of Jerusalem (Acts 15), at which the disciples unanimously agreed that strict adherence to the law was not required of Gentiles, are scarcely mentioned at all, even though according to the New Testament they were crucial for both developments. The one exception to this is where Usmani explains the findings of the Council as a temporary concession in order to facilitate the conversion of Gentiles, and holds that 'there was no difference of opinion amongst the disciples on the obligatory nature of the Law of Torah. All agreed that this law was in itself obligatory' (pp. 58–60).

Shafaat addresses the issues of the status of the law and the universalization of religion in the context of the relationship between the Abrahamic religions. He feels that one of the most valuable services rendered by Christianity was to broaden the circulation of the Old Testament, thus helping to provide a context for the Islamic revelation which had a 'greater affinity with the Old Testament religion than did Christianity' (p. 29). He observes that 'Islam established in the world a developed and integrated form of many of the doctrines, practices, and laws found in the Jewish scripture, such as respectively, monotheism, circumcision, and abstinence from pork' (p. 79). If for Shafaat the continuity between Judaism and Islam on the question of law makes Christianity appear aberrant by comparison, the same does not apply to the question of universalization. Here he feels that Christianity did make a positive contribution, in that it was one of two stages, Islam being the second, by which religion became detached from the nationalistic aspirations of the Jews (p. 77).

Christianity and Western Civilization

'Ata ur-Rahim expresses a commonly held view when he argues that 'the Christianity of today is inseparable from the culture of the West' (p. 205). The view of Christianity as Western (and of the West as intrinsically inhospitable to Islam) may be traced right back to the earliest period of Christianity. Thus, Jameelah writes that 'Christianity and Western civilization have been inseparable from each other ever since the time of St. Paul', the latter having transplanted Christianity from Semitic to Graeco-Roman soil (p. 351). While the Christians of Western Asia and North Africa were quick to embrace Islam, Europe by contrast evinced 'hostility and resistance to the spread of Islam', and since then 'the interests of Islam and Western civilization have always conflicted with each other' (p. 352).

A racial element is sometimes interjected. Jameelah holds that 'Christianity cannot appeal to the African or the Asian because it has always been identified in his mind (and rightly so) as the white man's religion. Christianity, the notion of the superiority of the white race and its inseparability from the aims of European imperialism are irrefutable when taken in the context of history' (pp. 362–3). She rejects any suggestion that Christianity is not a Western religion, since 'it is rather late in the day to proclaim Christianity as a religion of Asia and Africa or attempt to disentangle it from the development of Western civilization' (p. 363), and quotes a Muslim source which claims that outside Europe and the New World, 'the number of Christians is negligible' (p. 394). Only in two instances is there any reference to non-Western Christianity: Jameelah cites Ethiopia as an example of a backward Christian country in order to counter claims that Islam is responsible for the 'present-day decadence of Muslims' (p. 316), while Bewley, in support of his belief that the future of Europe is for Islam, argues that 'there is no logical reason to propose that Christianity is any more European than Islam since both have their origins in exactly the same part of the world' (p. 38).

A related theme is that of a moribund Christianity; several feel that 'Christianity is dying today in her own homelands'.[52] The lack of religion in Western countries is sometimes overstated; Ajijola, writing in 1979, claims that 'today the majority of the population in Europe and America is either agnostic, atheist or existentialist' (p. 81). The irreligion of the West may in turn be used to argue for the hypocrisy of Christian missions to non-Western countries; as Jameelah puts it, 'if the Christian missionaries were sincere, they would find more than enough work to do at home' (p. 203).

Despite the close identification of Christianity with the West, it is usually denied that the achievements of Western civilization are in any way attributable to Christianity. Jameelah accounts for these achievements as follows: 'Only the resurgence of the paganism, atheism and secular humanism of ancient Greece and Rome during the 'Renaissance', stimulated by the intellectual activity of the Muslim scientists and philosophers and the *violent rebellion against the Church*, brought about the social, economic and scientific revolution which has brought the West to its present world domination' (her italics, p. 317). Even in the presence of a fairly ubiquitous underlying anti-Westernism, in cases where a distinction is to be drawn between Christianity and the West the latter may be considered the lesser of the two evils. Thus, it is suggested that 'it is not Christianity that has civilized Europe but Europe . . . that has civilized Christianity', and it is generally held that 'the West made no progress as long as it was in the grip of Christianity'.[53] Azhar seems to wish to attribute all evils to Christianity when he claims simultaneously that 'the Emancipation of Women . . . is a Christian concept' (p. 115) and that 'in a true Christian society woman has no status whatever' (p. 97). Only Bewley portrays the decline of Christianity as detrimental to Western society, since it represented a shift in emphasis from the Creator to the created, but he goes on to argue that this decline is irreversible and only Islam can fill the resulting vacuum (pp. 35, 44).

Azhar illustrates some of the ambivalence one encounters on this theme. He is openly admiring of the achievements of Western civilization, which he describes as 'undoubtedly humane' (p. 5); further, 'the Christian world today is admittedly resplendent, the Muslim world – if you please – rotten' (p. 28), but this admiration coexists with occasional spirited anti-Western statements.[54] In contrast to some other writers, Azhar tends to overestimate the role of Christianity in the West; he describes the latter as 'Christianity-obsessed' (p. 16) and claims that it is 'afraid to offend Christianity'. This is 'because the West is so aggressive in *action* that it needs a psychologic [*sic*] compensation in *thought* . . . Both benefit from the union, both secure immunity from public censure' (his italics, p. 11). He believes that 'it is now considered axiomatic in the West that Christianity is the fountainhead of all humanizing institutions' (p. 168), and that 'the civilization that reigns today is by its artful authors presented to the helplessly imitating Eastern world as *Christian*' (his italics, p. 2). Despite such reasoning Azhar, like others, not infrequently conflates Christianity and Western civilization by using the term 'Christendom'.

There are frequent references to the West's civilizational debt to Islam, as well as to the fact that this has been insufficiently acknowledged in the West. Azhar, who has most to say on this subject, emphasizes Christian backwardness at the time of Muslims' greatest enlightenment: 'The Muslim Civilization taught these dark-age Christian Europeans all the arts and sciences forbidden at the height of Christianity; it taught them how to wash and how to spend; how to read and write and how to behave; indeed how to live'.[55] He argues that in ascending to the 'pedestal of knowledge' from which the Muslims have fallen, Europeans have in fact 'given up true Christianity – and adopted the spirit of Islam' (p. 171); the Westerner adopted 'the spirit of the Islamic progress, but with the label "Christian". The adversary had converted himself to Islam in all but *name*' (his italics, p. 166). However, the drive for knowledge in the West is motivated by greed rather than a genuine thirst for knowledge, while in the case of the Islamic civilization 'Muslims thought only of knowledge' (p. 181).

One important aspect of civilizational achievement is that of scientific discovery. Christianity's inimicality to science, both historically and intrinsically, is a common theme. Writers do not necessarily confine themselves to the enumeration of specific occasions when the Church persecuted scientists (notably Galileo), but may generalize further, for example claiming that 'in no instance did the Christian Church encourage the pursuit of knowledge' and that 'whenever anyone conceived a new idea or propounded a new theory, he was condemned by the Church as a heretic and subjugated to inhuman tortures'.[56] Ajijola claims that Christianity 'has proved an irreconcilable enemy of human advancement. It crushed science as long as it had the powers to do so and it would do the same today if the modern world allowed it' (p. 127).

Christian belief is frequently depicted as inherently irrational; its central doctrines constitute an 'unintelligible dogma' which is 'implacably hostile to reason' and 'cannot be acceptable to any person with a rational mind'.[57] Ajijola claims that Christian doctrine 'paralyzes the intellect' since 'it is based on mysteries and miracles' (p. 128); this is in contrast to Islam, whose creed is 'so simple and rational that its fundamentals cannot be easily attacked' (p. 144), and which appeals to 'reason and conscience' (p. 180). Maqsood believes that it is the habitual experience of converts from Christianity to Islam that 'logic and reason sweep in' (p. 4).

Clearly, many areas of potential or alleged contradiction between religion and science would apply equally to Islam and Christianity; in the light of this several writers attempt to explain why scientific discoveries are more problematic for Christianity than for Islam. Ahmed seeks to demonstrate that 'scientific thinking in Europe could only have been possible through cutting adrift from the tradition and control of orthodox Christianity' (p. 40). He claims that it was 'the special character of Christian Revelation which compelled scientists to eschew all references to the Supernatural', whereas 'as long as the Muslims were pioneers of science, such an attitude was not possible' (pp. 78–9). The doctrine of Incarnation, for example, 'has succeeded only in confusing the realms of the Supernatural and the Natural', which has in turn led to a division between 'Revealed Religion' and 'Natural Religion' (p. 53). The idea of original sin 'makes life on earth meaningless' (p. 151), causes a man to 'abdicate all responsibility' and to cease believing that progress is possible in history, and therefore Christianity had to be repudiated in order for any progress to be possible (pp. 51–2). Azhar maintains that in contrast to this the Islamic belief that man is born pure 'produces the self confidence that leads . . . to the spirit of inquiry and the conquest of Nature' (pp. 170–1). With reference to the Creation story, Ahmed refers to 'the retreat of Christian orthodoxy before science', but does not suggest why the creationist–evolutionist debate should have different implications for Islam (p. 75). The shift away from a geocentric universe, however, is felt to be more problematic for a religion 'where God himself becomes man and comes at a particular time in history' (p. 73).

Shafaat is the only writer to acknowledge a positive role for Christianity in the discoveries and achievements of modern Western civilization. He believes that the teaching of love in Christianity made it possible for Europe to build on the achievements of the Islamic civilization by creating 'a spirit of constructiveness which found expression in the use of science and technology for improving the lot of man'. This technology came to be seen as 'an instrument for realizing the Kingdom of God', and the Church therefore gave its support to such developments (pp. 60–1). However, he maintains that this was only possible after the Bible came to be considered less authoritative than before. For the greater part of Christian history, a different situation obtained, since 'various parts of the Christian scriptures often conflict so violently with one another that a spirit of learning, which at the very least would demand consistency in contents, would be fatal for faith'. Furthermore, Christian doctrines are not rooted in actual experience, whereas 'it is precisely such experience on which the spirit of learning is based' (p. 60). By contrast, the Islamic teaching of the Oneness of God is seen as providing 'an urge to unify and integrate observations and experiences', an urge which is 'probably the most important single impulse behind scientific developments' (p. 58).

One potential area of conflict between religion and science is that of miracles. Among those who broach the subject there is a broad spectrum of opinion, which even includes some who deny the possibility of miracles altogether, despite the fact that the Qur'an affirms, among other things, that Jesus cured lepers, healed the blind and brought the dead to life (3:49, 5:113). One explanation for this may be the belief expressed by Azhar among others that 'miracles are of the essence of Christianity; in a sense miracles *are* Christianity', which leads to the conclusion that 'if miracles are incredible, Christianity is false' (p. 54).

Ajijola argues that if Jesus had performed miracles, multitudes would have followed him (p. 20). Azhar believes that 'Jesus did not perform any miracles in the sense of an outside agency intervening and formally derogating [*sic*] the rules of nature. Nor did anybody else' (p. 67). He gives more than one explanation for the accounts of miracles contained in the Gospels; at one point he claims that they were interpolated by Paul (p. 58), while elsewhere he explains that such things as demon-possession were symptoms of hysteria or hypochondria, which could be cured by 'a mere touch of the physician'.[58] Elsewhere, Azhar speaks of 'the extreme simplicity of the minds of Jesus' disciples', who 'believed in phantoms', and 'imagined that they were surrounded by miracles; they were complete strangers to the positive science of the time' (p. 15); he even quotes with approval the opinion of Renan that Jesus believed in miracles because he *'had not the least idea of an order of Nature regulated by fixed laws'* (his italics, p. 60). He further cites Renan to the effect that the occurrence of miracles has never been scientifically verified (p. 65), and to ask why they only occur in Christian countries when the need should be greater in non-Christian countries, concluding on the latter question that 'such miracles and apparitions presuppose a quantum of credulity which is available only in Christian countries' (pp. 69–70). Among those who deny that Jesus performed any miracles, only Durrani makes any reference to the Qur'anic miracles of Jesus, and, interestingly, he singles out the one which is not contained in the Gospels, namely the creation of clay birds. He argues that this must be understood as a parable, since 'a prophet's dignity is much above such actions as the making of toy birds', and 'the act of creation is not attributable to any but the Divine Being' (p. 30).

The scepticism may extend beyond miracles to other supernatural phenomena. Ajijola rejects the idea that Jesus could have been tempted by Satan in the wilderness or ministered to by angels on the grounds that the laws of God are constant, and 'we do not have satans living visibly with men in this world, nor do we find angels doing visible services for men' (p. 114). As with the rejection of Jesus' miracles, this is surprising given that the Qur'an specifically speaks of Satan tempting people and angels fighting alongside the believers at Badr. Barelvi seems to deny any objective reality to alleged supernatural phenomena when he comments that angels 'were conceived by the Christians as real entities' (p. 32).

The authors differ as to whether Muhammad performed miracles; Azhar maintains that he didn't claim any miracles except that of the Qur'an (p. 55), and comments that 'Islam relies on truth itself, without the support of miracles'. In fact 'the miracle of Islam is rationalism'; this is in contrast to Christianity which 'lives on miracles and does not rest till every truth that it seeks to preach is buttressed by miracle' (pp. 172–3). Aziz-us-Samad quotes with approval the opinion that Muhammad did not 'delude' people with miracles (p. 109), while Meherally cites a source which mentions Muhammad's refusal to perform miracles because he 'taught respect for the world's incontrovertible order which was to awaken Muslim science before Christian' (p. 99). Durrani, on the other hand, believes that Muhammad performed many miracles but that 'Muslims did not flaunt it' (p. 31). Niazi accepts all the accounts of the miracles of Muhammad which are contained in the Hadith literature, including accounts of stones saluting him, a pillar weeping, and a tree uprooting itself and coming before him and bearing witness to the unity of God and the prophethood of Muhammad at his command (p. 35); these miracles are said to be superior to those of Jesus because they 'defy all rational explanation' (p. 36). However, Niazi, like others, sees the miracle of the Qur'an as excelling all others, since it is a miracle of intellect rather than sensual perception (p. 34).

Some seek to detract from the significance of Jesus' miracles as did the medieval writers, by referring to the fact that certain Old Testament prophets also performed miracles.[59] Others do this by offering a critique of miracles, for example by pointing out that they appeal only to an audience limited in time and place.[60] Azhar states that they appeal to the superstitious and credulous, and constitute a form of bribery to induce belief (pp. 56, 68), that they risk becoming ends in themselves instead of an aid to moral teachings, and that they become a reactionary force by offering compensation to the downtrodden (p. 61).

The attitude to the supernatural may also affect the belief in the virgin birth. Even though this is more unanimously believed by Muslims than Christians, since the Qur'an depicts Mary as saying: 'How shall I have a son when no man has touched me?' (3:47, 19:20), a few appear to deny it. Azhar, for example, states that 'the Quran has nowhere positively affirmed that Isa was born of Maryam without a human father' (p. 48). Those who draw parallels between mystery religions and Christianity in order to deny any originality to the latter often mention virgin birth as a feature in common; Barelvi, for example, after citing instances of alleged virgin births in pagan religions states that Christians 'adopted the same theory to account for the birth of Jesus' (p. 35). Durrani is ambivalent; on the one hand he vehemently objects to Christian belief, asserting that 'the lying dogma of birth by a Virgin Mother is filthily prurient and insulting in its very basis', and 'the Christian doctrines of celestial impregnation and divine begetting must be inexpressibly revolting and most hideously blasphemous' (p. 16); he attributes to Christians the belief that 'Jesus, son of Mary was born through intercourse with the Holy Ghost' (p. 17). He also asks 'What is there more degraded in male parentage than female?', echoing the Qur'anic castigation of those who attribute daughters to Allah and prefer sons for themselves (52:39). On the other hand, he seems to accept that Jesus was born without a human father when he concurs with most of the medieval and modern Muslim writers that 'the birth of Jesus is similar to the birth of Adam', and that both births simply 'manifest God's power of creation' (p. 16).

Contemporary Christianity

References to contemporary Christianity as it is practised are relatively infrequent, suggesting a largely theoretical rather than empirical approach on the part of the authors. Two recurrent themes are that Christianity is in decline and lacks the resources with which to face the modern world, and that it is fickle and changeable, having no genuine, immutable core.

Abd al-Qadir as-Sufi provides some of the most sweeping statements on the demise of Christianity in the introduction to 'Ata ur-Rahim's *Jesus, Prophet of Islam*. He writes that 'today Christianity as a body of metaphysics is frankly non-existent . . . Christianity is over. The myth has finally exploded . . . At the end of the day, Christianity was, simply, Europe. And Europe is finished' (pp. 3–6). Elaborating on its lack of spiritual resources, as-Sufi asserts that because of the 'trinitarian lie' Christianity has never been able to produce a pure gnostic tradition, and 'the result is that the spiritual impulse in this pseudo-religion is shot through with sadism, masochism, and incest'. The Church therefore is still 'grasping at every hint of spirituality outside it and trying to annexe it (e.g. Christian Zen and Jung's suggested Christian yoga)' (pp. 5–6). In short, present-day Christianity is 'a religion which at the popular level celebrates its two central rites by tying gifts to a fir tree and rolling eggs down the hill, and at the intellectual level no longer exists at all' (p. 6).

'Ata ur-Rahim refers to 'the total sickness of Christianity today' due the fact that it 'lacks a science of social behaviour': as a consequence 'the churches of the world are emptying – the mosques of Islam are filling up' (p. 205). Several others take up the theme of Christianity having nothing to offer for the guidance of society. Ajijola points out that Christianity 'never had and never will have a programme for the welfare of mankind'; it 'offers no solution to the material side of life . . . to industrial relations, family life, nor does it advocate any economic doctrine. Christianity has no social philosophy'. This is because it views the Law as a curse, therefore any definite programme 'will be part of the Law and hence a curse'.[61]

Some feel that Christianity is irrelevant to the needs of modern-day humanity. Ajijola, for example, believes that a religion such as Christianity which depends on 'magic and miracles' will 'lose its hold over the living world and will become a dead weight of obsolete rites. Its rituals and ceremonies and even its prayers will not be better than a repetition of meaningless incantations and such a religion in modern times is bound to meet with decay and death' (p. 191). Furthermore, 'Christianity is irreconcilable with modern ideas of democracy and equality of man', and its doctrines 'cannot expect any reasonable allegiance from the advanced nations of the world as it is a religion of primitive people'. It therefore 'ceases to exist in the land of culture and advancement . . . That is why education is alienating the human mind from the Church' (pp. 126–7). On an intellectual level, Christian belief 'no longer satisfies the modern mind . . . The God man of Christianity has become incredible to civilized man' (p. 193). Bewley feels that Christianity had a certain efficacy in the medieval world, but that the Christian tradition has now suffered 'irreparable damage', having capitulated to Godless ideologies; it 'has proved itself powerless to stem the flood of moral decline and there is now no way that the moral authority of Christianity can be restored in such a way as to enable it to become an effective force in the re-establishment of a balanced, safe, human society' (p. 44). He feels that only Islam can cope with the demands of the modern world, for 'the other spiritual traditions are only archaeological fragments, incomplete or altered teachings, intended for other peoples and former times' (p. 35). Bucaille maintains that 'Judaism and Christianity make no secret of their inability to cope with the tide of materialism and invasion of the West by atheism. Both of them are completely taken off guard' (p. 117). Many express the opinion that although Christianity has been obliged to give way to secularism, this is inconceivable in the case of Islam.[62]

One of the elements of Christian weakness is seen to be its disunity: because Christians do not share a divine Law or a unified mode of worship, Jameelah feels that they lack the sense of solidarity which Muslims have, so that Christians from different nations are foreigners to one another (pp. 202, 342). Christianity, or the Church, is seen by many as 'an organisation fragmented in sects beyond any sane motivation'.[63] Christians may be seen not only as disunited amongst themselves, but as holding divisive or exclusivist beliefs which are not conducive to good interfaith relations. In the words of Ajijola, 'the Christian is brought up to believe that his is the only true religion, with Judaism as a preparation for Christianity, and that all other religions are false' (p. 3). In recounting the process of her conversion to Islam Maqsood describes her growing conviction that all religions were paths to God, mentioning the well-known story of the blind men and the elephant, and her consequent rejection of Christianity since she 'could not accept that *any* one group of believers could take upon itself the right to specify by what criteria God alone would judge his people' (her italics, p. x). Nevertheless, none of the authors advocate religious pluralism as such, and none doubt that Christians have gone astray or that Islam is the true religion. Maqsood, for example, writes that 'Muslims and Jews . . . are alike in condemning trinitarian beliefs as a tragic error, a misunderstanding of reality' (p. 3), while Shafaat understands the Qur'an as saying that 'the trinitarian Christians, who deify Jesus have no hope of salvation (5:57–76) even though they may at the same time somehow affirm the unity of God (cf. 3:64)' (p. 32).

It is generally felt that there is little to choose between Protestantism and Catholicism, although saint- and idol-worship are sometimes mentioned in connection with the latter, and there is an occasional negative reference to the doctrine of papal infallibility.[64] Bucaille is highly appreciative of recent efforts on the part of the Catholic Church to initiate a *rapprochement* with Muslims, and feels there has been a genuine change of attitude (pp. ii–iv), while 'Abd al-Qadir al-Sufi, in complete contrast, describes the Vatican as 'mouthing declarations of friendship with Muslims' while at the same time being 'involved in an intellectual programme of ruthless censorship, repression and distortion of the message of Islam, of which, regrettably, we have collated powerful evidence' (pp. 4–5). The evidence is unforthcoming.

Although the Reformation is generally understood as 'the inevitable reaction against the corruption and tyranny of the Roman Catholic

Church',[65] many feel, like Qadri, that the cure was worse than the disease, since Protestantism turned out to be equally intolerant (pp. 33–4). Several express disappointment that Protestantism retained the central Christian doctrines, and that, in 'Ata ur-Rahim's words, 'Luther's revolt left Christianity essentially undisturbed' (p. 13). Some identify negative consequences of the Reformation. Jameelah states that 'the rebellion . . . against the authority of the Pope, the elimination of the priestly hierarchy, saint-worship, the use of images for worship, some of the sacraments and the abolition of monasticism have tempted some modernist Muslim thinkers to regard Protestantism as proof that Christianity is evolving closer to Islam'. However, she describes this as unjustified optimism, since the substitution of the authority of the scriptures for that of the Church 'gave every individual the license to interpret the Bible exactly as he wished, choosing and discarding according to whim, convenience and circumstance'.[66] Furthermore, the translation of the Bible into local vernaculars subjected it to 'even more corruption', while the rejection of the Pope's authority strengthened the cause of secular nationalism (p. 332). Bewley sees Luther as 'positing the supremacy of the individual over divine revelation', and thus opening the door to 'situational ethics whereby anything at all can be right or wrong according to the situation' (p. 7), while Jameelah similarly views the idea of the priesthood of all believers as having led to permissiveness and freedom to do as one pleases (p. 201). Only Barelvi speaks at all positively of Luther and his reforms, describing him, for example, as 'an honest, impetuous, heavy-set German, who linked conviction immediately and, as a matter of course, with appropriate action' (p. 199), but this diminishes in significance when one finds that the relevant passages are reproduced directly from a Western source.[67]

Christianity is often characterized as being flexible to the point of being unprincipled; 'Ata ur-Rahim remarks that 'to unbelievers and to people of other religions, it always appeared baffling how the Christians could accommodate themselves to every power-nexus that appeared' (p. 3), while Ajijola claims that Christianity is 'the ally of the successful and the victorious . . . [Christians'] faith is thus like a wax model which may be moulded into any desired shape' (p. 128). The idea that Christianity has 'sold out' to the modern world is a prevalent one. This is seen as a phenomenon that dates back to the earliest period when, according to Barelvi, it 'adopted the policy of making converts by adapting itself to their views', and 'took over everything it possibly could and gave [a]

Christian explanation for the pagan festivals, philosophy etc. In this way, the simple faith of the early Christians became swamped with the foreign ideas' (p. 28). Jameelah asserts that 'as Christianity accepted the innovations from the pagan past, so must it now tolerate with utmost permissiveness the inroads of present-day atheism' (p. 35). 'Ata ur-Rahim says that 'there are as many versions of Christianity today as there are Christians', and talks of 'the Pauline church's longstanding tradition of compromise by all means'. Touching on issues which are of concern to many contemporary Christians, he remarks that 'the Church has greatly accommodated itself to . . . new trends in the culture of the West', and that this compromise 'has resulted both in the continued absorption of the Church into the culture, and of the re-absorption of the culture into this changing structure of the Church'. He complains that 'the life-style of those who call themselves Christians closely resembles the life-styles of those who claim to be agnostics, humanists or atheists' (pp. 203–5).

Jameelah refers to the commercialization of modern Christianity, which attempts to sell itself 'by pandering to the tastes of the common mass . . . transforming the churches into cinema halls and social clubs and . . . making the whole church business more business-like'.[68] She comments that 'the church councils in America and England go even so far as to condone the practice of pre-marital sex' and cites Christian legitimation of homosexuality (pp. 347–8), leading to the conclusion that 'the Christian Church today does not lead society but merely refects its debased values' (p. 349). Innovations in Christian worship are often found to be particularly objectionable; Jameelah considers that the Protestant church service in particular is obviously 'entirely man-made', in contrast to Muslim worship which is based on 'the infallible and unchangeable *Sunnah* of the Prophet who condemned all innovation in matters of faith as tantamount to apostasy' (p. 341). She regrets that the 'vulgarity of modernism' has invaded the Church, for example with the use of modern styles of music such as jazz and rock and roll (pp. 342–4); Azhar considers this to be 'pandering to the lowest nature in men and women, if only such entertainment will "sell" Christianity to them' (p. 7).

Some writers object to specific elements of Christian worship; Jameelah comments that '*shirk* (associating partners with God) is characteristic of all Christian prayers and worship' (p. 277). After reproducing certain unexceptional Christian hymns and prayers, she contrasts their 'mawkish sentimentality' with the 'virile language of the *Salat* [ritual prayer]' (p. 279). Ajijola feels that the use of singing, music and the burning of incense in Christian worship is intended 'to create a sort of rapture in the mind' (p. 129); by contrast, 'for Muslims, prayers have no aesthetic paraphernalia' (p. 145). He is the only one to mention intercessory prayer, through which 'Christians beg God through Jesus Christ to grant them worldly favours' (p. 128). Some Christians might go some way to agreeing with Jameelah that 'Christmas in Europe and America is no more than a neo-pagan ritual of permissive affluence', but might be less ready to concede that for 'the average Christian in the West today', its main significance lies in 'food, presents, television and headache' (pp. 216–7). She conveys a rather gloomy picture of contemporary Christian religiosity via anecdotal material, including excerpts from two autobiographies in which one author describes his Methodist uncle's morbid propensity to dwell on the horrors of hell-fire, while another describes how his Seventh-Day Adventist grandmother's rigid adherence to the Sabbath blighted his childhood (pp. 295–8).

With reference to liberal developments in Christian theology, Jameelah comments: 'What a reduced and emasculated faith the Christian modernists preach which can scarcely appeal to anybody, much less the non-European peoples' (p. 340), but at the same time expresses the view that traditional Christianity 'cannot . . . survive the scientific and historical criticism' (p. 337). She sees recent intellectual developments as an attempt 'to rationalise Christianity by weeding out all that is objectionable to the modern scientific view, which, though it may temporarily succeed in deceiving people, actually ends in the virtual negation of Christian verities' (p. 345). According to Ansari, the 'drastic recasting and reforming of Christianity . . . is a proof by itself that Christianity is false', and 'once the historical and textual criticism of the Bible is accepted, the whole case for Christianity collapses automatically' (p. 141).

On the other hand, there are some who approve of the liberal trends in modern Christian thought; Bucaille feels that biblical criticism has not gone far enough, and complains that Christians 'hardly seem disposed to study [the scriptures] in the light of modern knowledge', but welcomes the fact that there is now 'a genuine body of textual criticism' (p. 19). Ajijola, who believes that the deity of Jesus is 'inconsistent with the development in modern science' and that 'Christian leaders must take steps to reject the deity of Jesus', since only then could there be unity between the three Abrahamic faiths (pp. 193–4), comments that 'no modern Christian scholar of any repute any longer considers Jesus to be divine in any other sense than as a man who best expressed what God wanted to be [*sic*] in his own time' (p. 189). Durrani similarly envisages a narrowing of the gap between Muslims and Christians 'especially these days when the Modernist view of Christianity is clearing the ground so courageously and producing such encouraging results' (p. 8).

Conclusions

Many of the comments that could be made on the material presented above are really general observations on the nature of polemic. Their constant footnote citation of Western scholarly works makes an implicit claim to academic status, and in fact several do see themselves as making an original contribution to scholarship.[69] However, the claim is not borne out in fact, owing to various features which amount to a consistently negative bias both in selection of data to be presented and in interpretation of that data. While at times one comes across statements which are rather disconcerting because they are seemingly groundless (such as the assertion that at the time of his death Jesus had only twelve followers) it is not strictly necessary to include factual errors in order to mislead, when selective presentation of material can convey false impressions just as surely. In fact, polemical writing almost always has a basis of truth; it is, for example, true that according to certain passages of the New Testament St Paul had, on more than one occasion, disagreements with individual disciples, but a straightforward reading of the New Testament as a whole does not support the complete break that several authors assert or imply.

Two themes that recur fairly frequently, but which it was not possible to accommodate in this chapter due to limitations of space, are the history of Christianity and the status of women. The first provides an example of how individual facts can be synthesized to present a distorted overall view. This is sometimes done by cataloguing the most bloodthirsty events in Christian history, which Christians themselves would see as aberrations (even where atrocities were carried out in the name of Christianity), and presenting them as a comprehensive history of Christianity or the Church.[70] Thomson, who gives the most detailed historical treatment, concludes that 'genocide has been a constant element in Christianity' (p. 346). Jameelah says frankly: 'As a child at the mere mention of the word "Christianity", I could only conjure up in my mind the horrors of the Spanish inquisition, the Crusades, the "pogroms" in Russia and Poland and the genocide of the Jews under Nazism which the Christian authorities did not attempt to resist or even protest' (p. 202); she does not leave the reader with the impression that anything she learned as an adult caused her to change her view. When speaking of the Muslims of Andalusia, Thomson offers an insight that might usefully be applied by some of the Muslims in this chapter to the study of Christian history: 'the fact that little attention is usually paid in official histories to people who live simple, peaceful and uncomplicated lives, does not mean that they are any less important than the people who are given all the coverage in official histories'.[71]

The status of women is the area which best demonstrates the close relationship between Islamic apologetic and anti-Christian polemic, since all authors who deal with the subject contrast the benefits brought to women by Islam with the alleged misogyny of Christianity. It also provides one of the clearest examples of the regurgitation of accusations that have been levelled against Muslims, sometimes by Christians. Thus, one author claims that 'the Bible teaches that the woman was made for the pleasure and convenience of man; it broadly asserts, as a fundamental principle, the subjection and inferiority of woman', while another states that 'in Christianity the treatment of the feminine could in a sense be viewed to partake of the canine'.[72]

Sources are often used selectively. From the broad spectrum of opinion which is represented in Western scholarship, it is often the extreme end of the spectrum which is chosen; in this way authors can usually find what they set out to look for. An example of this would be the dating of doctrinal formation or canonical collection as late as possible. In several areas, Muslims are more in harmony with the biblical scholarship of a century or so ago than with that of today – in fact the most oft-quoted theologian and biblical scholar is Adolph von Harnack (d. 1930), who is selectively used for his liberal opinions, mainly from *What is Christianity?*. The 'quest for the historical Jesus' is one in which Muslims become involved when they seek to demonstrate that the historical Jesus is to be identified with Jesus as portrayed in the Qur'an. However, as with many Western studies, especially in the nineteenth century, the application of external criteria in the attempt to reconstruct the Jesus of the Gospels in accordance with particular ideals runs counter to an organic approach which allows issues to arise from the text of the New Testament itself. The downgrading of St Paul's Jewish roots and the emphasis on the Hellenistic elements of his thought is reminiscent of nineteenth- and early twentieth-century scholarship (Bousset and Loisy are sometimes referred to by Muslim authors) which has been superseded by more recent studies such as those of W. D. Davies and E. P. Sanders. The identification of pagan influences on Christian doctrine is one in which far more caution is exercised in Western scholarship today than several decades ago. Muslims who address this subject do not refer to recent studies such as those by Nock and Wedderburn, but observe similarities between Christianity and the mystery religions while ignoring important differences, making uncritical use of outdated sources such as Edward Carpenter's *Pagan and Christian Creeds* or J. M. Robertson's *Pagan Christians*, in addition to the aforementioned Bousset and Loisy.

Religious knowledge is often regarded by Muslims as common property and something to be freely shared; the borrowing which one often finds between sources is not therefore considered plagiaristic or dishonest in any way, but it does make it difficult to trace the genealogies of ideas.[73] Relatively few of the authors in this chapter read Arabic, but many of them know Urdu; one would therefore expect at least some of them to have been exposed to Rahmatullah's *Izhar al-Haqq*, which preserves much of the medieval material, particularly on the subjects of scriptural falsification, doctrinal error, and prophecies of Muhammad in the Bible. Yet the fact is that Rahmatullah's book is seldom, if ever, cited in bibliographies or footnotes, even though the books often have some material in common with it. By contrast, Western sources are, for apologetic reasons, constantly quoted, the most prominent being Edward Gibbon's *Decline and Fall of the Roman Empire*, perhaps because it describes fairly graphically some of the blacker pages of Christian history. Mostly the sources are selectively used for particular purposes: Edward Carpenter crops up fairly regularly on the pagan origins of Christianity; J. M. Robertson is cited on generally anti-Christian points, particularly to support the view that Christianity is opposed to civilization; Bertrand Russell's *Why I am not a Christian* is another popular source, usually quoted on the reactionary history of the Church; Ernest Renan is used for his criticism of the New Testament and for his anti-supernaturalism; and Robert Briffault and William Draper are quoted on the West's civilizational debt to Islam.[74] A very common feature is the quoting of Christian critical scholars who have expressed views considered by the Muslim authors to discredit Christianity, although it is often (but not always) the case that the same views are largely acceptable to Christians. An example of this would be the acknowledgement of the human element in the formation of doctrine and the scriptural canon.

Notwithstanding a degree of uniformity which is engendered both by polemical concerns and an Islamic doctrinal framework, it emerges that there is plenty of scope for diversity of opinion on quite important issues, not least on the character and teachings of Jesus. The view of Jesus as an ascetic, espoused by 'Ata ur-Rahim and Thomson, contrasts with the mainstream Muslim view of prophets as activists rather than ascetics; Barelvi explicitly denies that Jesus was an ascetic or an Essene, since 'he was too sensitive to his social duty to go into monastic seclusion' (p. 171). Similarly, Maqsood offers a possible alternative view to the more usual acceptance at face value of Jesus' criticisms of Pharisaic legalism. Contrasting attitudes to the Sermon on the Mount and to the miracles of Jesus provide further examples of diversity of opinion. The treatment of miracles not only reflects the way in which the authors' views of Islam affect their views of Christianity, as for example in the case of Barelvi's anti-supernaturalism, but also provides one of the clearest examples of the way in which polemical concerns can outweigh other considerations, even in some cases fairly central Islamic beliefs. In relation to the spectrum of possible Muslim beliefs about Jesus, one tends to find in these works a minimalist interpretation of Jesus, prompted perhaps by a sense of religious rivalry.

The view of Christianity as a Western phenomenon is considerably outdated, although it should be remembered that some of the sources are two or three decades old. In fact, the empirical study of contemporary Christianity, including its forms of organization, worship, spirituality and so on, is largely omitted in these sources in favour of generalizations or references to isolated incidents and anecdotes seen as discrediting Christianity. In this respect these writers fall short of medieval Muslim scholarship, which sometimes demonstrated a detailed knowledge of the contrasting beliefs and practices of different Christian sects.

Methodological issues aside, Muslims are obviously not alone in criticizing certain areas of weakness in the Christian tradition past and present. Many, if not all, of the criticisms which may be taken as serious have been and are being addressed by Christians themselves. These include issues such as Christian disunity, shortcomings or aberrations in the history of the Church, and the decline of some Churches in the contemporary West. Conservative evangelical Christians are likely to share Muslim distaste for liberal developments in Christian thinking in the areas of ethics, theology or biblical criticism. However, since this criticism on the part of Muslims is not actually addressed to Christians, and since it is usually made in a spirit of aggression, it cannot really be called constructive. Were it otherwise, Muslims might be in a position to present a unique external critical view by virtue of their own religious and cultural experience. This could, potentially, make a useful contribution to Christian thought, to the extent that Christians were willing to learn from the views of outsiders and 'see themselves as others see them'.[75]

The topical organization of this chapter has made it difficult to do justice to the level of individuality that one finds in some of the works. On the whole, those by Western converts are the most original, although one might add 'Ata ur-Rahim (who acknowledges the help of converts), Shafaat and Ahmed to the list. The remainder of the works demonstrate a relatively high degree of continuity with the concerns and style of the medieval tradition, which, for example, tends to deal with the biblical text on an atomistic level, drawing conclusions from individual verses, in contrast to the more holistic approach employed by Bucaille, Maqsood and Shafaat. 'Ata ur-Rahim, Thomson, Ahmed and Bewley all attempt historical reconstructions with varying degrees of efficacy. The two latter sources incorporate some moderately sophisticated critique of the history of modern Western thought, drawing on modern Western sociological and epistemological scholarship.

The sources listed in bibliographies can be misleading. Some of the books which include the most up-to-date and mainstream sources in their bibliographies – Jameelah, Ajijola, and 'Ata ur-Rahim – are in fact among the most polemical. 'Ata ur-Rahim uses the sources mainly to supply a modicum of factual input, while supplying his own interpretive framework in the form of an alternative history which owes little to mainstream sources, while it is not at all clear what use Ajijola has made of his sources. Jameelah, on the other hand, is distinguished by the fact that she does not use her sources selectively but frequently reproduces long quotations from recognized Christian scholars, who are not necessarily from the liberal end of the spectrum. Many of these quotations do not appear on the face of it to be detrimental to Christianity at all (although her interpretations of them often are). Yet she is, in other respects, the most confrontational writer, and she ends her book with an appeal to fellow Muslims: 'We must crush the conspiracies of Zionism, free-masonry, Orientalism and foreign missions both with the pen and with the sword. We cannot afford peace and reconciliation with the *Ahl al-Kitab* until we can humble them and gain the upper hand' (p. 412).

Da'wah does not seem to be the primary aim of most of the works, although at least six of the authors – Ahmed, Ansari, Barelvi, Bewley, Jameelah and Shafaat – express some kind of missionary or expansionist hope. Some of the reasons for, and functions of, polemic in the present-day context have already been suggested in the introductory section of this chapter. One might also tentatively suggest a cultural dimension; where the honour of Islam is felt to be at stake, its defence takes on an urgency which overrides academic concerns. Ironically, some of those who are concerned about the misrepresentation of Islam in the West are themselves involved (whether knowingly or not) in a process of disinformation.

Some of the problems relate to the flow of information. Muslim anti-Christian polemic goes relatively unnoticed, even in the age of the mass media, because it occurs within an almost exclusively Muslim market, and is rarely subjected to critical scrutiny. Where Muslim bookshops stock books on Christianity authored by non-Muslims, they tend to be selected titles, often bestsellers, which are deemed either to cast aspersions on the origins of Christianity or to reflect badly on Christians by exposing some scandal. In addition, such works might offer incidental support for selected Muslim beliefs, especially the view that the scriptures have been corrupted.[76] So long as such outlets continue to be selective in this way, and to stock the works of Ahmed Deedat to the exclusion of books which provide accurate objective information on Christianity, and so long as Muslims do not in any significant numbers acquire such information by other means, the process of disinformation will continue. One encouraging initiative, which may or may not be followed by others, has been undertaken by the Islamic Foundation in Leicester, England, which has published an annotated bibliography of recommended books on Christianity, on the basis that 'the best approach to studying Christianity is via its own source materials, to think through and analyse the arguments of its adherents, instead of indulging in cheap polemics – as, regrettably, some Muslim writers have done in the past'.[77]

Notes

1. See Charfi, 'Polémiques islamo-chrétiennes à l'époque mediévale'. A fuller treatment can be found in his *Al-Fikr al-Islāmī fi'l-Radd 'ala al-Naṣārā ila Nihāyat al-Qarn al-Rābi'*.
2. This verse was originally revealed in connection with a religious dispute between the Prophet and a deputation of Christians from Najran.
3. Slomp, 'The Gospel in Dispute', p. 74.

4. For examples, see Jomier, 'L'Evangile selon Barnabe', pp. 212–25.
5. For Muslim rejections of the Gospel, see Ayoub, 'Muslim Views of Christianity', p. 66, and those referred to by Slomp in 'The Gospel in Dispute', p. 68 (fn. 1).
6. Of the eighteen main authors whose works are reviewed for this chapter, at least eight refer to it, and none question its authenticity.
7. A. Deedat, *Is the Bible God's Word?* (Birmingham: Islamic Propagation Centre International, 1990), p. 64.
8. Ibid., p. 64.
9. A. Deedat, *Combat Kit against Bible Thumpers* (Birmingham: Islamic Propagation Centre International, 1992), pp. 2–3.
10. A. Deedat, *What is His Name?* (Birmingham: Islamic Propagation Centre International, 1990), p. 13.
11. Shorrosh, *Islam Revealed*, incorporating a transcript of the debate: 'Is Jesus God?', pp. 257, 263–4 and 254 respectively.
12. For a brief description of Pfander's work, see p. 96.
13. Pp. 50, 51; Deedat's *Combat Kit against Bible Thumpers* contains an A to Z of allegedly embarrassing sections of the Bible with which to confront evangelists.
14. Muslim criticism of Christian doctrine is dealt with in chapter 4.
15. The last two works were originally published under slightly different titles: *Islam and Christianity* and *Islam and its Contemporary Faiths* respectively.
16. See, e.g., Qadri, *Dimensions of Christianity*, p. 119.
17. See, e.g., Ajijola, *Myth of the Cross*, p. 93.
18. For a Muslim treatment which draws parallels between the Scrolls and the Gospel of Barnabas, see M. A. Yusseff, *The Dead Sea Scrolls, the Gospel of Barnabas and the New Testament* (Indianapolis: American Trust Publications, 1990).
19. See, e.g., Niazi, *Mirror of Trinity*, chapter 7, and Meherally, *Understanding the Bible*, chapter 16; a more substantial treatment is contained in 'Abdu'l-Ahad Dawud, *Muhammad in the Bible* (New Delhi: International Islamic Publishers, 1993). On the medieval period, see Lazarus-Yafeh, *Intertwined Worlds*, chapter 4.
20. Qadri, *Dimensions of Christianity*, p. 123; for another such list see Ajijola, *Myth of the Cross*, pp. 111–13.
21. See, e.g., J. Ahmed, *Christianity*, pp. 45–6; Usmani, *What is Christianity?*, p. 40; Aziz-us-Samad, *Comparative Study*, pp. 76–7.
22. See, in addition to the references in the last note, Meherally, *Understanding the Bible*, pp. 103–7; Aziz-us-Samad, *Comparative Study*, pp. 41–3, 76–7.
23. 'Ata ur-Rahim, *Jesus, Prophet of Islam*, p. 71; Thomson, *Blood on the Cross,* pp. 5–6; Qadri, *Dimensions of Christianity*, p. 12.
24. Bucaille, *The Bible, the Qur'an and Science*, p. 138; see p. 160 for a similar point.
25. A detailed evangelical Christian response to Bucaille is W. Campbell's *The Qur'an and the Bible in the Light of History and Science* (Loughborough: Arab World Ministries, 1986).
26. Works on Pharisees which are cited or which appear in the bibliography include those by Finkelstein, Bowker, Finkel, and Neusner; she also uses Sanders, Vermes, and Davies.
27. Apart from Maqsood, Shafaat is the only other writer to do this: see p. 71.

28. Azhar, *Christianity in History*, p. 23; the same point is made in Durrani, *The Qur'anic Facts about Jesus*, p. 6.

29. Ajijola, *Myth of the Cross*, p. 40. See also Niazi, *Mirror of Trinity*, pp. 62–3; Durrani, *The Qur'anic Facts about Jesus*, p. 12; Azhar, *Christianity in History*, p. 114.

30. Niazi, *Mirror of Trinity*, pp. 41–2; see also Azhar, *Christianity in History*, pp. 85–6.

31. 'Ata ur-Rahim, *Jesus, Prophet of Islam*, pp. 35–6. Another extended reconstruction of Jesus' life, but one based much more closely on the Gospels, is A. Shafaat's *The Gospel According to Islam* (New York: Vantage Press, 1979), described in Goddard, 'Modern Pakistani and Indian Muslim Perceptions of Christianity', pp. 168–71.

32. *Dimensions of Christianity*, p. 86. Although it is not entirely clear, there is room here to suppose that the absurdity would apply only if Jesus is the redeemer that Christians claim him to be.

33. J. Ahmed, *Christianity*, p. 7; Aziz-us-Samad, *Comparative Study*, p. 173.

34. Aziz-us-Samad, *Comparative Study*, pp. 55–6; see also Durrani, *The Qur'anic Facts about Jesus*, p. 37; Jameelah, *Islam Versus Ahl al-Kitab*, p. 402.

35. *Comparative Study*, p. 62; see also Niazi, *Mirror of Trinity*, pp. 43–4.

36. E.g., Azhar, *Christianity in History*, p. 149.

37. Maqsood, *The Separated Ones*, pp. 156–7. Maqsood does however mention that the woman could not in any case have been condemned without witnesses, and if these were lacking the accusers were themselves guilty of false accusation of unchastity.

38. See, e.g., Meherally, *Understanding the Bible*, p. 86; Ajijola, *Myth of the Cross*, pp. 4–5.

39. Aziz-us-Samad, *Comparative Study*, p. 40, and Maqsood, *The Separated Ones*, p. 159.

40. Jameelah, *Islam Versus Ahl al-Kitab*, p. 208.

41. 'Ata ur-Rahim, *Jesus, Prophet of Islam*, pp. 12, 69.

42. Qadri, *Dimensions of Christianity*, p. 79.

43. Ibid., p. 75. For other treatments of the pagan origins of Christianity, see Ansari, *Islam and Christianity*, chapter 3; Aziz-us-Samad, *Comparative Study*, chapter 5; Jameelah, *Islam Versus Ahl al-Kitab*, pp. 210ff.

44. Aziz-us-Samad, *Comparative Study*, p. 116.

45. See, e.g., 'Ata ur-Rahim, *Jesus, Prophet of Islam*, p. 64; Thomson, *Blood on the Cross*, p. 51; Usmani, *What is Christianity?*, p. 56.

46. Qadri, *Dimensions of Christianity*, p. 41.

47. See, e.g., Ajijola, *Myth of the Cross*, p. 90; Qadri, *Dimensions of Christianity*, p. 12; 'Ata ur-Rahim, *Jesus, Prophet of Islam*, p. 71.

48. Meherally, *Understanding the Bible*, p. 65; 'Ata ur-Rahim, *Jesus, Prophet of Islam*, p. 57.

49. Usmani, *What is Christianity?*, p. 52; Qadri, *Dimensions of Christianity*, pp. 91–2; 'Ata ur-Rahim, *Jesus, Prophet of Islam*, p. 72; Thomson, *Blood on the Cross*, p. 2.

50. *Myth of the Cross*, p. 90; see also Azhar, *Christianity in History*, p. 58; Qadri, *Dimensions of Christianity*, p. 93.

Muslims and Christians Face to Face

51. *Blood on the Cross*, p. 9; see also Qadri, *Dimensions of Christianity*, p. 74; Aziz-us-Samad, *Comparative Study*, p. 71.

52. Ansari, *Islam and Christianity*, p. 23.

53. Qadri, *Dimensions of Christianity*, p. 40 (citing J. M. Robertson's *A Short History of Christianity*); Ajijola, *Myth of the Cross*, p. 127.

54. For example, the statement that Muslims are ignorant of their own history is followed by the remark: 'The clever Western teacher has seen to that' (*Christianity in History*, p. 14).

55. *Christianity in History*, p. 28; Azhar expounds on the low standards of hygiene in present-day Europe on pp. 159–61.

56. For the first quotation see Ajijola, *Myth of the Cross*, p. 80, and Qadri, *Dimensions of Christianity*, p. 35; for the second, see Aziz-us-Samad, *Comparative Study*, pp. 166–7.

57. Ahmed, *Christianity*, p. 54; Niazi, *Mirror of Trinity*, p. 117.

58. *Christianity in History*, p. 67; cf. Barelvi, *Islam and World Religions*, p. 172, and Durrani, *The Qur'anic Facts about Jesus*, p. 33, where much of Azhar is reproduced verbatim.

59. See, e.g., Durrani, *The Qur'anic Facts about Jesus*, p. 28; Meherally, *Understanding the Bible*, p. 98.

60. Aziz-us-Samad, *Comparative Study*, pp. 143–4.

61. *Myth of the Cross*, pp. 127–8; cf. Azhar, *Christianity in History*, p. 78.

62. See, e.g., Azhar, *Christianity in History*, p. 79; Ahmed, *Christianity*, p. 84; Jameelah, *Islam Versus Ahl al-Kitab*, p. 404.

63. 'Ata ur-Rahim, *Jesus, Prophet of Islam*, pp. 5–6.

64. For references to idol-worship, see Azhar, *Christianity in History*, p. 171; Jameelah, *Islam Versus Ahl al-Kitab*, p. 272; Ajijola, *Myth of the Cross*, p. 129. On papal infallibility, see Jameelah, p. 323; 'Ata ur-Rahim, *Jesus, Prophet of Islam*, p. 201.

65. Jameelah, *Islam versus Ahl al-Kitab*, p. 328.

66. Ibid., p. 332. Usmani similarly sees the fact that Luther 'arrogated to himself the interpretation of the Bible' as the thin end of the wedge which ultimately led to rationalist biblical criticism (*What is Christianity?*, p. 34).

67. See Noss, *Man's Religions*, p. 470; the source is mentioned in Barelvi's bibliography but not explicitly quoted.

68. *Islam Versus Ahl al-Kitab*, p. 345; see also 'Ata ur-Rahim, *Jesus, Prophet of Islam*, p. 203.

69. Among those who are explicit about this are Azhar for the history of Christianity (*Christianity in History*, pp. 18–19), Bucaille for the scientific interpretation of the Bible (*The Bible, Qur'an and Science*, p. 20), and 'Ata ur-Rahim for the life of Jesus (*Jesus, Prophet of Islam*, p. 1).

70. See, e.g., Qadri, *Dimensions of Christianity*, pp. 9–41.

71. *Blood on the Cross*, p. 165. Once again, Maqsood takes a different view, writing that 'Christians have always been known for their love and devotion to God, to their example – Jesus – and to humanity: they have died for that love in their millions; they have earned the gratitude, admiration and respect of the millions who have been helped by their urge to live in service of God' (*The Separated Ones*, p. 3).

72. Barelvi, *Islam and World Religions*, pp. 15–16; Azhar, *Christianity in History*, p. 127. Azhar devotes two whole chapters to this subject, while Aziz-us-Samad and Jameelah devote special sections to it: see *Comparative Study*, pp. 148–56 and *Islam Versus Ahl al-Kitab*, pp. 299–309 respectively.

73. For examples of such borrowing, see Ajijola's dependence on Aziz-us-Samad, *Myth of the Cross*, pp. 174–5 and *Comparative Study*, pp. 98–102 respectively, and Durrani's dependence on Azhar on the subject of miracles. It is not unusual to find identical quotations from a Western author such as Bertrand Russell or Ernest Renan in two or more Muslim sources.

74. Several of these sources are mentioned by Anawati as recurring in Muslim writings on Christianity in Arabic: see 'Polémique, apologie et dialogue', p. 449.

75. Several Christians feel that there are lessons to be learned from Muslims' views of Christians or Christianity. See, e.g., P. Griffiths (ed.), *Christianity through Non-Christian Eyes* (Maryknoll, NY: Orbis, 1990); C. Lamb, *Jesus through Other Eyes: Christology in Multi-Faith Context* (Oxford: Latimer House, 1982).

76. Examples of these are B. Mack, *The Lost Gospel*; P. De Rosa, *Vicars of Christ*; K. Salibi, *Who Was Jesus?*; R. Eisenman and M. Wise, *The Dead Sea Scrolls Uncovered*; R. Leigh and M. Baigent, *The Dead Sea Scrolls Deception*.

77. Von Denffer and Siddiqui, *Christian Literature for Muslims*, p. 5. The same organization has recently begun publication of *Encounters: Journal of Inter-Cultural Perspectives*, which devotes some space to interfaith issues.

three

PROTESTANT MISSIONARY LITERATURE ON ISLAM

In Muslim sources, missionaries are almost universally regarded as agents of colonialism, Westernization and secularism. Most contemporary missionaries are at pains to distance themselves from any identification with Western political interests, but Muslims continue to be sceptical; in this area, perhaps more than in any other, there is a marked divide between Muslim and Christian perceptions. For Muslims, partly by analogy with *da'wah* which aims not just at individual conversion but at Islamization, Christian mission is a political phenomenon; for those who engage in it, it is a spiritual imperative. Missionaries will invariably explain their vocation in terms similar to those used by Patricia St John (d. 1993), whose life straddled an era in which attitudes towards mission among the British public underwent a considerable change. Returning to England as an elderly woman after decades of missionary work among Muslim and other peoples, she was confronted with the following accusation: 'I think you missionaries do a great deal of harm. These people have their own religion, and by trying to impose your views upon them, you're forcing them into a different culture, dividing them, and introducing unnecessary problems. Why can't you leave them alone?' In response, she asks: 'do we really believe that Christ is so eternally precious that he is worth infinitely more to them than all that they may lose, even life itself? . . . If we do, let us press on; if not, by all means, let us leave them alone.' [1]

Approximately two per cent of missionaries are currently deployed in mission to Muslims, who make up about a sixth of the world's population. A perusal of the biographies of some of these missionaries shows that often a lifetime's effort yielded at most a handful of converts; a former missionary to Indonesia writes that 'mission among Muslims demands a high degree of persevering endurance in the midst of indifference, open hostility and usually unyielding resistance to the message of Jesus Christ'.[2] Owing to the difficulties involved, it is sometimes suggested that the paucity of visible results in the Muslim context has a purifying effect on missionary motivation.[3] Missionary organizations have often preferred to plough their resources into more fruitful fields, to the dismay of those who argue that Muslimness should not disqualify any from hearing the 'good news', and that numbers should not be the sole criterion for measuring the growth of the Kingdom.[4] The restrictions or bans on missionary activity in most Muslim countries, and the fact that any 'success' will inevitably bring its own rather acute difficulties and dilemmas, add to the impression that this is not a mission field for the faint-hearted.

The word 'missionary' has a rather old-fashioned ring to it; some alternative such as 'Christian worker' may be preferred, especially in a Muslim context. Broadly speaking, missionary work usually involves some kind of combination of 'proclamation' (i.e. preaching the gospel) and 'service' (i.e. social and relief work). The two are usually seen as not just complementary but inseparable – the latter representing the practical outworking of the former. Being a textual study, this chapter will be concerned only with 'proclamation', but it should be borne in mind that in Muslim contexts that represents a smaller than usual proportion of the missionary's activity, for obvious pragmatic and diplomatic reasons.[5]

Now that numerous translations of the primary sources of Islam are freely available, it is arguably no longer necessary for missionaries to be academic specialists in order to write books on Islam, whose foremost aim is, in any case, not to undertake original research but to further the cause of 'sharing the gospel' with Muslims. Today, the 'scholar-missionary' is an increasingly rare phenomenon, although Kenneth Cragg provides an outstanding contemporary example among Protestants. In the past, however, there were a number of missionaries to Muslims who were academic authorities on Islam in their day. Among them one can discern different strands of thought and ways of engaging with Islam or Muslims.

Some have shied away from religious controversy as a means of appealing to or 'reaching' Muslims. The English missionary to India

---

Henry Martyn (d. 1812) wrote in his journal: 'I lay not much stress upon clear arguments. The work of God is seldom wrought in this way.'[6] More recently, others have engaged in a sympathetic scholarship, sometimes finding in Sufism a kindred or congenial spirit. Temple Gairdner's *Al-Ghazzālī's Mishkāt al-Anwār ('The Niche for Lights'): A Translation with Introduction* (1924) showed an appreciation of al-Ghazālī's mystical thought, and Constance Padwick's *Muslim Devotions* (1960) was the fruit of many years of gathering Sufi prayer tracts.[7] Lewis Bevan Jones' *The People of the Mosque* (1932) attempted to portray Islamic beliefs and practices accurately and sympathetically, and 'to see Islam through Muslim eyes'.[8] All shared a devotion to the indigenous languages and (to a great extent) cultures with which they had to do.

Others have focused on more confrontational areas. Carl Gottlieb Pfander (d. 1865) and William St Clair Tisdall (d. 1928) were missionaries to India with the Church Missionary Society (CMS). Pfander was a German Lutheran who is remembered, among other things, for his participation in public Christian–Muslim debates (*munāẓarāt*) in India, most famously at Agra in 1854.[9] His best-known work is *The Balance of Truth* (also known by its Arabic title, the *Mīzān ul-Ḥaqq*), the three main concerns of which are to defend the authenticity of the Bible, to expound Christian truths to Muslims, and to cast doubt on Muslim claims about Muhammad and the Qur'an. Pfander's method involves using Christian criteria to evaluate Islam, for example as to what constitutes 'true revelation',[10] and consequently finding Islam wanting. His style is geared to the needs of religious disputation, and to some extent reflects the methods and rational emphasis of his Muslim opponents.

Tisdall adopted a generally more irenic approach than Pfander, although he did feel exposing the weaknesses of Islam to be a potentially fruitful mission strategy and he revised and enlarged the latter's *The Balance of Truth*. One of his main areas of interest was the origins of Islam. *The Sources of Islam*, which attempts to trace parallels between the Qur'an or Hadith and other sources, including Arabian pagan, biblical, and Judaeo-Christian heretical or apocryphal material, has been described as constituting his most accomplished and original scholarship.[11] Tisdall asserts, regarding the Qur'an, that 'if we can trace the teaching of any part of it to an earthly source, or to human systems existing prior to the Prophet's age, then Islam at once falls to the ground'.[12] His scholarly contribution consists of the identification of obvious parallels, particularly with rabbinical and New Testament apocryphal writings;[13] some of his 'parallels', however, are somewhat speculative, and recent research seems inclined to credit the Qur'an with more originality (in form if not in content) and less direct dependence on external sources.[14] The work of Pfander and Tisdall is still sometimes referred to by missionaries who consider religious polemic and debate to be a desirable method of evangelism.[15]

More prolific than either of the above was Zwemer, a minister of the Reformed Church of America who spent most of his missionary career in Arabia and Egypt, and who founded the periodical *The Moslem World* (now *The Muslim World*) in 1911.[16] Themes in his work that have had lasting influence among missionaries include the need to understand Islam not just through its textual sources but through living contact with Muslims;[17] the veneration of Muhammad, which was felt to have evolved among Muslims as a substitute for Christ; and theological comparisons between Christianity and Islam, focusing on contrasting elements.

The writings of Pfander, Tisdall and Zwemer reflect many of the assumptions that were prevalant in the nineteenth and early twentieth centuries: that Muslims worshipped a different God,[18] that Muhammad was insincere and opportunistic in the Medinan if not the Meccan phase of his mission, and that controversy, so long as it did not degenerate into discourtesy, was an appropriate method of Muslim evangelism. At the same time, there is a discernible shift of emphasis in their writings vis-à-vis the medieval refutation of Islam as wholly false, to an approach which acknowledges some of its achievements (e.g. the replacement of polytheism with monotheism) while emphasizing the ways in which it 'falls short of' Christianity. They tended to see Islam and Christianity in terms of rival civilizations, and to detect in contemporary developments the decline of Islam (one of Zwemer's books was entitled *The Disintegration of Islam*), a decline which would open the way not for Islamic reform but for the spreading of the gospel in Muslim countries. Contemporary missionary-minded Christians tend to be more sober in their estimations, in the light of a more critical view of Western civilization and the now obvious durability and resilience of Islam, in its social and political as well as religious (in the narrower Western sense) dimensions.

Most missionary works on Islam now abjure an aggressive confrontational approach; a former missionary to Sudan observes that 'the natural reaction of any man when his beliefs are attacked is to maintain them the more resolutely and even to discover better reasons for doing so . . . The results of missionary preaching during the past century and a half demonstrate with tragic clearness how unproductive such a method really is.'[19] Many express regret for the excesses of the past,[20] and most feel that Pfander's work is outdated, and are critical of the subjectivist, rationalist and polemical methods that his work exemplifies.[21] Contemporary missionaries often feel that to disparage Muhammad is both unnecessary and counter-productive, and those who focus on practical ways of 'reaching' Muslims sometimes point out that to win an argument may mean to lose a friend. In a study of other faiths a notable missionary thinker, Stephen Neill, urges the Christian to 'expose himself to the full force of these other faiths in all that is most convincing and alluring',[22] while former missionary Colin Chapman refers to the need to avoid comparing 'the worst in Islam with the best in Christianity', or 'judging the history of Islam in previous centuries by the moral standards of the 20th century'.[23] Even the more confrontational writers acknowledge the importance of accurately perceiving the insider view before proceeding to criticize it.[24]

A relatively small proportion of works, generally authored by evangelists rather than cross-cultural missionaries, do, however, adopt an aggressive approach. One of the most scurrilous examples is a book recently published in the United States, by the title of *The Islamic Invasion* (1992). Like the works of Ahmad Deedat on Christianity, it employs ridicule and abuse, and invariably puts the most pejorative interpretation possible on the 'facts', many of which are inaccurate. An appendix culls Hadiths from an English translation of al-Bukhārī, selecting those which are felt to convey a distasteful impression of Muhammad, including one which states that he had headlice, as if this represented a disqualification for prophethood on either Judaeo-Christian or Islamic grounds. Presumably, at least some Christians will acquire their entire knowledge of Islam from such a source.[25]

One significant new development is the appearance of Christian-authored books which are straightforward, non-interpretive, and generally sympathetic, and which aim to educate Christians about Islam. The writers are usually involved in some kind of work with or 'outreach' to Muslims; since these books are not really distinguishable from non-Christian works in what they actually say about the Islamic religion, they have not been dealt with in this chapter, which concentrates on those which provide a more explicitly Christian view of Islam.[26]

The typical Christian missionary manual on Islam contains several elements: the imparting of information about Islam, particularly in so far as it is seen to contrast with Christianity, practical advice on how to evangelize Muslims, and Christian apologetic focusing on areas that are problematic for Muslims; there may also be explicit refutation of Muslim beliefs. In accordance with the aims of this book, the emphasis here is on the way in which Islam is viewed, both in itself and in comparison to Christianity. Those areas that reflect specific Christian apologetic concerns, such as the refutation of the Gospel of Barnabas and of predictions of Muhammad in the Bible, and the defence of Christian doctrines and the textual integrity of the Bible, are not dealt with except in so far as they arise in the context of comparison between Islam and Christianity.

There is a good deal of overlap between the different missionary publications, which tend to deal with the same topics and sometimes refer to the same Christian Islamicists. Although they differ in style, tone, and scholarly accomplishment, they reflect a high level of agreement on the essential differences between Islam and Christianity, and the structure of this chapter reflects the primarily theological concerns of the authors. Priority has been given to those works which are more substantial or which appear to have the widest circulation. Although Cragg treats many of these themes in his work, he has not been included here, on the grounds that there is a qualitative difference between his writings, which contain original scholarly and creative thought, and these, which are largely, and avowedly, derivative. Those familiar with Cragg's books will discern frequent echoes of his ideas, reflecting the fact that his works have become a kind of common property among Christian missionaries to Muslims.

The authors whose works form the basis for this chapter are, with one or two exceptions, current or retired missionaries and evangelists; several now lecture in Bible or missionary colleges, or work for missionary organizations. Their mission-fields have included Bangladesh and the Philippines (Phil Parshall), Egypt and the Lebanon (Bill Musk, Colin Chapman), the Sudan and Jordan (David Brown, d. 1982), and North Africa (Sam Schlorff). John Gilchrist is a South African lawyer and evangelist who has written tracts in reply to those of Ahmed Deedat, while Abdiyah Akbar Abdul-Haqq is now a travelling evangelist, originally from the Punjab and the son of a well-known Indian apologist and convert from Islam, Padri Abdul-Haqq. Chawkat Moucarry is a Syrian Christian who currently teaches in a British missionary training college, while Ida Glaser, also based in Britain, is currently affiliated to the Bible Church Missionary Society (BCMS). Norman Geisler is dean of a Bible college and his co-author, Abdul Saleeb (a pseudonym) is described only as a 'former Muslim'.

Their academic qualifications vary: most have had some formal training in Islamic studies, usually from Christian educational institutions. Abdul-Haqq is described as being conversant with several Muslim languages, and Gilchrist seems to have sufficient linguistic competence to make use of primary Arabic sources. Among the more highly qualified in Islamic studies are Chapman, who has an M.Phil., and Moucarry, Glaser, and Musk, who hold doctorates in areas related to Islamic studies. Brown was the Bishop of Guildford and, in association with the British Council of Churches, the author of the influential *A New Threshold: Guidelines for the Churches in their Relations with Muslim Communities* (London: British Council of Churches,1976), which was fairly radical at the time in suggesting that 'understanding other faiths . . . involves a willingness to believe that many of those who practise other faiths have a living relationship with God and know the power of his grace in their lives' (pp. 22–3). Geisler, Saleeb, Parshall, Abdul-Haqq and Schlorff are based in the United States, Gilchrist in South Africa, and the others are based in Britain. There are six other writers who receive an occasional mention in this chapter: Anis Shorrosh, a Palestinian Arab who has engaged in public debate with Ahmad Deedat; Norman Anderson (d. 1994), former missionary to Egypt and academic specialist in Islamic law; J. Dudley Woodberry and Martin Goldsmith, who have both taught in Bible colleges after retiring from the mission field; Salim Haddad, who seems to be a largely self-taught retired neurosurgeon of Palestinian origin; and Michael Nazir-Ali, an Anglican bishop of Pakistani origin and former head of CMS.

In cases where only one main work is cited for a given author, page references in the text will be given without reference to the title. This applies to the following: Abdul-Haqq, *Sharing your Faith with a Muslim* (1980); Brown, *The Way of the Prophet* (1962); Geisler and Saleeb, *Answering Islam: The Crescent in the Light of the Cross* (1994); Goldsmith, *Islam and Christian Witness* (1982); Haddad, *The Principles of Belief in the Qur'an and the Bible* (1992); and Moucarry, *Islam and Christianity at the Crossroads* (1988).

As will become apparent, the approaches of these authors vary. At one end of the spectrum are works which aim to refute Islam by various means, while at the other end are those which genuinely seek to understand the appeal of Islam or which undertake non-polemical comparisons between Muslim and Christian beliefs. The more confrontational approach, which tends to rely on rational or evidential methods, is illustrated by Geisler and Saleeb who introduce their work by saying that 'since both orthodox Islam and Christianity claim to be the true religion, it is incumbent upon thinking persons to examine carefully the evidence offered by both and to make their own decision in view of the evidence' (p. 10). Such a view personifies the two religions and presents them as conterminous, engaged in battle and resorting to the same weapons, as it were. Others prefer a less robust approach. Parshall, for example, draws attention to the limitations of the rational approach, asking: 'If Christianity stood only on unquestionable and totally verifiable propositions, what need would there be for a humble faith linkage between the created and the Creator?'[27]

Islam and the Qur'an

In this literature there is relatively little reflection on why God may have allowed Islam to exist and to flourish. For most, Islam, with its continuing vigour and relatively high level of resistance to missionary efforts, represents a particular challenge. Reflecting on this may induce a mood of introspection; Goldsmith writes that 'the fortress of Islam remains intact and stands as a constant indictment of the failure of the Christian Church' (p. 33).

There are some who hint that there may have been a demonic element in the revelatory process, and who emphasize Muhammad's original fears concerning the source of the revelations.[28] However, in the missionary-authored works reviewed here there is no suggestion of an apocalyptic role for Islam, as found in certain evangelical sources which see the current revival as a sign of the 'end times'.[29] Chapman warns against identifying the forces of evil with any particular political or religious system in view of the biblical teaching that such forces are located 'in the heavenly realms'.[30]

Among missionary writers there are those who see Islam as a possible preparation for the gospel, and who may therefore appeal to common ground between Islam and Christianity, and, conversely, those who see Islam as a barrier to true knowledge of God, and who refer almost exclusively to differences between the two religions. Chapman inclines to the former position, and refers to the biblical affirmation of the worship offered to God by the not-yet-Christian Cornelius (Acts 10:4ff), and to the way in which Paul in his testimony to the Greeks in Athens appealed to their belief in a god, even if 'unknown' (Acts 17).[31] On the question of the salvation of Muslims, he refers to the distinction between general (i.e. natural) and special (i.e. biblical) revelation, in the light of which one could say that 'if Muhammad was a sincere seeker after God, any revelation he received was no different in principle from that given to a man like Cornelius before his conversion'; he furthermore expresses the opinion that 'God had real personal dealings with Muhammad'.[32] Similarly, Nazir-Ali feels that 'at least in some parts of the Qur'an . . . there seems to be a genuine encounter with the Supreme Reality of the universe'.[33] Brown believes that God is present 'long before the Christian arrives on the scene, caring for the Muslim no less than for the Christian', and suggests that God may be using Islam to inculcate in people 'a recognition of God's presence' (p. 94). Rather than seeing Islam as an impediment, then, some missionaries may see it as having the potential to convey some, albeit imperfect or incomplete, awareness of and knowledge about God.

A small minority see Islam as explicitly anti-Christian. For them, even common ground is likely to be seen as a hindrance; the nineteenth-century orientalist William Muir complained that Islam contained 'just so much truth . . . as to direct attention from the need for more'.[34] Because of its rejection of specific tenets of the gospel, Schlorff sees Islam as repressing even a person's natural knowledge of God which they may otherwise have been able to acquire through general revelation.[35] He feels it is pointless to seek out common ground between Islam and Christianity, since the similarities are only on a superficial level, while at a more fundamental level 'the ideology of Islam runs *counter* to that of Biblical Christianity' (his italics).[36]

A related issue is the appropriateness or otherwise of using the Qur'an, or Islamic teachings, as a 'bridge' to Christian faith, which has theological implications for the continuity or discontinuity of Christianity with other religions. Those in favour of this approach point to the existence of a small number of former Muslims who were attracted to the figure of Christ as a result of their reading of the Qur'an, and stress that God can work through whatever channels He chooses.[37] This often involves interpreting the Qur'an in accordance with Christian beliefs; Abdul-Haqq, for example, interprets the Qur'an as supporting the divinity of Christ since it refers to him as 'the Word of God' and the

'Messiah', among other things (chapter 7), while Haddad finds in it support for the doctrine of original sin (chapters 11 and 12). Opponents, such as Schlorff, argue that such methods constitute an implicit recognition of the authority of the Qur'an, thereby compromising that of the Bible, and that any specifically Christian interpretation of the Qur'an, apart from being academically questionable, gives Muslims a corresponding right to interpret the Bible according to their own beliefs.[38]

Notwithstanding the insistence on essential theological differences, some missionaries do feel free to express appreciation of certain aspects of Islam. A positive attitude towards elements of Islamic culture is encouraged by the increasingly prevalent awareness that the gospel can be 'incarnated' in different cultures, and that Christianity is no longer a primarily Western phenomenon; in fact several make a plea for a disassociation of the gospel from Western culture.[39] 'Contextualization' has become an important theme in contemporary missiological thinking; its advocates seek to minimize the cultural dislocation of converts to Christianity by retaining or adapting indigenous cultural and even religious practices in so far as these are considered not to conflict with the gospel.[40]

Parshall is one of the most active proponents of contextualization in the Islamic context,[41] and his appreciation of Islamic cultural forms extends to forms of worship. He feels that it is important for Christians not only to observe Muslim rituals but also to 'probe deeper and enter into the *meaning* of each external observance', and sees 'God-awareness' as the central feature of Islam.[42] He comments on the sense of awe and humility which is visible in the performance of the five daily prayers, and mentions the 'reverential beauty and sublimity illustrated by a great mass of people bowing with faces to the ground in prayerful adoration of their Creator'.[43] Indeed, Muslims are said to be more biblical in their forms of worship than Christians, since the Bible mentions prostration as well as several other of the positions used by Muslims in prayer.[44] Parshall is able to express such admiration partly because of the diversity in forms of worship which is permissible in Christianity, and partly because he distinguishes between external forms and theological underpinnings: 'stripped of its legalisms and theological aberrations, perhaps the ideal of Muslim prayer has a challenge for the devout Christian.'[45]

An appreciation of certain aspects of Muslim culture is often coupled with a critical attitude towards Western culture. Parshall lists eleven areas in which the Muslim worldview is closer to that of the Old

Testament Hebrews than is that of Western Christians.[46] These include a greater emphasis on family solidarity, a more comprehensive view of life, and a corresponding rejection of individualism and secularism. Musk unfavourably compares the Western Christian reluctance to bring matters of faith into the public sphere with Islam's 'holistic worldview', and concedes the validity of much of the Islamists' diagnosis of Western civilization as materialistic and suffering from moral and social breakdown.[47]

Musk's *Touching the Soul of Islam* draws on anthropological and literary sources to explore various cultural themes, including 'male and female', 'family and individual', 'honour and shame', and 'time and space'. He acknowledges the plurality of Muslim cultures, and the fact that not all aspects of these cultures derive from Islamic sources (p. 17). The book aims among other things to challenge Westerners' ethnocentrism and to remove psychological barriers and negative stereotypes; the author acknowledges, for example, that the veil is often a matter of choice for Muslim women rather than something imposed on them, giving them 'a secure sense of place and identity in the public, "outside" world' (p. 27). Musk hopes that through this book 'the "giant" of Islam will not seem so large or so alarming as it is often portrayed in both the Christian and secular media', and that 'many of the Muslim's qualities will come to be accepted, even admired' (pp. 19, 20).

The elements of Muslim culture that Musk admires include emotional spontaneity and openness, particularly on the part of males; the emphasis on hospitality; the 'dignity and poise' of Middle Eastern peoples; and the people-centred, rather than achievement-oriented or materialistic approach to life (pp. 147, 90ff., 179, 111ff., 126). Even patronage is viewed sympathetically as a preference for interacting 'on a personal level in which people are far more important than certificates' (p. 167). He doesn't necessarily refrain from discussing cultural features that may appear less attractive, such as the forms which violence may take in different societies, but overall the selection of anecdotal and literary material seems geared towards conveying accurate insights and a balanced overview rather than towards portraying a negative or positive image of Muslim or Middle Eastern culture.[48]

Like Parshall, Musk draws attention to biblical parallels with Muslim culture, such as the importance of the concept of honour in the Old Testament and in Jesus' cultural milieu, and the way in which this is reflected in biblical stories and parables (pp. 83–5). He also observes that the God of the Old Testament was apparently willing to work through Semitic patriarchal cultural norms without necessarily condemning them (p. 58).

As in much secular scholarship, the assumption that Islam is not of divine origin leads to an assumption that the Qur'an and the Islamic religious cult were the result of specific influences to which Muhammad was exposed. Some Christian writers are confident that these can be traced, and assume direct borrowing, in contrast to the more usual Western scholarly opinion that Muhammad had no direct access to the Christian scriptures.[49] Geisler and Saleeb maintain that 'it is common knowledge that Islam borrowed many of its beliefs and practices from other religions', and that 'the vast majority of ideas in the Qur'an have known sources, whether Jewish, Christian, pagan or otherwise' (pp. 166, 156). Gilchrist states that 'there is nothing in the Qur'an which is genuinely original or which cannot be shown to have parallels in the varying religious convictions found throughout the region'.[50] Brown believes that it would be easy to refute the Qur'an by comparing its versions of biblical stories with those in the Old Testament, of which he feels they are 'imperfectly remembered versions . . . together with a great deal of Rabbinic legend and imaginative reconstruction', but he does not in fact deem this to be a desirable way of relating to or reaching Muslims (p. 89).

A certain (albeit decreasing) amount of missionary effort is aimed at refuting the textual integrity of the Qur'an, whether by questioning the process of redaction or by referring to alleged errors or contradictions in the text; this material provides a fairly close parallel to the Muslim material on the text of the Bible. To the extent that missionary authors are not academic authorities in Arabic or Islamic studies, they are dependent on secondary sources. On the question of the redaction of the Qur'an, Parshall comments that 'Islamic vulnerability at this point seems obvious to most Western scholars', and he and others complain of Muslim reluctance to acknowledge or address this problem.[51] The most comprehensive contemporary missionary work on the collection of the Qur'an is Gilchrist's *Jam'al-Qur'an: The Codification of the Qur'an Text*. The author's list of sources consulted includes the primary Muslim Arabic sources, including the main Hadith collections and the works of Sira (biography of the Prophet), as well as the works of orientalists such as Jeffery, Nöldeke, Watt and Margoliouth (pp. 11–15).

Gilchrist aims to refute only 'the Muslim hypothesis of a perfect text' which has 'been preserved to perfection without variations of any kind' (pp. 134–5). He therefore emphasizes the various aspects of diversity to which the sources (mainly the Hadith accounts) refer: the use of different dialects in the early period, the existence of variant codices (such as those of 'Abdullah ibn Mas'ūd and 'Ubayy ibn Ka'b) before 'Uthman's standardization, and the existence of variant readings both before and after the 'Uthmanic recension. He also refers to accounts of 'missing verses' such as the famous 'verses of stoning for adultery' which, according to the Hadith, 'Umar claimed to have formed part of the revelation. He dismisses Muslim attempts to explain these and other verses as 'abrogated' (*mansūkh*), on the grounds that they were not replaced by anything else and their legal force remained (pp. 91–9).

Gilchrist argues that Zayd ibn Thabit's codification, which remained essentially a private copy of the Qur'an until 'Uthman imposed it as the standard version, was simply one of a number of more or less equally authoritative versions, and that 'Uthman resorted to it as a version that had not yet been widely circulated, and which was therefore not involved in any of the controversies that had prompted his standardization in the first place (p. 45). 'Uthman's reason for ordering the destruction of any variants was therefore a pragmatic one: 'not . . . because they were considered unreliable but rather to prevent future dissension among the inhabitants of the different provinces' (p. 44).

Gilchrist concludes that 'the single text as it stands today was only arrived at through an extended process of amendments, recensions, eliminations and an imposed standardization of a preferred text at the initiative of a subsequent caliph and not by prophetic direction or divine decree' (p. 137). Interestingly, he adds that 'the Qur'an is an authentic text to the extent that it largely retains the material initially delivered by Muhammad'. He is therefore able to confirm the 'relative authenticity of the text', and finds no evidence of any significant post-Muhammadan additions (pp. 137–8). This is in line with the acceptance on the part of most missionaries and secular scholars that the current recension is in fact the 'Uthmanic one, which does not depart significantly from the Qur'an as collected soon after Muhammad's death.[52]

Gilchrist also challenges the rationale underlying the Muslim belief in the need for a perfect text. He argues that 'if a book never was the Word of God in the first place, no amount of proof that it has been absolutely and perfectly preserved will make it the Word of God.

Conversely, if a book was indeed the Word of God at the time when it was first inscribed, the later existence of a few suspect passages and variant readings which do not affect the overall content of the text would not negate its original divine authenticity' (p. 125). In this he appears to be partially undermining his own efforts, in that a 'way out' is offered to Muslims; however, it is one which is almost never taken.

Some missionaries explicitly relate this issue to the Muslim tradition of impugning the biblical text. Several writers express the opinion that the main difference between the fixing of the biblical and the Qur'anic texts is that Christians preserved early (although not the original) variant manuscripts, whereas 'Uthman's standardization aborted the possibility of critical appraisal of the earliest manuscripts.[53] It is not, therefore, that there is necessarily felt to be any great divergence between the biblical and the Qur'anic canonical processes (although the shorter time-scale is generally acknowledged for the latter), but rather that Muslim claims for the Qur'anic text are seen as excessive, and that Muslims are accused of being inconsistent in criticizing the biblical canon while assuming *a priori* the authenticity of the Qur'anic text.

Geisler and Saleeb refer to internal textual criteria in order to question the divine origin of the Qur'an, such as its literary quality and alleged grammatical errors, contradictions, and factual or scientific inaccuracies (chapter 8). Since they do not know Arabic, the literary excellence of the Qur'an is questioned on the basis of a reading of the Qur'an in translation, notwithstanding Muslims' insistence that the Qur'an is essentially untranslatable and can only be fully appreciated in the original Arabic (pp. 92, 189). In fact, they reproduce several passages in English and invite readers to 'judge for themselves'. They doubt whether in fact the Qur'an is qualitatively different from the best of pre-Islamic poetry, or for that matter from the best of Western literature (pp. 158, 187), and regard literary quality as in any case an arbitrary and subjective criterion for establishing divine authorship (pp. 187, 188).[54] Parshall, on the other hand, does acknowledge the powerful effect that the Qur'an can have on Muslims, and that it has sometimes played a part in the conversion of Westerners to Islam.[55]

There is little specifically on alleged linguistic and factual errors in the Qur'an, although these have been a theme in orientalist scholarship in the past. Factual errors are primarily considered to be the particulars in which the Qur'anic stories depart from the biblical versions; the most commonly cited are the fact that the Qur'an refers to Mary the mother of

Jesus ('Maryam' in the Qur'an) as 'the sister of Aaron', allegedly confusing her with the biblical Miriam, sister of Moses and Aaron, and the fact that Haman seems to be placed a thousand years earlier in the Qur'an than in the Book of Esther.[56] Whether or not the Bible is supported by external historical sources, it is sometimes argued that its anteriority gives it priority as a historical source, contrary to the theologically based Muslim argument which claims the advantage for posteriority.[57] In some cases apparent contradictions in the Qur'anic text arise from a literalistic reading which would give similar results if applied to the Bible. For example, Geisler and Saleeb assert that the Qur'anic passages on the creation of the world, one of which mentions six days while another seems to refer to eight days in total, are irreconcilable, while simultaneously holding that the differing Gospel accounts of the number of angels who were present at the discovery of the empty tomb (Matthew having one, while John mentions two) are 'minor discrepancies' which constitute 'conflicts but not contradictions' (pp. 197, 239–40).

A more reflexive attitude is taken by Glaser, who acknowledges that for both Christians and Muslims there are obstacles to appreciating each other's scriptures: for the Christian, who is not used to the idea of a sacred language, 'the Qur'an has a monotonous and stylized form', and his or her Arabic is not usually adequate to appreciate its poetic qualities, while for the Muslim, 'most of the biblical writings are of obviously human origin, and do not resemble what he recognizes as divine revelation', especially in view of 'their failure to give clear guidelines on life-style'. She concludes that Muslims and Christians 'cannot understand each other's Book . . . by applying their own criteria to the other's revelation'.[58]

Muhammad

Moucarry speaks for nearly all evangelical Christians when he says that a Christian cannot endorse the second half of the Muslim profession of faith, which affirms Muhammad as the messenger of God, without denying his own faith (p. 105). Although some do acknowledge certain parallels between Muhammad and some of the Hebrew prophets, the fact that Muhammad came *after* Jesus means that he cannot be placed in the same theological category. Chapman perceives a 'striking resemblance' between Muhammad's career and that of Gideon in the Book of Judges in the Old Testament; he observes that such similarities may help

Christians to feel more sympathy for Muhammad's vision, but nevertheless feels that Muhammad, unlike Gideon, cannot be fitted into 'the total plan of biblical history from Adam to Jesus'.[59] Gilchrist expresses this by saying that: 'between those prophets and [Muhammad's] era stands a new dawn in human history when the man Jesus Christ projected a perfect human character and fulfilled God's revealed purposes for mankind once and for all'.[60]

However, the belief that Muhammad was not a prophet does not necessarily preclude a belief in his sincerity. Some, including Gilchrist, Geisler and Saleeb, point to Muhammad's obvious belief in his own divine mission; Gilchrist feels that 'the simplicity of his life . . . testifies to his personal sincerity'.[61] Parshall is slightly more hesitant; although he feels unable to declare Muhammad 'a purposeful impostor and deceiver', he believes that ultimately the matter of his sincerity has to be left to God, who alone knows the truth and is competent to judge.[62] Whether or not Muhammad deliberately rejected the gospel may have implications for the Christian's view of him. On the basis that the Qur'an seems to reject heretical beliefs such as tritheism or the physical sonship of Jesus, rather than mainstream Christian beliefs, and that Muhammad would not have had access to the Judaeo-Christian scriptures in his own language, it is often held that he was never properly exposed to the gospel message but only to a distorted form of it.[63] This view may enable those who hold it to refrain from seeing Muhammad as 'anti-Christian'.[64]

Moucarry warns against 'hasty judgements on Muhammad', especially those which find him to be 'an impostor, a false prophet and even an anti-Christ'. He believes that 'such judgements, far from being inspired by the teachings of Jesus and his apostles, betray a great ignorance of Islam and a lamentable lack of understanding of the biblical doctrine of revelation' (p. 97). Gilchrist, perhaps with more diplomatic considerations in mind, states that 'no Christian should be ignorant of his image in the hearts and lives of common Muslims and it is obvious that he should be respected and not be reviled in any way in conversation with Muslims'.[65]

Some missionaries express admiration for the extent of Muhammad's human accomplishments. Given the state of Arabia in Muhammad's day, Chapman feels that one 'cannot but feel genuine amazement and admiration for all that he achieved in his lifetime' in the areas of both political unification and religious reform.[66] Brown lays particular emphasis on the religious dimension: 'By any standard,

Muhammad's achievements were little short of miraculous, and are to be attributed not so much to courage and skill in battle, though these qualities played their part, as to the wisdom and clemency, the patience and perseverance with which Muhammad pursued his ends and called forth the loyalty of those who served him' (p. 61). His unification of Arabia was 'no mere military victory . . . but the achievement of a Prophet who spoke and acted in the name of God, and who inculcated into the proud, self-sufficient merchants of Mecca and the pagan Arabs of the desert alike, the humbling ever-present fear of God and the practices of piety, prayer, fasting and almsgiving'. He suggests that Christians might 'see in him the partial fulfilment of some of [their] own natural longings and desires' and recognize Islam as an originally Arab version of religious truth, were it not for the fact of the Crucifixion (p. 69).

Christians see neither Muhammad nor any other human being (with the exception of Jesus) as beyond moral reproach. Parshall says: 'Unequivocally we can and do declare Muhammad to be a sinner with no claims to deity or saviorhood. He simply is not to be categorized with Christ'.[67] Evidence is sometimes enlisted from the Qur'an or the Hadith to demonstrate that even in the Muslim view, Muhammad was not originally seen as sinless. Geisler and Saleeb cite Qur'anic verses which tell Muhammad to seek forgiveness (p. 173), while Haddad maintains that 'the claim of the sinlessness of the prophets is an outright contradiction of the Qur'an', and cites Qur'anic verses which appear to rebuke Muhammad (pp. 36, 39–40).

The appreciation of Muhammad's positive or admirable qualities is usually qualified by being expressed in terms of the context of his day. Moucarry describes him as 'probably the most zealous Arab of his generation in God's cause' (p. 105), while Anderson observes that 'his virtues outshone those of his contemporaries, while his failings can scarcely have provoked comment in his day and generation'.[68] Gilchrist describes Muhammad as 'one of the giants of human history' and 'a truly remarkable man', and states that 'judged relatively by the standards of his day . . . he appears worthy of much respect and a man of a generally unimpeachable character'.[69] However, he goes on to say that 'anyone who projects himself as the finest and greatest of all God's messengers in history immediately exposes himself to the most exacting scrutiny to prove his claims'; Muhammad must therefore be judged by absolute rather than relative standards, and furthermore he actually invites comparison with Jesus by claiming to be on an equal level with him.[70]

Geisler and Saleeb comment along similar lines that 'however much [of] an improvement Muhammad's morals may have been over many others of his day, he certainly seems to fall short of the perfect example for all men of all times that many Muslims claim for him' (p. 173).

It is perhaps unremarkable that the main areas in which Muhammad is criticized are those of military activity or violence, on the one hand, and his relations with women on the other. Although the authors are aware that there were Old Testament kings, prophets and godly men (all considered 'prophets' by Muslims) who engaged in warfare or polygamy, the Judaeo-Christian tradition portrays them as morally fallible and therefore their actions are not necessarily considered exemplary. Christian responses to Muhammad are often influenced by their vision of Jesus, who neither married nor bore arms, and the comparison between the two is sometimes explicit. Although Parshall believes that one should avoid attacking Muhammad's character, he suggests that he can be contrasted with Jesus, who, according to Muslims and Christians alike, 'neither sinned nor remained in an earthly grave'.[71] Gilchrist echoes the view of Muhammad and Jesus as different not just in degree but in kind when he says that 'Muhammad shows himself to be as much in need of the redeeming work of God's Saviour as any other person in history', and he contrasts the Qur'anic cursing of Muhammad's opponents with Jesus' command to love one's enemies.[72]

Actions which are seen as particularly reprehensible include the practice of raiding; the treatment of the Jews, particularly the killing of the men of Banu Qurayzah and the enslavement of their women and children;[73] the implementation of certain punishments such as amputations and floggings; and the ordering of the removal of opponents such as Ka'b ibn Ashraf and Abu Rafi, who both composed satirical verse against Muhammad, by assassination.[74] While Muslims defend such actions as tactically necessary for the preservation of the early Muslim polity, Geisler and Saleeb see them as a case of the end justifying the means, and evidence that Muhammad was not of 'flawless moral character' (pp. 175–6). Contrasting interpretations of events enlist contrasting vocabulary: what is for Gilchrist the 'slaughter' of Banu Qurayzah or of individual opponents is for Muslims their 'execution'.[75] Reporting the affair of Ka'b from the Hadith collections of al-Bukhārī and Muslim, and Ibn Sa'd's *Kitāb al-Ṭabaqāt al-Kabīr*, Gilchrist concludes that 'this whole affair had an atmosphere of conspiracy and intrigue, of deception and treachery, of murder and assassination'.[76]

Parshall, who bases his book *Inside the Community: Understanding Muslims through their Traditions* (1994) exclusively on al-Bukhārī's Hadith collection, concludes his chapter on 'Jihad and Violence' with the statement that 'Islamic belief and practice as stated in the Hadith undeniably affirm religious violence' (p. 111). This conclusion is not surprising, since Parshall gathers together in this and the following chapter on 'Punishments for Sin' a good number of relatively bloodthirsty Hadiths, such as the account of a tribe who apostasized and killed a Muslim shepherd, and who on Muhammad's orders were left to die after having their limbs cut off and nails driven into their eyes (p. 121). The theme of violence is further highlighted when in several places in this book he refers to contemporary acts of violence on the part of Muslims, one of which involved the killing of a 'close friend and colleague' (p. 14). For his part, Parshall professes to struggle with certain passages of the Old Testament, but believes that 'the world view of Christians has undergone a paradigm shift from the harshness of the Old Testament law to the New Testament emphasis on mercy and forgiveness', illustrating this point with reference to Jesus' forgiveness of the adulterous woman in John 8 (pp. 98–9, 112, 122).

If violence or the use of force is perceived as inherent in Islamic origins, then its use by Muslims in history may be interpreted as authentically Islamic, while the same violent acts perpetrated by Christians may be seen as a deviation from their faith. Parshall, mentioning the Crusades, admits that 'Islam does not stand alone in regard to the embarrassment flowing from the activities of religious zealots', but suggests that there is a closer scriptural connection in the case of Islam: 'Islamic scriptures are a source from which the extremists can selectively pick and choose, thus legitimizing their acts of violence'. He does however add that 'such fanatical deeds will continue to be denounced by other Muslim theologians and laypeople who see Islam in a different light' (pp. 98, 123). Haddad speaks for most contemporary Christians when he says that 'although Christ's message is universal . . . it was never intended to achieve world dominion. When organized Christianity aimed to subjugate the nations by force of arms, it did so in contradiction of what its God intended' (p. 97).

On the subject of Muhammad's domestic affairs, Parshall acknowledges that some Hadiths show evidence of 'a kind of good-natured camaraderie between Muhammad and his wives', but highlights the reports which speak of jealousy between wives and Muhammad's partiality to A'isha, and concludes that overall there was 'a distinct lack of harmony' in Muhammad's household.[77] Also censured are some of the marital arrangements which were practised or condoned (although not introduced) by Muhammad, in particular the practices of polygamy, concubinage and the sanctioning of temporary marriage (*mut'ah*) up until the late Medinan period.[78] With regard to polygamy, Geisler and Saleeb claim that God permitted it but did not command or approve it in the Old Testament, and contend that 'every polygamist in the Bible, including David and Solomon, paid dearly for their sins' (p. 170). Musk, on the other hand, does not detect any strong condemnation of polygamy in the Old Testament, but simply sees it as part of a 'fallible, human culture' through which the revelation came.[79]

The close relationship between Muhammad's marital affairs and certain revelations is sometimes the subject of adverse comment. The implication is that notwithstanding Muhammad's overall sincerity, there is an element of expediency, if not opportunism, in such revelations. Sometimes mentioned in this connection is the revelation which sanctioned Muhammad's marriage to Zaynab bint Jahsh, whose (not altogether happy) marriage to his freed slave and adopted son Zayd he had previously arranged.[80] The traditional account is that as a result of a chance encounter one day, Muhammad experienced a strong attraction for her. Zayd subsequently insisted on divorcing her, a move which Muhammad at first resisted but which was approved by a revelation (Qur'an 33:37).[81] Also greeted with scepticism are the revelations which allowed special marriage privileges to Muhammad, such as being permitted to retain all his wives when others were limited to four (implied in 33:30), not having to observe the strict order of rotation among wives whereby a night was to be spent with each in turn (33:51), and the relaxation of the rules governing betrothal (33:50).[82] While Muslims view such exceptions as justified by the peculiar circumstances attendant on Muhammad's prophetic role,[83] these writers view them as evidence that Muhammad contravened the regulations laid down in the Qur'an. Geisler and Saleeb ask in connection with the limitation of wives to four: 'how can someone be a perfect moral example for the whole human race and not even live by one of the basic laws he laid down as from God?' (p. 171).

Many missionaries comment on the great reverence, even veneration, which Muslims have for their Prophet, even though orthodox Islamic doctrine holds him to be purely human. Gilchrist, who has the fullest treatment of the subject, believes that although 'all Muslims will boldly state that they worship Allah alone and that their prophet was only a faithful messenger', yet Muhammad is 'absolutely central to the hopes, desires, convictions and yearnings of the average Muslim', for whom he has become almost 'an essential mediator'.[84]

Those who deal with this subject usually draw on the writings of Annemarie Schimmel, an authority on Sufism, who deals with the subject of the veneration of Muhammad particularly in . . . *And Muhammad is His Messenger* (Chapel Hill: University of North Carolina Press, 1985). Recurrent themes are the taking of Muhammad as exemplar even in small details; the sometimes elaborate celebrations of the Mawlid (the Prophet's birthday); Muhammad's role as intercessor; the calling down of blessings on him in prayer; the importance of dreams or visions of Muhammad; the conserving of relics; and the elevation of Muhammad, sometimes to the rank of deity, in Sufi poetry and doctrine.[85]

Sometimes a contrast is drawn between the Qur'an – which presents Muhammad as an ordinary human being, seems in places to deny the possibility of intercession, and rebukes those who ask for a miracle – and later Muslim tradition, which increasingly elaborated on the Qur'anic conception.[86] Gilchrist comments that the image of Muhammad evolved from that of 'a prophetic statesman and warrior' in the earlier period to that of 'a saint and mystical philanthropist' later on.[87] Several authors suggest, as does much secular scholarship, that the stories of Muhammad's miracles were promoted or embellished by Muslims in the context of Muslim–Christian theological controversy.[88]

On this issue the relationship between 'official' or 'normative' Islam on the one hand, and 'popular' or 'actual' Islam on the other, is perceived as one of osmosis. In illustration of his points Gilchrist sometimes cites examples of authoritative Muslim theologians such as Jalaluddin al-Suyūṭī, who claimed to have had a vision of the Prophet and who approved the celebration of the Mawlid as a 'good innovation' (*bid'ah hasanah*).[89] Parshall suggests that although orthodox Muslims would recoil at assertions of Muhammad's deity in Sufi poetry, nevertheless 'they would reason that the heresy is at least headed in the right direction. The heart of the Muslim in his devotion toward Muhammad takes him further than his theological orthodoxy would normally allow him to go.'[90] Gilchrist detects a similar tension, commenting that although the apotheosis of Muhammad 'is not immediately apparent in the face that Islam presents to the world', nevertheless it is a reality 'in the hearts and minds of most of the ordinary Muslims of the world'.[91]

The veneration of Muhammad is often interpreted as the fulfilment of a natural human need for a bridge or intercessor between humankind and God; Abdul-Haqq remarks that 'without this mediator mankind will always be under a spiritual constraint . . . to deify creatures'.[92] Nazir-Ali similarly sees this phenomenon as illustrating that 'human beings continually waver between their awe of God's holiness and their need for intimacy with the source of their being'.[93] In other words, Muslim apotheosis of Muhammad is a substitute for Christ, who alone can respond to the needs of the human heart. Gilchrist fears that the idealization of Muhammad is 'a great stumbling block to the Gospel and one which has somewhat confused the true image of Jesus who really was many of the things that have wishfully been attributed to the Prophet of Islam'.[94]

The Relationship between God and Humankind

When treating theological issues, missionaries and evangelists become more explicitly comparative: it is the perceived contrasts between Islam and Christianity that draw their attention, and it is presumably those contrasts that might conceivably provide the motivation for a person to choose one faith rather than the other. The theme of relationship itself is one which is arguably more central to Christians than Muslims; Glaser observes that 'the notion of relationship runs through a number of major areas of Christian doctrine', most notably that of the Trinity, according to which God Himself is 'in relationship in eternity'. Accordingly, 'a weakening of this notion will produce doctrines that come close to an Islamic understanding', so that, for example, to remove the concept of relatedness within the Godhead is to move towards the Islamic idea of God as a unity without plurality.[95]

In the past, the question of whether Muslims and Christians worship the same God was not uncommonly given a negative answer – in other words, 'Allah' was taken to be a conceptual idol. Nowadays missionaries tend to be more cautious in answering this question, and generally do so in the affirmative, albeit with some reservations. Geisler and Saleeb sum up the general feeling with a quote from Cragg: 'The differences, which undoubtedly exist, between the Muslim and the Christian understanding of God are far-reaching and must be patiently studied. But it would be fatal to all our mutual tasks to doubt that one and the same God over all was the reality in both' (p. 14). Parshall comments more forthrightly that 'Islam presents an inadequate and incomplete – but not totally misguided – view of God'.[96] Evidence adduced in support of this includes the testimony of converts from Islam to Christianity, who usually feel that there is some continuity in their relationship with God before and after their conversion, and the fact that Arab Christians use the word 'Allah' for God.[97]

Chapman feels that it is helpful to talk about common ground at least as a starting point: 'we want to see how far we can walk along the same road with the Muslim before we come to the fork where our paths diverge'.[98] He points out that both Muslims and Christians can assent to a series of simple propositions: 'God creates. God is one. God rules. God reveals. God loves. God judges. God forgives.' While there is no dispute between Muslims and Christians as to *whether* God does these things, however, there is a difference concerning *how* he accomplishes them.[99]

The theme of God's love is prominent in the Bible – especially the New Testament – and in Christian thought, and it is therefore a theme to which Christians often refer when relating to Islam. It is often acknowledged that the idea of God's closeness or even His love is not absent from the Qur'an; several missionaries cite the Qur'anic verse which describes God as being nearer to man than his jugular vein (50:16).[100] However, God's love in Islam is felt to be mitigated either by not being prior to His other attributes, or by being qualitatively different to His love in Christian teachings. Goldsmith expresses the former view when he says: 'while the Christian will insist that God's power is subject to his love and holiness, Islam will feel that God's love and holiness must never contradict his sovereign power' (p. 90). Brown acknowledges that Muslims, like Christians, see God as 'living and personal', but finds that the emphasis in the Qur'an is on His omnipotence and sovereignty rather than His love (pp. 73–4). He observes that the Qur'an speaks of God's mercy rather than His love, yet even so that mercy is 'only one quality among many others which God displays in dealing with men, and which may, at times, be overshadowed by other qualities of might and power'. This is contrasted with the portrayal of God's love in the New Testament as 'something constant and unchangeable, the very nature of God himself' (p. 75). Geisler and Saleeb cite Qur'anic verses which emphasize God's mercy, compassion and forgiveness, but find that ultimately the relationship between God and humankind in the Qur'an 'is described in terms of master (*rabb*) and slave (*'abd*). God is the sovereign Monarch who requires man to submit to him as an obedient slave' (p. 27). Chapman, however, warns against understanding this servant–master relationship in terms of servility or degradation.[101] According to Brown, the God of the Qur'an resembles 'a king exercising the prerogative of mercy', rather than 'a father who suffers with his child and loves him out of his disgrace' (p. 75), while Glaser comments that 'God's love may cause him to have mercy on his creatures, even to the extent of communicating with them; but it is a love that condescends in beneficence rather than a love that shares in relationship'.[102]

Some feel that the love of God as depicted in the Qur'an is conditional, since 'the Qur'an always speaks of God's love for the righteous or for the believers and never of his love for sinners'.[103] Chapman elaborates on this: while God loves 'certain kinds of people', including those who do right, the God-fearing, the patient, and those who do battle for His cause, 'God does *not* love certain other kinds of people: aggressors (2:190), the corrupt (5:64, 28:77), the evil unbelievers (2:276), the ungrateful (22:38)', etc.[104] Moucarry contrasts the Qur'anic view with the biblical account in which 'God loves all men equally, even those who disobey him, for his love is unconditional' (p. 48).

God's relative 'detachment' in Islam is attributed to various factors. While Christians stress the likeness between God and humankind as illustrated by the fact that God created man in His own image and then took on human form Himself at the Incarnation, Moucarry observes that Muslims, concerned to defend God's transcendence, conceive Him as 'radically other' than humankind, even if not necessarily distant (p. 47). Some refer in this connection to the Islamic theological doctrines of *mukhālafah* (difference) and *tanzīh* (elimination of anthropomorphism), which maintain that attributes predicated of God do not have the same content when predicated of humankind.[105]

This essential difference is often seen as entailing an ultimate agnosticism concerning the nature of God, since He is inscrutable both in His essence, which can never be known, and in the outworking of His will.[106] Geisler and Saleeb observe that the 'ninety-nine names' of God preserved in Muslim tradition contain epithets that appear to contradict each other (e.g. 'the One Who leads astray' and 'the One Who guides'). Although this can be explained by reference to the fact that they describe God's will rather than His essence, nevertheless they are understood to mean that ultimately, as far as humans are concerned, God's actions are arbitrary: 'the action of his will may be identified from its effects, but his will itself is inscrutable. From this it may be concluded that God is not necessarily loving, holy, and righteous in every situation' (p. 26).

Another aspect of God's detachment is His impassibility, i.e. the belief that God cannot experience pain or suffering, or, more extremely, emotions.[107] Citing relevant texts from the Qur'an and Hadith, Glaser states that Muslims feel that 'man cannot affect God, since this would detract from his power and self-sufficiency . . . he cannot cause him grief or joy', and concludes that 'although God has deigned to communicate with his creatures, and even to love them, the relationship cannot be mutual since man's response can make no difference to God', and 'the ultimate in relationship is willing submission rather than interaction'.[108] Schlorff seems not even to acknowledge this one-way affection from God to the creature, and states more categorically that according to Muslims 'God *has no feelings or affections* for any creature' (his italics). He is more in line with Muslim thinking when he continues: 'Were God to display emotions, this would make Him like men and would be a weakness . . . He gains nothing from our obedience and loses nothing from our rebellion.'[109]

According to Moucarry, 'bowing before God's unfathomable and transcendent nature, Muslims say *what* God is. Receiving his love . . . Christians confess *who* God is' (his italics, p. 49). The less personal conception of God in Islam is seen as being reflected in a lesser concern with God's character in the Qur'an than in the Bible. Geisler and Saleeb quote the eminent Muslim modernist scholar Fazlur Rahman, who claims that 'the Qur'an is no treatise about God and His nature: His existence, for the Qur'an, is strictly functional' (p. 19). They cite other Muslim authorities to demonstrate that 'whereas in Christianity Christ is believed to be the self-disclosure of God, in Islam the emphasis of the Qur'an is not on revealing God per se, but more important, on disclosing the commands of God'. Furthermore, 'according to orthodox Islam, the purpose of man is not to know God and become more conformed to his character, but to understand his will and become more obedient to his commands' (pp. 101, 47).

Without exception, Christians view themselves as monotheists, and do not consider that the concept of plurality within unity in the Godhead in any way contradicts this. Various analogies are used to try and convey this to the Muslim; among those used by Geisler and Saleeb are that of a person's mind, thoughts and words which have a unity but are still plural, and, perhaps slightly provocatively, that of Muhammad, who is at one and the same time husband, prophet and leader (pp. 263, 269). By contrast, Islam's monotheism may be described as 'rigid and inflexible'; Geisler and Saleeb believe that in its simple undifferentiated oneness it resembles a product of human reason rather than divine revelation (pp. 134–5). Moucarry also pursues the theme of the limitations of human reason; although he doesn't accept that the Qur'an itself is anti-trinitarian, since he believes that it rejects tritheism rather than trinitarianism (p. 82), he feels that later Muslim interpreters were, in the belief that 'human reason . . . is capable of grasping, by its own effort, the truth of its Creator. In the Christian view, this truth is inevitably too high above mankind to be grasped by our unaided reason. It therefore includes "mysteries" which the Scriptures reveal and which can be grasped only by faith' (p. 91). Haddad feels that the simplicity of absolute unity is unbecoming to God: 'the bare and solitary Oneness of God is easier to fathom than the nature of man himself . . . If God is a rigid unity, then he is less than his creature' (p. 58).

Some missionaries recruit philosophical arguments for plurality within the divine nature; these often echo the arguments which were used in the medieval Christian–Muslim theological debates. Moucarry asks: 'how can the universe be recognized as having a real existence unless the principle of "otherness" within the Creator is acknowledged?', and feels that only a plural monotheism 'permits a qualitative distinction between God and man, conferring on man a separate and real identity' (pp. 88–9). Abdul-Haqq develops this idea, maintaining that the denial of any multiplicity within God may lead to the view that all of creation is 'against the fundamental nature of God', and in this light the Qur'anic statement: 'everything will perish save His countenance' (28:88) would mean that even heaven and hell will cease, leaving 'no promise of life everlasting for the creature' (p. 183). Some draw attention to the parallel between the Christian doctrine of the Incarnation and the Islamic theological doctrine of the eternal speech of God, as 'inlibrated' in the Qur'an. Abdul-Haqq states that 'it is no exaggeration to say that Muslims claim for the Koran what Christians have always testified about the Lord Jesus Christ' (p. 62), while Geisler and Saleeb reason that 'if speech is an eternal attribute of God that is not identical to God but is somehow distinguishable from him, then does not this allow the very kind of plurality within unity that Christians claim for the Trinity?' (p. 136). Abdul-Haqq makes a similar point concerning God's attributes: 'if they are considered outside His nature . . . [this] will amount to "Shirk" (Associationism) . . . On the other hand, if these qualities belong to the divine nature, the absolute unity of God . . . is removed' (p. 182).

'Singular monotheism' is seen as entailing certain risks, for which evidence is sometimes furnished from Islamic history. Abdul-Haqq sees Muslims as gravitating to the two extremes of 'practical Deism', as represented by orthodoxy, and pantheism, as represented by Sufism (p. 183). Moucarry has a similar conception of the 'twin dangers' facing Islam. On the one hand, the blurring of the distinction between God and humankind leads not only to pantheism (or 'fusional spiritualism') but also to fatalism, since it undermines the idea of free will (p. 88). The opposite danger, legalism or 'an activism which tames God's power and reduces faith to its merely horizontal dimension' (p. 89), ensues from the absence of a personal relationship with God. However, he acknowledges that 'plural monotheism' carries its own dangers, as witnessed by various heretical beliefs which have been held by some Christians, such as tritheism or the deification of humankind (p. 90). A concomitant of singular monotheism is the absence of a doctrine of incarnation in Islam. Abdul-Haqq maintains that 'in the absence of belief in the mediator between God and creation, Muslims have been struggling to satisfactorily reconcile the two opposite poles of divine transcendence and immanence' (p. 183). Goldsmith holds that 'if there is no mediating Son of God, then God must either be stripped of his absolute glory in order to relate to man or he will remain in isolated splendour with such glory that man cannot approach him' (p. 36).

Sufism is often cited as a tradition within Islam which seeks a closer relationship between God and humankind and lays greater emphasis on love;[110] it is almost always seen as a reaction to and compensation for the dryness of orthodox Islam, since 'the daily ritual of Islam and the stern demands of the law provide little to quicken the pulse or fire the emotions'.[111] However, the Sufi path is not necessarily seen as being in harmony with the Christian way. Because of Islam's singular monotheism, the attempt to achieve communion with God may have undesirable consequences; Moucarry states that 'some Muslim mystics, seeking an intimate communion with God, crossed the dividing line between God and man, and thus jeopardized the divine transcendence' (p. 88). Parshall wishes to uphold what for the Christian is an important distinction between absorption in God and being filled with God (i.e. the Holy Spirit), while Schlorff holds that the 'goal of absorption is just as foreign and inimical to the Gospel message as is orthodox Islam'.[112] Furthermore, progress along the Sufi path is seen as dependent on human effort rather than God's initiative: Schlorff states that for the Sufi, union with God 'is achieved by man's striving upward, and not by the coming down of the Holy Spirit to dwell in their hearts'.[113] Abdul-Haqq similarly comments on the fact that Sufis endeavour to attain experience of God 'by human devices', and believes that as a result 'Sufism stumbled on the rocks of Buddhistic nihilism ("Fana fi Allah" – losing oneself in God) and Hindu pantheism ("Baqa bi Allah" – finding oneself through identity with God)' (p. 172). The emphasis on experience may be seen as a further hazard: Chapman quotes Gairdner as saying that the Sufi's 'experimental gnosis is an intellectual agnosis'.[114]

The concept of sin is pivotal to the Christian view of salvation history. Understood in the generic sense (innate or 'original' sin), it forms an essential part of both the Christian account of universal history, beginning with the creation of the universe and of humankind, and of a particular view of metaphysics, representing as it does a pathological human condition which requires the remedy of a sacrifice or a redemption. The Christian who examines what the Qur'an has to say on this subject therefore often feels that something is missing, or that it lacks cohesion.[115]

Glaser recognizes that the Muslim view of sin forms part of a coherent set of beliefs, and is aware that the contrasting teachings of Christianity and Islam are likely to lead to 'accusations of denigration of humanity from the one side, and of self-righteousness from the other'.[116] She views the way in which the differing attitudes of Islam and Christianity towards sin function in the wider context of their respective faiths, stressing the implications for her chosen theme of 'relationship'. While in Islam, sin is conceived as a 'violation of the law', Christianity conceives it in relational terms as 'a state of separation rather than a series of violations of his [God's] regulations'. While in Islam sin affects humans and their eternal destiny, in Christianity it also affects God, offending and grieving Him. Since the Muslim does not see himself as fallen, 'he will not seek the restoration of a relationship which he does not believe ever existed'.[117] Schlorff elaborates on this theme: while both Christianity and Islam envisage the possibility of separation between humans and God, in Islam this is a permanent state of affairs due to an irremovable metaphysical difference, while in Christianity the separation is a temporary aberration restorable through acceptance of redemption through Christ.[118] By claiming that in Islam 'both man's separation from God and his present condition are traced back to God himself, not to man, and are thus made normative', he reverses the common Muslim accusation that Christians are pessimistic about the human condition.[119]

The different views of sin are seen as having consequences for both soteriology and ethics. Abdul-Haqq maintains that in Islam 'salvation is a release in the hereafter from the punishment of sin and not a present freedom from its hold upon the mind and heart of a believer' (p. 162). Glaser cites a Muslim scholar, Muhamed Abul Quasem, to the effect that while the Christian seeks salvation from the state of sin itself, the Muslim seeks salvation from punishment for sin. Following on from this is a different view of ethical behaviour, which Glaser expresses as follows: while in Islam, it is obedience which precedes and is the cause of God's acceptance, in Christianity it is God's acceptance which enables the believer to conform to His will.[120] Geisler and Saleeb feel that the Qur'anic view of sin has given rise to a 'nominalistic view of ethics' among Muslim theologians, referring to the widely accepted Ash'arite position that acts are not intrinsically right or wrong, but only so because God has declared them as such (p. 44). Schlorff appears to attribute moral relativism to Islam when he says that 'no act or attitude is inherently sinful . . . but is only sinful in circumstances in which it is declared to be *ḥarām* (forbidden) in the religious law, while it may not be sinful in other circumstances'.[121]

It is often felt that sin is viewed too lightly by Muslims. Geisler and Saleeb observe that according to the understanding of most Muslims, the Qur'an presents Adam and Eve's disobedience as a minor infringement which is soon forgiven, with no dire consequences (pp. 42–3). According to Schlorff, if 'man's basic problem is ignorance, rather than sin', then 'man's basic need is for knowledge of the law, for sin is basically erring from the true religious law'. He maintains that 'by denying the moral nature of man's problem and by substituting for it a mere problem of cognition', the Islamic teaching 'cuts off the Muslim from a consciousness of sin and of his need for salvation'.[122]

Several remark on what they see as a concern with external actions rather than inner intentions. Goldsmith feels that 'ethics based on commands rather than on the character of God face the constant danger of degenerating into legalism' (p. 51). The Christian concept of 'sanctification', i.e. the process by which the believer is gradually made holy or transformed into the image of God, having its completion in the afterlife, is seen as lacking in Islam: 'Islam believes in a God who helps men in particular situations, but it seems to have little stress on God's work in changing the very nature of man from within or . . . of growth in spirituality, holiness and love'.[123] Abdul-Haqq does not find 'concern about the purity of secret thoughts and imaginations' particularly prominent in the Islamic sources and comments that these 'were not to occupy too much attention of the believers' (p. 162). Brown relates this externality to the events of the Sira, where 'the story of the Hijra and of Badr focuses our attention on the outward actions of Muhammad and his enemies', and contrasts this with the Crucifixion which 'forces men to consider [their] inner sinfulness' (p. 79). Those who emphasize the externality or legalistic nature of Islamic ethics do not usually mention the importance in the Shari'a of the concept of *niyyah*, or right intention, which is considered essential in performing acts of worship, among other things.[124]

The way in which sin is viewed also has consequences for beliefs about forgiveness: Glaser cites a Muslim scholar to the effect that in the Qur'an, 'punishment is not the necessary and unavoidable consequence of sin. If there is repentance then any sin, however grave it may be, can be forgiven by the mercy of God.' Since Islam does not envisage a complete incompatibility between God's holiness and sin, which would make it a metaphysical necessity that sin should be judged, 'the Christian means to salvation are quite simply unnecessary. God can forgive sin without sacrifice or mediator.'[125] Chapman observes that 'in Islam, when people repent, God forgives, as it were, by a word', contrasting this with the costliness of forgiveness in both the Old and New Testaments.[126] In this connection he asks: 'If God is . . . the personal Creator who has made man in his own image, would we not expect his way of forgiving to have more in common with forgiveness between people as we know it than with the pardon extended by an all-powerful ruler to his subjects at little or no cost to himself?'[127]

Some, while aware of the mainstream Muslim view of the nature of humankind as essentially good, point out that many texts seem to support a more pessimistic view of human nature, thus presenting the possibility of narrowing the gap between Christian and Muslim beliefs. Woodberry, who treats this subject at some length in an article entitled: 'Different Diagnoses of the Human Condition', observes that Muslims, who do not believe that humans are fallen beings, 'are only looking for right guidance, not the transformation of their natures', and expresses the hope that they might, 'on the basis of their own writings . . . search for a more drastic solution' (p. 149). He draws attention to the angels' prediction at the time of humankind's creation that humans would cause corruption in the earth (2:30), and Satan's promise to pervert humankind until the Day of Judgement (15:39) (p. 151). He discerns the fulfilment of the latter in the many Qur'anic passages which recount the rejection of past prophets and the wickedness and unrighteousness of past generations, which sometimes led God to destroy whole communities. Furthermore, he observes that the Qur'an refers to humankind as 'sinful . . . (14:4), foolish (33:72), ungrateful (14:34), weak (4:28), despairing or boastful (11:9–10), quarrelsome (16:4), and rebellious (96:6)' (p. 155). Other texts considered of particular significance are the Qur'anic verse which states that 'if God were to punish men for their wrongdoing . . . he would not leave on earth a single creature' (16:61), and a Hadith from al-Bukhārī's collection to the effect that 'Satan touches every child when it is born, whereupon it starts crying loudly, except Mary and her son'(6:54) (pp. 155, 157).

Woodberry believes that the mainstream Muslim understanding of the 'descent' from paradise, as a physical movement rather than a moral fall, depends on a somewhat selective interpretation which emphasizes Adam's forgetfulness rather than his disobedience, and he attributes this in part to the Muslim belief that Adam was the first of the prophets, who are generally regarded in Islamic doctrine as protected from committing major sins, at least (p. 150). While Woodberry observes that *some* Muslims have interpreted the Qur'anic account of Adam and Eve's disobedience as having ramifications for the rest of humankind along the Christian lines of the Fall (pp. 152–4), Haddad goes further, believing that when properly understood the Qur'an fully supports the Christian view of humankind's sinfulness, including the Fall (chapters 11 and 12).

While most missionaries emphasize the legalistic nature of the Islamic view of sin, Woodberry follows up some of the other aspects of the Qur'anic teaching on sin, one of which is '*proud self-assertion* on the part of humans . . . When humans become anthropocentric as in the "tribal humanism" of pre-Islamic Arabia, rather than theocentric, it is sin' (his italics, p. 156). He suggests that other types of sin, such as disbelief and transgression of the law, can be seen as areas of common ground with the Bible, even if the New Testament sees the function of the law differently (pp. 156–7).

Conclusions

As people whose life's work involves immersing themselves in other cultures, communication and understanding are increasingly missionary concerns.[128] Most of the works cited quote extensively from books on Islam written by Muslims, and many refer to diversity of interpretation among Muslims. At the very least, the authors could be said to have made a serious attempt to engage with Islam as professed by Muslims. Although there does exist some poor quality evangelistic literature, as was indicated in the introductory section of this chapter, it appears to represent a relatively small proportion of the market and tends to be authored by those who have not lived in Muslim countries. Missionary literature does not usually lay claim either to neutrality (one might say that it has the merit of being explicit about the faith commitment and presuppositions which underpin it) or to academic status, and should not therefore be evaluated on purely academic grounds.

Christian missionaries share many areas of concern with Muslims, such as an interest in establishing whether or not the Qur'an is the word of God and in evaluating Muhammad's moral character. As with Muslims, this evaluation is likely to be on the basis of avowedly universal norms, in contrast to some more secular Western scholarship which seeks to soften its judgement by viewing Muhammad's actions in the context of seventh-century Arabian norms.[129] Like many modern Muslims, Christian missionaries often approach the source materials directly, without reference to subsequent Muslim interpretation. These works cover many areas of inquiry which are becoming increasingly rare in the academic study of Islam, for example the more controversial aspects of Muhammad's life (again, in common with Muslim apologists), subjective evaluation of the Qur'an's literary style and the tracing of parallels between the Qur'an and Judaeo-Christian extra-biblical sources. Of course, there are still some secular scholars who consider these to be legitimate areas of academic endeavour. Maxime Rodinson, for example, regrets that 'any criticisms of the Prophet's moral attitudes' are becoming increasingly taboo,[130] and Andrew Rippin believes that the predominance of the irenic approach in religious studies 'has led to the unfortunate result of a reluctance on the part of many scholars to follow all the way through with their insights and results', particularly concerning 'the historical dimensions of a faith that conceives itself as having a stake in that very history'.[131]

Like Islamists, missionaries may promote a fairly unitary view of orthodox Islam – one has to have something definable whether one wishes to refute or defend it.[132] To the extent that both are encroaching on the same territory, as it were, conflict is inevitable. Yet from a Muslim point of view, these writers may be said to have the virtue of taking Islam seriously. Parshall says: 'I personally cannot affirm [Muhammad] as a true prophet. If I did, I would be forced to accept his revelations as from God and therefore binding on all men', while Chapman replies to Muslim enquiries as to his view of Muhammad: 'if I *did* believe that he was a prophet, I would be a Muslim'.[133] This simple logic is closer to the thinking of most Muslims than is a more sophisticated liberal theological stance which seeks to accommodate the 'prophethood' of Muhammad, albeit not in Muslim terms, even if such initiatives are sometimes welcomed by Muslims for obvious reasons.

Many missionaries draw a distinction, whether implicitly or explicitly, between 'Islam' on the one hand, aspects of which they may censure, and 'Muslims' on the other, for whom they may profess 'a deep and constraining love'.[134] For a missionary, it would not necessarily be a contradiction in terms to say that censure of Islam was motivated by a concern for Muslims, even if in practice the censure is often attenuated by the desire nòt to offend or alienate. Most Muslims would not appreciate the distinction; for them, Islamicity is felt to be such an integral part of identity that aspersions cast on Islam are likely to be taken personally.

In certain areas, particularly concerning Islamic origins, one is dealing with mutually exclusive views which tend to argue their respective positions on grounds that are unlikely to appeal to the other. Some of the supposed 'inadequacies' of the Qur'an arise from the imposition of Christian criteria for scriptural authenticity. Geisler and Saleeb, for example, refer to the Qur'an's lack of accurate prophecies,[135] and others criticize the Qur'an for a lack of originality, although Muslims do not in fact claim 'originality' for the content of the Qur'an.[136] Many things that may appear self-evident to missionaries are effectively neutralized on the Muslim side by internal or circular arguments which cannot be invalidated without undermining fundamental assumptions. Muslims do, of course, have their own explanation for discrepancies between the Qur'anic and biblical accounts of particular stories (i.e., alleged distortion in the latter). Those elements of Islam assumed to be of pagan origin by some Christian commentators, such as the rites connected with the pilgrimage,[137] are also incorporated into Islam's account of itself, which sees these rites as instituted by Abraham and restored to their original monotheistic purity by Muhammad. Presumably, the immediate Muslim response to the existence of parallels between Qur'anic passages and rabbinical or apocryphal material which pre-dates Islam would be the theologically based argument that attributes the parallelism to the fact that they come from the same (divine) source, with the implication that such apocryphal material derives from the original and genuine revelation from God that was mistakenly (or deliberately) discarded in the canonical process. However, to date, Muslims have not attempted to explore this academically. The imputation of linguistic errors to the Qur'an is likely to be countered by the argument that the grammatical rules of Arabic as they were elaborated in the early centuries of Islam were, in fact, based primarily upon the usage of the Qur'an (as well as pre-Islamic poetry), and cannot therefore be used to impugn its correctness.[138]

As far as relating the events of Muhammad's life is concerned, missionaries depend, like everyone else, on the earliest Muslim sources, many of which are available in translation: the Qur'an, the Sira and the Hadith. Although some doubts may be expressed as to the authenticity of the Hadith,[139] the broad picture of Muhammad as conveyed in that literature seems to be accepted. Parshall, who deals with the Hadith most extensively, treats them as a package, in that when Hadiths which might be a potential cause of embarrassment are related, there is no suggestion that individual Muslims might be able to exercise discretion by rejecting certain Hadiths (even if they are contained in the prestigious collections of al-Bukhārī or Muslim).[140] Referring to certain 'medical' Hadiths, such as the one in which Muhammad recommends the drinking of camel's urine, he implies that the knowledge of such Hadiths is sometimes concealed by Imams for fear of undermining Muslims' faith.[141]

Even if there is agreement on the basic framework of Muhammad's life and certain events and facts, there is inevitably some leeway for interpretation of these events or of Muhammad's motivation. There are certainly occasions when an unfavourable interpretation is chosen, as where Parshall questions the propriety of Muhammad's visiting a female acquaintance, Umm Haram bint Milhan, who would serve him food and check his hair for lice. Parshall asks 'Why did Muhammad repeatedly visit this married woman?', and concludes that 'this familiarity seems to exceed the boundaries of decorum set by Muhammad himself'.[142] Some problems of interpretation arise from relying on translations and viewing them in isolation from Muslim commentary; Parshall understands a Hadith (al-Bukhārī 3:535) which mentions different punishments for a male and female who have indulged in illicit sexual relations (a hundred lashes and a year's exile, and death by stoning respectively) as a case of sexual discrimination, seemingly unaware that Muslims explain the contrast on the basis of the distinction between married and unmarried offenders.[143]

Muslims will agree with many of the theological distinctions identified by Christians, even if they articulate them slightly differently; elsewhere in this book Muslims are quoted as saying that the Qur'an reveals God's will rather than His character, and that it is guidance or education, rather than salvation, that humans need (see chapter 4). Few Muslims would wish to defend the idea of God's unconditional love.[144] It is when these differences are taken to alleged, sometimes forced, logical conclusions that they risk becoming a distortion of Muslim beliefs. Schlorff's opinion that God can have no real affection for humans even though the Qur'an talks of God's 'loving' or 'liking' them, on the grounds that 'these attributes do not mean what they would mean when predicated of man',[145] may accord with the opinions of some medieval theologians but most contemporary Muslims' understanding of the Qur'an will not be filtered through such abstract philosophical concepts. Similarly, the assertion that Islam supports moral relativism may owe something to Ash'arite theology and a small number of Hadiths which permit lying in specific circumstances,[146] but most Muslims reading the Qur'an are likely to conclude that certain things are right or wrong regardless of their context.

On matters related to the Muslim emphasis on God's transcendence, it is usually the case that issues *between* the two faith traditions are also issues *within* them. Many of the doctrines which were evolved to guard God's transcendence in Islam, such as nominalism and atomism, had their Christian precedents in those strands of the tradition which emphasized the ineffability of God and the inadequacy of human language to describe Him, such as the *via negativa* or the apophatic way. Nevertheless, such concepts are less central to Christianity than Islam, and, in the former, are apt to lead to heresy if taken too far; and while Neoplatonism influenced both Christian and Islamic theology, the belief in the Incarnation meant that the former was generally less receptive to singular monotheism and agnosticism.[147] On the question of singular versus plural monotheism, although most educated Muslims today would probably defend the idea of absolute unity, it should be observed that mainstream Islamic theology, culminating in al-Ghazālī, defended a relative rather than an absolute unity, in that God's attributes were declared (*contra* the Mu'tazila) to have real existence.[148] When Christians argue that the Muslim view of God's attributes (or the Uncreated Qur'an) allows plurality into the Godhead and is analagous to the Trinity, it is classical Muslim theology that they have in mind; when they argue against singular monotheism, they are refuting popular Muslim perceptions. The charge of agnosticism must be qualified by the observation that mainstream Islamic opinion believed that to divest God of all real qualities (*ta'ṭīl*) was a heretical extreme to be avoided along with its opposite, anthropomorphism (*tashbīh*). What to Christians may appear as 'agnosticism' may be viewed by Muslims as humility or lack of presumption, and Muslims may point out that to consider God's actions as being beyond human understanding or unfathomable is not the same thing as considering them arbitrary or meaningless.

While much of the criticism directed against Islam in these writings could be said to arise fairly automatically from a Christian frame of reference, some of it appears to go beyond this, sometimes betraying a lack of sympathy. It seems unduly cynical, for example, to describe the equality of the pilgrims on the Hajj as 'a brief interlude from reality', and more than a little wide of the mark to speak of Muslims' 'overt and blatant worship' of the black stone.[149] Geisler and Saleeb imply that Islam cannot stand up to any kind of objective examination when they conclude their chapter 'An Evaluation of the Qur'an' with the words: 'one can continue to *believe* in the divine origin of the Qur'an without evidence to support it. But those who seek a reasonable faith will have to look elsewhere' (p. 204). Such remarks seem to disregard the fact that there are intelligent and educated human beings who are Muslims.

Nevertheless, there are some missionaries who seem genuinely desirous of fostering a spirit of open communication. Musk talks of the need to 'break open the closed circles of self-contained, self-affirming worldviews', which are characteristic of Westerners no less than Middle Easterners; in view of a universal human fallibility, he believes that this can only be achieved by God's initiative.[150] Glaser feels that Christians and Muslims should 'seek to recognize and understand fundamental differences in ways of thinking and then . . . take the different way of thinking seriously . . . The two religions are different, and disagreement is inevitable. But let it be a disagreement based on understanding and respect, and not on ignorance.'[151]

Notes

1.   *Patricia St John Tells her own Story*, p. 115.
2.   Goldsmith, *Islam and Christian Witness*, p. 32.
3.   See, e.g., Padwick, 'North African Reverie', p. 353.
4.   Goldsmith, *Islam and Christian Witness*, pp. 32–3; N. Anderson, *The World's Religions*, p. 98; Miller, *A Christian Response to Islam*, pp. 155ff.
5.   Most missionaries to Muslims are of necessity 'tentmakers', that is to say they have full-time secular jobs in the country of residence. Radio broadcasting is often the main form which 'proclamation' *per se* takes in Muslim countries.
6.   Cragg, *Troubled by Truth*, p. 23.
7.   The work of Gairdner (d. 1928) is described in Vander Werff, *Christian Mission to Muslims*, pp. 200–24; on Padwick (d. 1968) see Cragg, *Troubled by Truth*, chapter 3.
8.   Bennett, 'The Legacy of Lewis Bevan Jones', p. 127. Bevan Jones died in 1960.
9.   See Powell, *Muslims and Missionaries in Pre-Mutiny India*, pp. 242ff. for a description of the debate, and chapter 5 on the *Mīzān ul-Ḥaqq*. See also on Pfander: Gaudeul, *Encounters and Clashes*, vol. 1, pp. 256–9, and Vander Werff, *Christian Mission to Muslims*, pp. 41–4.
10. *The Mīzān ul-Ḥaqq*, pp. 25ff.
11. Bennett discusses Tisdall's life and work in *Victorian Images of Islam*, chapter 6; for this point, see p. 141.
12. Tisdall, *The Sources of Islam*, p. 2.
13. For example, between the stories of Solomon and Sheba as told in the second Targum of the Book of Esther and in the Qur'an (*The Sources of Islam*, pp. 24–8).
14. See, e.g., Fueck, 'The Originality of the Arabian Prophet'; Kronholm, 'Dependence and Prophetic Originality in the Koran'.
15. Their works, and those of Samuel Zwemer, referred to below, are still being reprinted and circulated in both European and oriental languages by the Light of Life press and other organizations which operate from PO Box addresses in central Europe.
16. On Zwemer see Vander Werff, *Christian Mission to Muslims*, pp. 232ff. and the sections on him in Ipema, 'The Islam Interpretations of Duncan B. McDonald and Samuel M. Zwemer, A. Kenneth Cragg and Wilfred C. Smith'.
17. Several of his works therefore focus on 'folk' or 'popular' Islam; see especially *The Influence of Animism on Islam* (London: SPCK, 1920) and *Studies in Popular Islam* (London: The Sheldon Press, 1939).
18. Zwemer in his later writings, however, accepted that Muslims worshipped the same God and did not shift their allegiance on conversion to Christianity: see 'The Allah of Islam and the God revealed in Jesus Christ', p. 309.
19. Brown, *The Way of the Prophet*, p. 90.
20. Several authors stress the need to overcome prejudices and negative stereotypes. See, e.g., Cooper (ed.), *Ishmael, My Brother*, p. 9; Musk, *Touching the Soul of Islam*, p. 207.
21. See, e.g., Chapman, 'Rethinking the Gospel for Muslims', p. 118, and *Cross and*

Crescent, p. 213; Schlorff, *Discipleship in Islamic Society*, p. 15; Vander Werff, *Christian Mission to Muslims*, pp. 41–2.

22. Neill, *Crises of Belief*, p. 32.
23. Chapman, 'Going Soft on Islam?', pp. 20–1.
24. E.g. Geisler and Saleeb, *Answering Islam*, pp. 61, 131.
25. The author, a Dr R. Morey, has also written works in refutation of Mormonism, Jehovah's Witnesses, Freemasonry, reincarnation and astrology.
26. Some examples are Cooper, *Ishmael, My Brother*; C. Kimball, *Striving Together: A Way Forward in Christian–Muslim Relations* (Maryknoll, NY: Orbis, 1990); G. Marrison, *The Christian Approach to the Muslim*, 4th ed. (London: Lutterworth Press, 1971); C. Fry and J. King, *Islam: A Survey of the Muslim Faith* (Grand Rapids: Baker Books, 1980); B. Haines and F. Cooley, *Christians and Muslims Together* (Philadelphia: Geneva Press, 1987).
27. Parshall, *The Cross and the Crescent*, p. 208.
28. See, e.g., Gilchrist, *Muhammad: The Prophet of Islam*, pp. 88–9, 90, 95; Geisler and Saleeb, *Answering Islam*, pp. 155–6.
29. See, e.g., G. Otis Jr., *The Last of the Giants: Lifting the Veil on Islam and the End Times* (Grand Rapids: Baker Books, 1991); Shorrosh, *Islam Revealed*, p. 189. Shorrosh is an evangelist rather than a missionary.
30. Chapman, 'Biblication Foundations of Praying for Muslims', p. 319.
31. Chapman, 'Thinking Biblically about Islam', p. 72.
32. Chapman, 'Going Soft on Islam?', p. 18.
33. Nazir-Ali, *Frontiers in Muslim–Christian Encounter*, p. 128.
34. Muir, *The Life of Muhammad*, p. 522.
35. Schlorff, *Discipleship in Islamic Society*, p. 39.
36. Ibid., p. 17.
37. See, e.g., F. Accad, 'The Qur'an: A Bridge to Christian Faith' (*Missiology*, 4, 1976), and Parshall, *Beyond the Mosque*, pp. 198–9.
38. S. Schlorff, 'The Hermeneutical Crisis in Muslim Evangelization' (*Evangelical Review of Theology*, 5, 1981).
39. See, e.g., Brown, *The Way of the Prophet*, p. 97; Musk, *The Unseen Face of Islam*, p. 260; Parshall, *The Fortress and the Fire*, p. 83.
40. A seminal work on the subject is D. Hesselgrave, *Communicating Christ Cross-Culturally* (Grand Rapids: Zondervan, 1991). In view of the special difficulties attending Muslim conversion, the issues become especially pointed in the Islamic context; these and other related issues are discussed in the publications issuing from missionary conferences, such as McCurry (ed.), *The Gospel and Islam*; Woodberry (ed.), *Muslims and Christians on the Emmaus Road*.
41. See especially his *New Paths in Muslim Evangelism*.
42. *The Cross and the Crescent*, pp. 24ff.
43. Parshall, *Inside the Community*, p. 68; see also p. 62 and *The Cross and the Crescent*, p. 67.
44. *The Cross and the Crescent*, p. 70.
45. *Inside the Community*, p. 73.
46. Parshall, *New Paths in Muslim Evangelism*, pp. 64–73. See also Musk's comparison between the Western secular humanist's human-centred worldview and

the Muslim's God-centred worldview (*Passionate Believing*, pp. 34–5), and D. Burnett's comparison between the 'Western worldview' and the 'Middle Eastern worldview', in Cooper (ed.), *Ishmael, My Brother*, pp. 156–7.

47. Musk, *Passionate Believing*, p. 213. Western Christians are also said to have too easily capitulated to secularization and liberal theological trends.

48. Other, briefer attempts to characterize Muslim culture or an Islamic 'worldview' can be found in Burnett, *Clash of Worlds*, pp. 107–12; Cooper (ed.), *Ishmael, My Brother*, pp. 143–58; F. Iliff, *Salam Alekum! Understanding Muslim Culture* (London: Interserve, 1995). Christine Mallouhi's *Mini-Skirts, Mothers and Muslims: Modelling Spiritual Values in Muslim Culture* (Tunbridge Wells: Spear, 1994), which focuses on issues relating to the position of women, pleads for cultural sensitivity on the part of Western Christians in general and missionaries to Muslims in particular.

49. Watt, for example, maintains that 'Muhammad received his knowledge of Biblical conceptions in general . . . from the intellectual environment of Mecca and not from reading or from the communication of specific individuals' (*Muhammad: Prophet and Statesman*, p. 41).

50. Gilchrist, *Muhammad: The Prophet of Islam*, p. 8.

51. *Inside the Community*, p. 23; see also Geisler and Saleeb, *Answering Islam*, p. 309.

52. Recently, a very few missionaries have drawn on revisionist scholarship, particularly that of John Wansborough, Patricia Crone and Michael Cook, to suggest that the Qur'anic redaction may have taken up to two hundred, as opposed to just thirty, years. As far as I am aware this material has as yet only been published on the Internet.

53. See, e.g., Geisler and Saleeb, *Answering Islam*, p. 303; Parshall, *The Cross and the Crescent*, p. 52; Moucarry, *Islam and Christianity at the Crossroads*, p. 41; Nazir-Ali, review of Akhtar's *A Faith for all Seasons* (*ICMR*, 2, 1991), p. 297.

54. A few Muslims also question this as a criterion for Qur'anic inimitability: see, e.g., Akhtar, *A Faith for all Seasons*, pp. 43–7.

55. *The Cross and the Crescent*, pp. 46–8.

56. Shorrosh, *Islam Revealed*, pp. 213, 209.

57. Ibid., p. 206.

58. Glaser, 'Towards a Mutual Understanding of Christian and Islamic Concepts of Revelation', p. 22.

59. 'Thinking Biblically about Islam', p. 70.

60. *Muhammad: The Prophet of Islam*, p. 69.

61. Ibid., p. 57; Geisler and Saleeb, *Answering Islam*, p. 147.

62. *The Cross and the Crescent*, p. 183.

63. Abdul-Haqq, *Sharing your Faith with a Muslim*, pp. 185, 187; Chapman, 'Thinking Biblically about Islam', p. 70; Brown, *The Way of the Prophet*, p. 80.

64. Chapman, for example, questions whether in the light of this Christians can view Muhammad as simply 'a post-Christian heretic' ('Thinking Biblically about Islam', p. 70).

65. *Muhammad: The Prophet of Islam*, p. 126.

66. 'Thinking Biblically about Islam', p. 70.

67. *The Cross and the Crescent*, p. 183. Geisler and Saleeb suggest that 'unlike the Jesus of the Gospels, he certainly would not want to challenge his foes with the question: "Which of you convicts Me of sin?"' (*Answering Islam*, p. 173).

68. N. Anderson, *Islam in the Modern World*, p. 9.

69. *Muhammad: The Prophet of Islam*, pp. 58, 59.

70. Ibid., pp. 59, 60. In fact while some Hadiths elevate Muhammad over other prophets, others portray Muhammad as rebuking his followers for promoting him over Abraham.

71. *Inside the Community*, p. 50.

72. *Muhammad: The Prophet of Islam*, pp. 68–9.

73. The sources state that this took place following Banu Qurayzah's co-operation with the Muslims' enemies during the Battle of the Trench (5 AH/627), which violated the terms of the Constitution of Medina; most accounts portray Muhammad not as initiating this but as acquiescing in the decision of Sa'd ibn Mu'adh, who was appointed as an arbiter at the request of the Banu Qurayzah.

74. See, e.g., Geisler and Saleeb, *Answering Islam*, pp. 173–6; Gilchrist, *Muhammad: The Prophet of Islam*, chapter 3; Parshall, *Inside the Community*, pp. 104–5, 116–21.

75. Gilchrist, *Muhammad: The Prophet of Islam*, pp. 75, 66–7.

76. Ibid., p. 65.

77. *Inside the Community*, pp. 183, 184–5, 190. For similar points made by Gilchrist, see *Muhammad: The Prophet of Islam*, pp. 81–5.

78. See, e.g., N. Anderson, *Islam in the Modern World*, pp. 31–4; Geisler and Saleeb, *Answering Islam*, pp. 170–2; Gilchrist, *Muhammad: The Prophet of Islam*, chapter 4; Parshall, *Inside the Community*, p. 176.

79. Musk, *Touching the Soul of Islam*, p. 37.

80. This is dealt with in Gilchrist, *Muhammad: The Prophet of Islam*, pp. 80–1; Geisler and Saleeb, *Answering Islam*, pp. 171–2; Parshall, *The Cross and the Crescent*, p. 181.

81. See, e.g., Lings, *Muhammad: His Life Based on the Earliest Sources*, pp. 212–3. The Qur'anic verse represents this as a practical enactment of a new legal ruling (i.e. that it was now permissible to marry the former wife of one's adopted, as opposed to natural, son) which would serve to break down old taboos.

82. Geisler and Saleeb, *Answering Islam*, p. 172; Gilchrist, *Muhammad: The Prophet of Islam*, p. 84; Nazir-Ali, *Islam: A Christian Perspective*, p. 33; Parshall, *Inside the Community*, p. 187.

83. See, e.g., Yusuf Ali's commentary on the following verses of Sura 33:28, 30–2, 50–1, 53.

84. *Muhammad: The Prophet of Islam*, p. 121.

85. See Geisler and Saleeb, *Answering Islam*, pp. 80–8; Parshall, *The Cross and the Crescent*, pp. 173–80; Gilchrist, *Muhammad:The Prophet of Islam*, chapter 5.

86. See Geisler and Saleeb, *Answering Islam*, pp. 83–5; Gilchrist, *Muhammad: The Prophet of Islam*, pp. 119, 133–4.

87. *Muhammad: The Prophet of Islam*, p. 112.

88. Abdul-Haqq, *Sharing your Faith with a Muslim*, pp. 103–4; Geisler and Saleeb, *Answering Islam*, p. 166; Gilchrist, *Muhammad: The Prophet of Islam*, p. 136.

89. *Muhammad: The Prophet of Islam*, pp. 125–6, 131.
90. *The Cross and the Crescent*, p. 174.
91. *Muhammad: The Prophet of Islam*, p. 137.
92. Abdul-Haqq, *Sharing Your Faith with a Muslim*, p. 184.
93. Nazir-Ali, *Frontiers in Christian–Muslim Encounter*, p. 137.
94. *Muhammad: The Prophet of Islam*, p. 126.
95. Glaser, 'The Concept of Relationship', pp. 57–8.
96. *The Cross and the Crescent*, p. 24.
97. Geisler and Saleeb, *Answering Islam*, p. 15; Goldsmith, *Islam and Christian Witness*, p. 15; Parshall, *The Cross and the Crescent*, pp. 23–4.
98. Chapman, 'The God Who Reveals', p. 127.
99. 'Rethinking the Gospel for Muslims', p. 122; here Chapman is explicitly citing an oft-expressed idea of Cragg's.
100. Geisler and Saleeb, *Answering Islam*, p. 27; Goldsmith, *Islam and Christian Witness*, p. 89; Moucarry, *Islam and Christianity at the Crossroads*, p. 47.
101. 'Biblical Foundations of Praying for Muslims', p. 307.
102. 'The Concept of Relationship', p. 58.
103. Nazir-Ali, *Islam: A Christian Perspective*, p. 62.
104. 'The God Who Reveals', p. 138.
105. N. Anderson, *Islam in the Modern World*, p. 25, and *God's Law and God's Love*, pp. 101–2; Goldsmith, *Islam and Christian Witness*, p. 89.
106. Geisler and Saleeb, *Answering Islam*, pp. 137ff; Schlorff, *Discipleship in Islamic Society*, p. 19.
107. Christians have sometimes expressed a belief in God's impassibility, but in view of the belief in the Incarnation this is usually understood to mean not that God is incapable of suffering or feeling, but that humans cannot actually inflict pain on Him at will.
108. 'The Concept of Relationship', pp. 58, 59. Glaser does however observe that expressions of mutual love can be found in the Sufi tradition: ibid., p. 60, fn. 7.
109. *Discipleship in Islamic Society*, p. 20.
110. N. See, e.g., Moucarry, *Islam and Christianity at the Crossroads*, pp. 51–2; Parshall, *The Cross and the Crescent*, p. 26.
111. N. Anderson, *God's Law and God's Love*, p. 102.
112. Parshall, *Bridges to Islam*, p. 111; Schlorff, *Discipleship in Islamic Society*, p. 27.
113. *Discipleship in Islamic Society*, p. 29.
114. Chapman, 'Rethinking the Gospel for Muslims', pp. 118–9.
115. The Christian scholar Stanton described the Qur'anic teaching on sin as 'very sparse' (*The Teachings of the Koran*, p. 56); Abdul-Haqq comments that 'the Koranic position on the nature of sin and forgiveness consists of strands of teaching. It is difficult to weave them into a harmonious pattern' (*Sharing your Faith with a Muslim*, p. 157).
116. Glaser, 'Qur'anic Challenges for Genesis', forthcoming in *Journal for the Study of the Old Testament*.
117. This and the foregoing points are from Glaser, 'The Concept of Relationship', p. 59.
118. Schlorff, *Discipleship in Islamic Society*, pp. 22–3.

119. Ibid., p. 24.
120. 'The Concept of Relationship', p. 59.
121. *Discipleship in Islamic Society*, p. 24. Schlorff attributes Islam's moral relativism to the orthodox theological view that nothing can be binding on God: 'since God is absolutely free and unbound by moral absolutes, man has also no transcendent standard for morality. In sum, truth and morality are relativistic' (ibid., p. 21).
122. Ibid, p. 24.
123. Goldsmith, *Islam and Christian Witness*, p. 102. Cf. Abdul-Haqq, *Sharing your Faith with a Muslim*, p. 162; Parshall, *New Paths in Muslim Evangelism*, p. 79.
124. However, Woodberry and Parshall do refer to the importance of this inner dimension: see Woodberry, 'Different Diagnoses of the Human Condition', p. 157, and Parshall, *The Cross and the Crescent*, pp. 145–6.
125. Glaser, 'The Concept of Relationship', p. 60.
126. 'Rethinking the Gospel for Muslims', p. 124.
127. 'Thinking Biblically about Islam', p. 75.
128. 'Cross-cultural mission' is a much discussed phenomenon. It is now no longer a case of 'the West to the rest', as an increasingly high proportion of Protestant missionaries are of non-Western origin – up to forty per cent, according to P. Johnstone, *Operation World* (Carlisle: OM Publishing, 1993), p. 643.
129. This is done explicitly by Watt in *Muhammad at Medina* (see chapter 5), and Armstrong, *Muhammad: A Biography of the Prophet*, where for example the author states that the 'massacre of Qurayzah . . . was not as great a crime as it would be today' (p. 208).
130. Rodinson, 'The Western Image and Western Studies of Islam', p. 59.
131. Rippin, 'Literary Analysis of *Qur'ān, Tafsīr*, and *Sīra*', p. 159.
132. This needs to be qualified by the observation that several missionaries, including Musk and Parshall, do emphasize 'folk' Islam in their writings, and some feel that it is statistically more significant than normative Islam.
133. Parshall, *The Cross and the Crescent*, p. 183; Chapman, 'Going Soft on Islam?', p. 20.
134. Parshall, *Inside the Community*, p. 14. This is somewhat reminiscent of the old Christian adage: 'Love the sinner and hate the sin'.
135. In fact, they refute the traditional Muslim claims to identify such prophecies in the Qur'an, while maintaining that the Bible contains 'clear and specific predictive prophecies', notwithstanding the fact that biblical prophecy is a relatively controversial hermeneutical area: see Geisler and Saleeb, *Answering Islam*, pp. 162–3.
136. E.g., Gilchrist, *Muhammad: The Prophet of Islam*, p. 8; Shorrosh, *Islam Revealed*, p. 194.
137. See, e.g., Parshall, *Inside the Community*, pp. 84ff.
138. Qur'anic exegetes such as al-Zamakhsharī (d. 538 AH/1144) in his *al-Kashshāf 'ān Haqā'iq Ghawāmiḍ al-Tanzīl* made extensive efforts to explain the rhetorical effect of seemingly irregular usages in the Qur'an.
139. E.g., Geisler and Saleeb, *Answering Islam*, p. 165.
140. It is true that in practice Muslim scholars highly respect these collections and rarely impugn the authenticity of the Hadiths contained in them, but strictly speaking it is not an essential matter of faith for Muslims to accept all of them. A

distinction is commonly made between a minority of Hadiths which are supported by multiple chains of narration (known as *mutawātir*), and those which are not
(known as *āhād*). The former cannot be rejected.

141. Parshall, *Inside the Community*, pp. 202–3. He feels that such Hadiths pose serious problems for Muslims, and that 'it is possible to undercut the authority of the
Hadith by emphasizing these problem areas' (although he does not recommend
this as an evangelistic method) (p. 211).

142. Ibid., p. 168.

143. Ibid., p. 118.

144. Daud Rahbar, writing as a Muslim in a semantic study of the nature of God in the
Qur'an, finds that 'unqualified Divine Love for mankind is an idea completely
alien to the Qur'an', and that in most cases the Arabic verb *ahabba* denotes liking or approval rather than love (*God of Justice*, p. 172).

145. *Discipleship in Islamic Society*, p. 20.

146. Cf. Geisler and Saleeb, *Answering Islam*, p. 174; Gilchrist, *Muhammad: The
Prophet of Islam*, pp. 63ff; Parshall, *Inside the Community*, p. 218.

147. Sweetman, *Islam and Christian Theology*, vol. 2, p. 317.

148. Wolfson, *The Philosophy of the Kalam*, p. 138.

149. Parshall, *Inside the Community*, p. 88. This is surprising in view of Parshall's
appreciation of other aspects of Islamic worship, described above. In fairness it
should be pointed out that he has a somewhat ebullient style and is sometimes
facetious in the Christian context as well, as when he describes how the vision of
heaven as a jewelled city as depicted in Revelation could appear as 'truly a cap-
italist fantasy come alive' (*The Cross and the Crescent*, p. 200).

150. *Touching the Soul of Islam*, pp. 208, 205.

151. Glaser, 'Towards a Mutual Understanding', p. 22.

four

THE STUDY OF
CHRISTIANITY BY
MUSLIM INTELLECTUALS

Over two decades ago, a Lebanese scholar regretted that 'there has never been a single Muslim who dedicated his whole life to the study of Christianity and who . . . could write a single authoritative work on Christianity that would be accepted by the Church or by recognized Christian scholars . . . This self-isolation of Islam from Christianity is one of the most important acts of radical discontinuity that occurred in history.' He went on to suggest that the Muslim who, whether out of curiosity or a desire to explore his or her own roots, studied such disciplines as the archaeology of the Middle East, bibilical or Christian languages, the lives of the saints, and Jewish and Christian theology, spent time living among Christians, and then offered his or her own authentic Islamic interpretation, 'would be a new creature, quite different from any the world has known so far'.[1] Today, these statements hardly stand in need of modification. The contemporary study of Christianity by Muslims does not measure up to the level it attained in the medieval period, when Muslims were among the most accomplished historians of religion: al-Shahrastānī (d. AH 548/1153) has been described as the author of 'the first history of religion'.[2]

It is difficult to appreciate the extent of Muslim study of other religions in the past because the relevant material is contained in different types of work and scholarly genres: Qur'an and Hadith commentaries, theological treatises, works of *fiqh* (jurisprudence), heresiography and polemical works proper, historical and geographical compendiums, *belles lettres* and even poetry.[3] No doubt this accounts in part for the fact that this area has not received as much attention as it might have done in Western scholarship on Islam. Among the more distinguished Muslim scholars of religions are many luminaries who are best known for their work in other areas, including al-Mas'ūdī (d. AH 345/956), al-Bāqillānī (d. AH 403/1013), al-Bīrūnī (d. AH 442/1050), Ibn Ḥazm (d. AH 456 /1064), al-Ghazālī (d. AH 505/1111) and Ibn Qayyim al-Jawziyya (d. AH 751 /1350). These scholars are sometimes described as 'polemicists' because of their concern to refute other religions, but it should be noted that this concern did not necessarily exclude a full and accurate exposition of others' religious beliefs, which was sometimes apparently motivated by a genuine disinterested curiosity.

From the ninth century onwards, when Muslims acquired the tools of Greek philosophical thought, there was a lively polemic between Muslims and Christians who were relatively evenly matched, in which communication was greatly facilitated by the fact that they shared many intellectual resources.[4] There was often an awareness of the need to present the doctrines and religious arguments of others on their own terms before refuting them; a Muslim scholar might, for example, describe the relationship between the three hypostases of the Trinity using Christian illustrations such as the analogy of the sun, from which light and heat emanate.[5] Some demonstrated a detailed knowledge of the often subtle variations of belief between one Christian group or sect and another, a knowledge sometimes based on personal contact with Christians.[6]

In the past, as in the present, it was the more rationally minded Muslims who undertook systematic refutations of Christian doctrine, the same Muslims whose rationalism sometimes caused them to fall foul of Islamic orthodoxy, as in the case of the Mu'tazila. The Greek philosophical tools which were employed against Christianity could be a two-edged sword, and gave cause for concern when applied to Islamic thought. An example of this is the use of Greek philosophical categories to refute the Trinity, which had implications for the question of God's attributes in Islam; it was not always easy to uphold the distinction between the latter and the Christian hypostases.[7] Underlying this intellectual activity was an assumption, especially on the Muslim side, that the categories of Aristotelian logic were sufficient to evaluate religious belief;[8] while this assumption may be open to question, the high level of sophistication of individual Muslims who utilized those categories is not.

Several Muslims have regretted the dearth of Muslim specialists in the study of Christianity in the contemporary period, and express the hope that this will change in the future. Because of this dearth, there was little need for selection criteria in this chapter; its structure was largely dictated by the materials available. Thematically, there has been some rationalization for the sake of coherence, and it has not been possible to accommodate certain topics which have been treated in depth by particular individuals.[9] Of the scholars cited in this chapter, very few can be said to have made an in-depth study of Christianity or Christian thought, and none are conversant with New Testament Greek or Old Testament Hebrew.

Isma'il al-Faruqi (b. 1921) was a Palestianian exile who spent most of his academic career in the United States. He combined a Western training in philosophy and the study of religion (he worked under Wilfred Cantwell Smith for a time) with an Islamic education, having spent time at the Azhar and the Institute of Islamic Research in Karachi. In 1986 he and his wife were tragically murdered at home; the killer was apprehended but the motive was not definitely established. Al-Faruqi has produced by far the most exhaustive treatment of Christianity, and as a result his contributions tend to dominate this chapter; there seems little point in quoting others on matters with which al-Faruqi deals more thoroughly and more competently. His writings demonstrate a twofold interest: exploring the origins of Christianity in order to rediscover its true essence on the one hand, and critiquing the subsequent development of Christian theology, both traditional and modern, on the other. His *Christian Ethics: A Historical and Systematic Analysis of its Dominant Ideas* (1967), based on his doctoral thesis, has been described as 'perhaps the first sustained critique by a modern Muslim of Christianity in general and Christian ethics in particular',[10] and nothing of a comparable standard has been produced by a Muslim since. Despite his often confrontational style, he was an active participant in and promoter of Muslim–Christian dialogue and was keen to further practical co-operation between Muslims and Christians on ethical issues.[11]

Shabbir Akhtar, a British Muslim with a philosophy degree and a doctorate in the philosophy of religion, shows greater familiarity in his numerous books with Christian than Islamic thought. In recent years he has been teaching at the International Islamic University in Malaysia. His most learned work on Christianity, *The Light in the Enlightenment: Christianity and the Secular Heritage* is a critique of modern Christian theologians, but of more relevance here is his thinking on Christian doctrine as expounded mainly in *A Faith for all Seasons: Islam and the Challenge of the Modern World*, and on the respective stances of Islam and Christianity to social and political issues as expounded in *The Final Imperative: An Islamic Theology of Liberation*.

Also worthy of mention in terms of erudition is Frithjof Schuon, a German convert to Sufi Islam and one of the major proponents of the 'perennial philosophy', which is the eternal wisdom believed to be contained in all religions. His writings on Christianity represent his attempt to interpret its true 'essence'; to this end he writes imaginatively on Christian rites and liturgy, and defends traditionalism vis-à-vis modernism in Christianity as in Islam.[12] However, since he does not write about Christianity from an explicitly Islamic point of view, he does not figure prominently here. Seyyed Hossein Nasr, an Iranian Shi'ite and a Muslim scholar of international repute living in the USA, has been strongly influenced by Schuon and shares his philosophy of religion and attraction to gnosticism. Although he has not written at length on Christianity, his views may be considered more relevant for the purposes of the present study by virtue of the fact that he is more active in, and attuned to, the Islamic mainstream.

Other contributors include Professor Syed Naquib al-Attas, an eminent Malaysian academic who has been active in the movement for the 'Islamization of Knowledge', in which al-Faruqi was a founding figure,[13] and the founder-director of the new International Institute of Islamic Thought and Culture at Kuala Lumpur; and the Bosnian president Alija Izetbegovic who, although better known as a politician than an Islamic thinker, has some interesting views on the relationship between Islam and Christianity.

Among the Muslims who have an irenic approach are some who have been active in interfaith dialogue such as Hasan Askari, Mohammed Arkoun and Ali Merad. Askari is an Indian Shi'ite Muslim who is strongly influenced by the mystical tradition; he gained his Ph.D. in Sociology at Osmania University in Hyderabad, and spent some years at the Centre for the Study of Islam and Christian–Muslim Relations at Selly Oak Colleges in Birmingham.[14] Arkoun and Merad are academics of Algerian origin who are resident in France; Arkoun is a professor of Islamics at the Sorbonne, while Merad is a retired professor of Arabic literature and civilization at the University of Lyon. Syed Vahiduddin, like Askari, is an Indian Muslim strongly influenced by the Sufi tradition.

He did his postgraduate research in religious studies in Germany under the eminent scholar of religions, Rudolph Otto, and later taught philosophy and comparative religion at the Universities of Hyderabad and Delhi.

As one would expect, there is considerable diversity in the Islamic standpoints of the authors, and these differences affect their views on Christianity. The main lines of division seem to fall between the mystically and the rationally inclined: Nasr, Askari and Vahiduddin participate in the Sufi tradition, while al-Faruqi and Akhtar have more vigorously embraced post-Enlightenment rationalism and empiricism. Nasr complains of al-Faruqi's neglect of Islamic philosophy and mysticism and his rationalist emphasis on God's transcendence at the expense of His immanence,[15] while al-Faruqi for his part believes that the esotericism of Nasr and Schuon inevitably corrupts religion, as he feels it can be arbitrarily used to validate any view and fails to provide the necessary guidance for the regulation of human conduct.[16] As a result of their respective Islamic stances, Nasr and Schuon admire what they perceive as the 'sapiential' tradition in Christianity, represented by Augustine among others, and defend this against modernizing and rationalizing tendencies,[17] while al-Faruqi admires the rationalist and philosophical strands represented by Aquinas and others over against the 'irrationality' of the Augustinian tradition.[18] Similarly, Nasr and Schuon's emphasis on spirituality leads them to appreciate Orthodox or Catholic forms of religiosity which give more space to the contemplative and the liturgical, in contrast to other Muslims who disapprove of Catholicism's tradition of using images and statues as well as its hierarchism.

Christianity as 'Proto-Islam' or Distinct Religious Tradition

Because Christianity represents the penultimate stage in the evolution of religions, of which Islam is the culmination, it is theoretically seen (in the positive sense) as agreeing with Islam in essentials, and (in the negative sense) as lacking certain qualities which Islam has. Within these assumptions, however, there is a wide diversity of opinion among Muslims. Several Muslim intellectuals feel that the original Christian teachings possess a certain distinctiveness vis-à-vis Islamic teachings, by dint of appearing in a different environment; since in the Muslim view the original revelation has not survived intact, there is considerable room for speculation as to what it may have consisted of.

Christianity as a historical religion which has evolved over the course of two millennia provides a vast field of study. As in the popular literature, almost all draw a sharp distinction between God's original revelation to Jesus, and historical Christianity with its accretions and innovations. In this connection it is to be noted that the Arabic/Islamic term for innovation, *bid‛ah*, is strongly pejorative when used in a religious context. Some Muslims coin special terms in order to distinguish historical Christianity from the original God-sent Christianity, such as 'pseudo-Christianity', 'Christianism', or 'Western Christianity' ('Western' here incorporating all three main Christian traditions regardless of geographical distribution, being a reference to Greek cultural influence in the formative period). The disjunction between the two is sometimes presented as total: 'there were, and still are from the Muslim point of view, two Christianities: the original and true one and the Western version of it'.[19]

Al-Faruqi gives a very full analysis of pristine Christianity and its place in the evolution of religions. He strongly affirms the view of Islam as both the primordial religion and the fulfilment and culmination of other religions. As primordial religion, Islam is described as the 'religion of nature' (*dīn al-fiṭrah*), which corresponds exactly to the innate religious faculty which God has implanted in human beings.[20] As such, and because 'the Islamic spirit . . . is none other than rationality itself', it supplies the criteria by which other religions can be judged.[21] The Abrahamic religions are viewed within the framework of the stream of 'Arab consciousness': this concept, elaborated in *On Arabism*, seems to denote a primarily spiritual and cultural phenomenon, although it sometimes acquires racial overtones. Pristine Judaism and Christianity represented 'moments' in this consciousness, but each subsequently subverted its true course and diluted its pure monotheism: Judaism, by introducing ethnic exclusivism, and Christianity, by distorting the true doctrine in ways which violated God's transcendence. Muslims can therefore be said to be the true Christians, since Muhammad's teachings represented a return to the authentic Arab stream of being which had survived only in heterodox Christian groups.[22] Among these religions, then, only mainstream Islam has succeeded in preserving its original and authentic character.[23]

Al-Faruqi refers to historical Christianity as 'Christianism' or 'the Christianist transvaluation' in order to distinguish it from God's original revelation. He believes that it is difficult but not impossible to 'sift' the message of Jesus from its 'unchristian accruements' in order to rediscover the 'essence' of Christianity.[24] To this end he proposes to identify an internally coherent body of sayings from among the four Gospels, which are not offensive to either moral or common sense and which should then be 'subjected to the further test of coherence with the history of revelation'.[25] By this he means the retrospective history of revelation as understood from an internal Islamic viewpoint, for he does not seek to apply conventional historical methods, which usually take as a starting point the chronologically earlier material.

Al-Faruqi's interpretation of the original mission of Christianity elaborates on the Qur'anic view considerably. In his opinion, the rationale behind the revelation brought by Jesus was twofold, consisting of the 'universalization of the message' (as a corrective to Jewish exclusivism) and the 'interiorization of ethics' (as a corrective to Pharisaic legalism). Here the originality of his thought is in evidence, since his view on the interiorization of ethics concurs with the Christian view that Jesus effectively abrogated the Judaic law in its externals, contrary to the usual Muslim view that he upheld it, or at the most modified it.

Al-Faruqi's interpretation of Jesus' teachings as portrayed in the Gospels is conditioned by these two factors. The Sabbath, for example, is interpreted as a shibboleth of Jewish separatism, so that Jesus' confrontations with the Pharisees regarding its observation become part of the universalization of the message.[26] Since he is at odds with majority Muslim opinion in both cases, he rejects as inauthentic those sayings of Jesus which are usually among the most frequently quoted by Muslims in order to criticize Christianity, such as those which seem to privilege Jews over Gentiles (e.g. Matt. 10:5–6), or those which speak of fulfilling rather than abolishing the law (e.g. Matt. 5:17–19).[27]

In *Christian Ethics*, al-Faruqi maintains that the 'ethical breakthrough' of Jesus was an 'antidote to the exteriorized, legalistic ethic of the Jews', and consisted in the fact that his teachings made possible a 'radical transformation of self' which was such as to dispense with the need for law (pp. 79–80). Al-Faruqi says of the moral law that 'it is not of its nature ever to become a legislation. Its nature defies all kinds of exteriorization', and he finds Jesus' elevation of the value of the individual over that of the community entirely commendable (p. 76). He feels that conscience rather than external law is the appropriate tribunal in moral issues, since the law cannot judge intent, and quotes with approval Augustine's famous saying: 'Love God and do as you like' (pp. 83, 81). Furthermore, he maintains that the impact of Jesus' message should be understood on a metaphysical rather than just an ethical level; the inner transformation required by Jesus constitutes a 'religious event' with ontological consequences in the form of a 'radical reorientation of one's soul to God' (pp. 84, 80).

Al-Faruqi's understanding of the nature of Jesus' mission leads him on several occasions to confirm certain aspects of his teachings which are usually denied by Muslims. 'World denial', for example, is seen as Jesus' corrective to Pharisaic materialism and as conducive to moral purification; it is rationalized in terms of Jesus' prioritizing 'higher' (i.e. moral) values over 'lower' ones (e.g. the pursuit of pleasure or power) which are, however, not necessarily wrong in themselves.[28] This leads al-Faruqi to authenticate biblical verses which are usually rejected by Muslims as encouraging a secularist division between the temporal and spiritual realms, or as unrealistic and impractical. The inwardness of the Kingdom of God, which is 'not of this world', is affirmed,[29] and monasticism is described as the 'only true theatre for Jesus' message'.[30] The ideals enshrined in the Sermon on the Mount, such as 'turning the other cheek', loving one's enemy, and refraining from judging others, are presented as the authentic teachings of Jesus.[31] Consequently, certain verses which are considered by al-Faruqi (but not by Christian interpreters) to be in contradiction to these, such as Jesus' sayings to the effect that one will be judged in the same way as one judges others (Matt. 7:2), or that he will deny before God those who deny him (Matt. 10:33) are rejected on the basis that Jesus 'would never repay evil with evil'.[32]

Ironically, given al-Faruqi's strong condemnation of the Jews for furnishing 'history's most rabid racialism',[33] he puts forward an essentially racialist theory for the subversion of the Christian message, namely Western people's obtuseness, 'contempt for everything cultured', 'spiritual flat-footedness', and 'brutalized' character, since they had not previously received any ethical teachings at all.[34] Furthermore, in an image which is perhaps more redolent of the twentieth century than the first, al-Faruqi remarks that Westerners were 'accustomed to pursue existence only at the cost of neighbour and nature', and speculates that if only Paul had travelled eastwards his distorted teachings would have fallen on arid soil, and would have come up against the '*largeur de coeur*' of the Arab spirit.[35] He elaborates on this thesis with linguistic arguments: while the 'Arab attitude of mind' is accustomed to poetic and metaphorical language, and as such would have no problem even with John's Gospel, Westerner's literalism led them to misunderstand the teachings of the Gospels.[36] With regard to the expression 'son of God', al-Faruqi comments that 'only a crude, naive, and, most important of all, a non-Arab mind could take it literally'.[37] Such a metaphorical approach to language would seem to offer the possibility of authenticating most, if not all, of the biblical text, but al-Faruqi does not take advantage of this.

In *Christian Ethics*, al-Faruqi advances a rationale for the coming of Islam and its supersession of Christianity; he feels that this was not out of a dissatisfaction with it *per se* but because of a change in the human situation and the rise of new circumstances (which he does not specify) 'which could not fall under the purview of Jesus' ethic' (p. 251). His explanation of this may come as a surprise to both Christians and Muslims: in contrast to Christianity, which was solely concerned with intentions, Islam insisted that a person 'must actually enter the world of real space and time, disturb its flow and equilibrium and bring about the real content of the act' (p. 252). The fact that this necessitated a reintroduction of religious law in the form of the Sharī'a leads al-Faruqi to draw a distinction between Pharisaic legalism and the Sharī'a, by claiming that the latter is not concerned with actual effects and consequences, but only 'with man's actual and effective transcendence of himself to the reality of space-time, with his disturbance of the ontological poise of the cosmos' (p. 253). He concludes that 'Jesus demanded that man should live purely, saintly, always dominated by the love of God, determined by His will alone. Islam confirmed all this and added that, in addition, man should live dangerously, should break forth into space-time, disturb it, and transfigure the universe into that divine pattern which is the Will of God' (p. 253). Despite al-Faruqi's radical (Islamically speaking) acceptance of certain aspects of Jesus' teachings, then, Islam is seen to have absorbed all that is of value in Christianity and indeed to have been solely responsible for preserving its true teachings intact.

Like al-Faruqi, Izetbegovic in his *Islam Between East and West* draws on Western academic sources on philosophy and the study of religion, using them to elaborate on and substantiate a view of the relationship between the Abrahamic religions that is of essentially Islamic inspiration. He points out that as the primordial religion, Islam has always existed (p. 87); expressing an idea which is reminiscent of 'anonymous Christianity',[38] he holds that since 'Islam represents man's natural potential, it must be found in imperfect form or in fragments wherever religious people think and work', and finds evidence of this particularly in the Anglo-Saxon world (p. xix). Islam is distinguished by 'bipolarity', in that it incorporates both rationalism and mysticism in a way that transcends Christian dualism, which inevitably engenders conflict between 'spirit and body, religion and science, and culture and civilization' (pp. xvii–xix). In a dialectical model which implicitly legitimizes contrasts between the Qur'an and the extant biblical text, the Qur'an is seen as a 'unique synthesis of the realism of the Old Testament and the idealism of the New Testament' (p. xvii). Moses, Jesus and Muhammad are 'the personifications of three primeval possibilities of all that is human' (p. 187). While the this-worldly emphasis of Judaism looked for a 'paradise on earth', and awaited a Messiah who would inaugurate a temporal kingdom, the gospel countered Jewish materialism by bringing 'the principles of asceticism, nonviolence, and nonresistance to evil' (pp. 188, 190).

Christianity, like Buddhism, represents for Izetbegovic what he terms 'pure religion', and like all pure religions has two ways or programmes, one for the élite and one for the lay people; this is epitomized in the rule of celibacy for the clergy, with marriage being seen as a compromise for ordinary people (p. 191). Christianity 'turned the human spirit in upon itself', and directed people's energies exclusively towards heaven; it therefore gave up 'any intention to change or to make the outside world perfect' (p. 190). It seeks to provide 'an answer to the question of how to live within oneself . . . not . . . how to live in the world and with other people. It is a temple on a mountain top, a shelter one must climb to in order to leave behind the emptiness of an unrepairable world governed solely by Lucifer' (p. 191).

Islam, by contrast, is 'Christianity reoriented toward the world' (pp. 192–3). Although Muhammad was an ascetic for a time in Mecca, he 'had to return from the cave' and it was in Medina that Islam reached its culmination. The Qur'an is described as 'a realistic, almost antiheroic book. Without man to apply it, Islam is incomprehensible and would not even exist in the true sense of the word' (pp. 193–4). Islamic mystics who retired from active life and political involvement effected a 'Christianization' of Islam, and 'a relapse . . . from Muhammad back to Jesus' (p. 199). Izetbegovic draws a contrast between Islam and Christianity on the basis of the contrasting vocabularies of their respective scriptures: words which occur frequently in the Gospels such as 'blessed, holy, angel, eternal life, heaven, pharisee, sin, love, repentance, forgiveness, mystery', are contrasted with the 'definite and realistic terms' of the Qur'an, such as 'reason, health, cleanliness, strength, buying, contract, pledge, writing, weapons, battle position, force, struggle, trade' (p. 196). Part of Muhammad's mission was to effect what Izetbegovic describes as a 'clarification' of the image of God: 'In the Gospels, God is father; in the Qur'an, God is master. In the Gospels, God is loved; in the Qur'an, God is respected' (pp. 194–5).

Although Izetbegovic does not distinguish terminologically between pristine and historical Christianity, he clearly feels there was a gulf between the original teachings and the historical evolution of Christianity: 'from the very beginning, Jesus was on one side, while Christianity was on the other' (p. 254). Since the otherworldliness of Christianity was intrinsic, its political empowerment on the conversion of the Emperor Constantine represented 'a decisive historical step toward [its] deformation' (p. 255).[39] The monastic orders could then be described as 'resulting from true religious inspiration', the real culprit for the perversion of Christianity being the established Church which sought to impose its dogma and transform Jesus' teachings into an 'ideology' (p. 256). In refutation of the Church's systemization of Christian teachings, Izetbegovic, quoting a Western author, endorses a strikingly Christian, as opposed to Islamic, view of Christ: 'There does not exist a system of moral values, or a religious attitude, or a life program which could be separated from Christ's personality and of which it could be said: This is Christianity. Christianity is He himself' (p. 256).

Syed Naquib al-Attas, in his *Islam, Secularism and the Philosophy of the Future*, is more in line with the mainstream in seeing authentic Christianity in essentially negative terms, and is less interested than al-Faruqi and Izetbegovic in speculating on its original nature. He believes that Jesus was sent as a messenger to Israel, 'charged with the mission of correcting their deviation from their covenant with God and of confirming that covenant with a second covenant', which was 'meant to be valid until the advent of Islam' (p. 25). Those who believed in the original teachings of Jesus, given the opportunity, would have become Muslims after the advent of Islam (p. 18). Jesus was not, however, charged with establishing a new religion, for otherwise he would have brought a new law; it was Paul and others who were responsible for this misunderstanding (pp. 25–6). Al-Attas suggests that Christians only belatedly realized that Christianity had the potential to become a universal religion, inspired in this by Jesus' sermons which mentioned a universal religion when referring to the coming of Islam (pp. 93–4). Christianity therefore enjoyed a 'borrowed and artificially created universality', which however took two millennia to realize, geographically speaking, in contrast to Islam's achievement of the same within less than a century (pp. 94–5).

Al-Attas holds that Christianity as an empirical phenomenon is not a revealed religion in the sense that Islam is, since its central doctrines are 'cultural creations' which are 'categorically denied by the Holy Qur'an' (pp. 25, 27). Al-Attas' critique of Christianity hinges on a distinction between divine and man-made religion; the former is not subject to change and can therefore be said to be absolute, while the latter evolves and is changed by the buffeting winds of history, having lost its original and true essence. He accordingly represents Islam in rather static terms: 'a revealed religion as we understand it is complete and perfect in its adequacy for mankind from the beginning', and 'since Islam is the religion which transcends the influences of human "evolution" and historicity, the values embodied in it are absolute' (pp. 27–8). This principle extends even to the scholarly elaboration of Islam, for 'there can be no relativism in the historical interpretation of Islam, so that knowledge about it is either right or wrong, or true or false' (p. 101). There is a completeness and self-sufficiency about Islam which is lacking in Christianity: Islam has 'its own ontological, cosmological, psychological interpretation of reality' and 'its own world view' (p. 28), whereas Christianity, lacking its own laws, had to 'assimilate' Roman laws, and lacking a coherent worldview, had to 'borrow' from Graeco-Roman thought and 'to construct out of it an elaborate theology and metaphysics' (p. 26). A clear contrast is thus presented between the purity of Islam, and the arbitrary or accidental contamination of Christianity by foreign or external elements.

A further dimension of 'absoluteness' is added when linguistic considerations are brought into play. The Arabic language was 'Islamized' by being made the vehicle of the divine revelation, and Arabic became 'the only divinely inspired living language'; given the close relationship between language, thought and reason, 'the islamization of language brings about the islamization of thought and reason'. The Arabic language is 'not subject to change and development nor governed by the vicissitudes of social change as in the case of all other languages which derive from culture and tradition', and therefore the meaning of any Islamic precept 'is governed by the semantic vocabulary of the Holy

Qur'an and not by social change, so that adequate knowledge about Islam is made possible for all at all times and generations'. The 'ethical, axiological, aesthetical and logical norms' of Islam are therefore 'an established matter, and not one that "evolves" and "develops" as man and history allegedly "evolve" and "develop"'. Conversely, 'deislamization is the infusion of alien concepts into the minds of Muslims, where they remain and influence thought and reasoning' (p. 43). In these views it is possible that al-Attas was inspired by al-Faruqi, who puts the matter more concisely: 'God sent, in the revelation of Muhammad, a verbatim-dictated, verbatim-transmitted, verbatim-preserved word of God in an untranslatable tongue, in order that the change of the categories of human consciousness might not provide occasion for change in the understanding of the divine word or in the apprehension of the values of which it is the conceptual expression.'[40] Such a view is wholly at odds with modern hermeneutical theory or the findings of the sociology of knowledge, which emphasize the inevitability of a subjective element in all understanding.

Christian Doctrine

The doctrines which are usually seen as the most central and distinctive to Christianity, such as the Incarnation, the Trinity, original sin and redemption, are those which are most problematic for Muslims. This in part accounts for the fact that even those Muslims who, like al-Faruqi, believe that it is both possible and desirable to exercise 'epoché', or the 'putting in brackets' of one's own beliefs, when studying another's faith,[41] find it difficult to describe Christian beliefs in a detached way, and indeed feel the need to explicitly refute them.

Of the authors under consideration, al-Faruqi gives the fullest treatment of Christian doctrine, and he expresses his objections to two main areas of belief using specially coined terms which are intended to be pejorative: 'peccatism', which refers to the doctrine of original sin, and 'saviourism', referring to the doctrine of redemption. He believes that the 'transvaluation' of the values of Jesus began with St Paul, who 'practically invented a wholly new religion',[42] and was continued by such figures as Tertullian, Athanasius and Augustine.[43] He implies in several places that the formulators of Christian orthodoxy were cynical deceivers, or that the formation of doctrine was an arbitrary process, dependent only on superior force: the promoters of what subsequently became orthodox

Christianity 'knew that what [they] taught was different from Jesus' teaching', and the 'deviationists' set up their own traditions as authoritative and 'elbowed imperialistically all other traditions out of existence'.[44]

The theological divisions in early Christianity provide an opportunity for al-Faruqi to distinguish between 'Arab Christianity' which was 'rationalistic, tolerant, affirmative, optimistic, purely monotheistic and universalistic', and 'Western Christianity' which was simply 'the opposite'.[45] Certain groups, in so far as they upheld the aforementioned principles, were 'extensions of the Arab spirit'; these are identified as the Ebionites, Gnostics, Marcionites, Manichaeans, Arians and Nestorians. On the other hand, groups seen as falling short of these ideals, for example the Montanists, Donatists and Athanasians, are seen as representing 'Western Christianity'.[46]

Seeking to trace the origins of the doctrine of 'peccatism', al-Faruqi examines the story of Adam and Eve as told in Genesis. He suggests that the naming of the tree from which they ate as the 'tree of the knowledge of good and evil'[47] was a fabrication of the Hebrews, since such knowledge challenged their racial exclusivism and their 'blind attachment to an empty monotheism devoid of ethical significance'.[48] Citing certain verses from the Psalms, such as 'enter not into judgement with thy servant, for in thy sight shall no man living be justified' (143:2), he maintains that the Jews increasingly emphasized the sinfulness of man in the exilic and post-exilic period under the influence of 'the empirical reality of evil around and within Jewish society'.[49] This idea was later developed by Christians, who 'universalized this "sin", made it hereditary, and declared it of the essence of humanity'.[50]

Al-Faruqi argues in *Christian Ethics* that the idea of original sin was in direct contradiction to the teachings of Jesus, who taught that 'ethical worth or unworth are functions of the conscious self's willing alone' (p. 201). He reacts against the Christian interpretation of events to the extent of denying that Adam sinned at all, describing him as 'the author of the first human mistake in ethical perception, committed with good intention, under enthusiasm for the good' (p. 202). While acknowledging the empirical reality of sin, al-Faruqi objects to what he sees as the Christian view of sin as a 'universal and necessary phenomenon' (p. 193). By means of syllogisms, al-Faruqi arrives at a characterization of Christian belief with which few Christians could agree: Christianity is said to hold a 'perfect absoluteness and necessity of evil', and even its desirability, since 'human lapse is that happy, fortunate event which brought about this . . . outpouring of divine love and mercy', and 'had man remained good, he would have upset the divine plan'. In view of this, 'no Christian can consistently maintain a thorough-going condemnation of sin and evil' (pp. 194–5). Since in the Christian view the mission of Jesus would be pointless without the existence of sin, sin is given 'metaphysical priority to everything else', and is even 'a presupposition of God'. Most Christians would agree with al-Faruqi in describing such assertions as 'blasphemous' (p. 196).

In *On Arabism*, al-Faruqi objects to 'saviourism' on metaphysical, rational, philosophical, ethical and theological grounds. The cardinal events of Creation, the Fall, the Crucifixion and Resurrection form a 'divine plan' which Christians have extrapolated from the Old Testament quite arbitrarily and with much 'fanciful imagination'; indeed he feels it to be 'the greatest monument to the histrionic genius of Western man'. However, he unwittingly undermines his own position as expositor of both Old and New Testaments when, in order to refute the Christian view of the Old Testament, he holds that priority should be given to the Jewish interpretation, since it is 'Jewish literature' (p. 91). He describes the plan as 'blasphemously unlikely' in that God does not need to resort to 'tricks' or 'means' in order to carry out His will (p. 97); indeed, he feels that 'it betrays a severe limitation of the Godhead to think that . . . He had to follow such a long, farfetched circuitous process' (p. 93). In his view this plan is 'incoherent in its inner structure' and 'has no claim to validity', but can only be justified by blind faith (p. 94).

The view of salvation as a *fait accompli* is, in al-Faruqi's view, 'the mortal enemy of morality', and he attributes the wrongs perpetrated by Christendom in both earlier and recent centuries to 'that self-righteousness which saviourism breeds and nourishes'.[51] 'Saviourism' is said to breed complacency, since salvation is for the Christian 'a blessing to be immediately dispensed' and 'an entry into the divine fellowship which nothing can interrupt or prevent'.[52] Reversing a saying of Wilfred Cantwell Smith, he insists that 'salvation must flow out of morality, not *vice versa*'.[53] Al-Faruqi perceives an element of self-indulgence in the doctrine of justification by faith, which he finds distasteful: it 'allows ample scope for the "heaving breast" to heave, for the wishful to wish and wish and wish in childlike intensity and innocence'.[54] This is a point of contrast with Islam, for unlike Christianity, 'Islam holds no sweet, immediate recompense to give its convert gratuitously upon conversion. On the contrary, it tells him point blank that his acceptance of Islam puts him squarely in the zero zone and lays out before him the arduous road of the Shari'ah . . . which he has yet to tread in order to lift himself out of the zero zone by his own efforts.'[55] As a result, 'the Muslim is . . . by nature moralistic, an activist, and a futurist; the Christian is by nature complacent, a passivist, and a proclaimer of an event past'. While the Muslim is compared to a 'tautly-drawn bow, ready for the arrow', the Christian is 'like the soldier whose chest and arm and feet are weighed down by the prizes of past victories'.[56] Both 'peccatism' and 'saviourism' are seen by al-Faruqi as derogatory to man's dignity and a denial of his freewill.[57] In contrast to 'the utterly powerless creature that salvation theory requires man to be',[58] man in Islam 'is not an object of salvation, but its subject; through his agency alone the moral part, which is the higher part of the will of God, enters, and is fulfilled in, creation'. It is this which constitutes 'man's cosmic station and significance'.[59]

Theologically, the events in the Christian story are seen as compromising God's transcendence and separateness from man. God must always remain 'ontologically disparate' from the whole realm of creation which includes humankind.[60] God 'does not reveal Himself to anyone in any way', but 'reveals only His will', since it is not possible to have 'complete transcendence and self-revelation at the same time'.[61] While agreeing with his Christian partners in dialogue that God cares about and is somehow involved with mankind, al-Faruqi, in harmony with majority Muslim belief, insists that it is not conceivable that he could be hurt.[62] The 'Christian fellowship of man with God . . . puts God in a position irreconcilable with his omniscience and omnipotence'.[63] In Islam, God 'is not man's fellow, but his Transcendent Creator and First Mover', whose nearness is not that of a fellow but 'the nearness of the ethically imperative'.[64]

Some of the arguments which al-Faruqi employs against Christianity are questionable from an Islamic point of view, or else assume dubious distinctions between Islam and Christianity. His emphasis on God's absolute justice leads him to take issue with 'the Christian claim that in God, mercy is higher than justice',[65] and to endorse the contrary view: in any conflict between justice and mercy, justice must take priority, for creation must be orderly, and 'order cannot proceed from, or be based upon, mercy. A cosmos in which mercy is the absolute law of being would not be a cosmos, but a chaos'.[66] One senses that it is with reluctance that al-Faruqi concedes that 'God may and does grant His grace to whomsoever He chooses', for he quickly passes on to talk of 'another divine grace which is not quite gratuitous', and which God dispenses 'only in deserving cases'.[67]

Al-Faruqi sometimes portrays a view of God in Islam and Christianity which seems to imply that God's omnipotence is actually more pronounced in the latter, as where he criticizes the 'historical determinism' of the divine plan according to Christianity, and rejects 'God's alleged interference in the processes of history' since 'the initiative in history is always with man'.[68] Islam, on the other hand, 'is safe against ever having to rely upon a deterministic theory of history in order to justify itself'; although God may act in history, these acts are to be interpreted as 'the reward of virtue or the punishment of vice'.[69] His argument that the Christian view of redemption is metaphysically impossible because it involves a change (from a state of sin to a state of innocence) on 'the level of nature', which 'belongs to reality from which there is no escape',[70] appears to confuse the immanent with the transcendent and, in fact, to compromise God's transcendence from both an Islamic and a Christian point of view.

In *Christian Ethics*, al-Faruqi expresses the view that the only way forward for the Christian in the modern age is to abandon the tenets that constitute 'Christianism'. Although 'after eighteen centuries of Dark Ages, the Christian mind is dazed by the light of day and stands utterly confused', he senses 'the dawn of a new age' in certain liberal Christian interpretations of these tenets (p. 180). However, these 'acrobatic efforts' are not sufficient, and he professes, as a brother in faith, to 'shudder at and bemoan' such 'futile sport' (p. 313). He regrets that in spite of the advent of biblical criticism and the rise of modern scientific knowledge, no Christian theologian has been 'bold enough to by-pass the tradition as final authority, and to bring its own relativities of history under judgement of the pristine faith of Jesus' (p. 312). In short, 'what is needed above all is for the Christian to realize his own predicament, namely, the impossibility of reconciling his traditionalist faith with either the pristine faith of Jesus or the demands of the modern mind and heart. What is needed is not less than a "Reformation"; a reformation which, unlike that of Luther . . . will be directed against the authority of the cumulative tradition' (p. 313). He feels that Muslims can help Christians in 'the rediscovery and reconstruction of the Christian faith' in a kind of 'mutual spiritual midwifery' (p. 314).

Al-Faruqi does in fact put forward some suggestions for a modification of Christian thought, intimating in several places that the key tenets are radically out of harmony with 'contemporary reality' or the worldview of 'the modern Muslim and Christian'.[71] He approves of the 'didactic' view of redemption as expressed by some liberal Christian thinkers.[72] This view sees redemption or salvation as the ultimate logical consequence of following Jesus' teachings, rather than as a metaphysical event which occurs during the believer's lifetime: 'it is not the fact of Jesus' passion and Crucifixion that constitute redemption, but the moral truth it was his special distinction to bring'. Like Muhammad, Jesus 'came but to show how man ought to live, how he ought to conduct himself *vis-à-vis* the world and existence'.[73] For al-Faruqi, the advantages of this view are that 'there would be no need for any mystery in redemption' and it would undermine the claim to Jesus' divinity. He argues that the vision of Jesus as an 'inspired man', in the sense that his life 'was saturated with the high personal, moral values of which his whole career is the expression', would be more effective and reach more people, since 'the person of the hero does far more to affect people in favour of heroism . . . than a whole pile of conceptual analyses of these values', just as a work of art affects people more than a dissertation on aesthetics.[74]

In his article 'Islam and Christianity: Diatribe or Dialogue', al-Faruqi suggests that the Christian view of sin could be reinterpreted as 'ethical misperception', in which case the Muslim could join him or her in acknowledging its universality, inasmuch as all humans make mistakes (p. 21). The cure for such misperception would then be found in education, which would enable people to 'surmount the sinful misperceptions', and which is described as no less than 'the unique processus of salvation' (p. 22). The Christian teaching on forgiveness is effective only for the few with 'strong ethical sensitivities', and the rest are likely to be 'encouraged and confirmed in their sinfulness'; education, on the other hand, is universal and 'ministers to everybody's need' (p. 20). Furthermore, while in the case of forgiveness 'its activity and effect are always erratic', education 'is always subject to deliberation, to critique and to planning' (p. 21).

Shabbir Akhtar, expounding his views mainly in *A Faith for all Seasons*, acknowledges to a far greater extent than al-Faruqi that the modern world poses challenges to both Muslims and Christians, and urges Muslims not to be complacent about the dangers of secularism (p. 11). He believes that Muslims have something to learn from Christians who have 'confronted the cold and riddling gaze of secular modernity longer and more self-consciously than any other extant religious tradition', and he goes so far as to describe nineteenth-century Protestant theology as 'possibly the finest essay in intellectual probity in the history of religious ideas' (p. 12). In particular, he admires the spirit of openness and self-criticism in liberal Protestant theology, and considers Christianity 'the only faith in the Semitic trio whose adherents still continue seriously to produce intellectual self-defence when challenged by the alien convictions of the contemporaneous age' (p. 13). In the circumstances he suggests that these faiths should join forces and become 'partners in adversity' (p. 14).

Akhtar recommends that Muslims should 'exercise imaginative sympathy' with Christian ideals and study Christianity as 'an autonomous expression of religiosity' (p. 182). The view that Christianity is a 'perversion' of Islam or that 'genuine Christianity is found only in Islam' should not absolve Muslims from 'the normal need for independent historical or rational support' (p. 181). He regrets that 'most Muslims, including educated ones, know next to nothing about Christology', and exhorts Muslims to take the trouble to inform themselves accurately about Christian belief: 'few Muslims can distinguish clearly between the view that a man claims to be divine – a blasphemy – and the entirely different view according to which God volunteers to become human – the orthodox Christian conviction' (p. 182).

Akhtar nevertheless believes that Muslims should have the right to draw attention to those areas in which Christianity is weak and Islam strong, which for him include the areas of 'intellectual appeal' and 'canonical formulation' (pp. 189–90). He feels that Islam has 'somewhat fewer scandals to the secular intellect' than Christianity (p. 10), and that to embrace Christianity 'requires assent to the largest collection of highly implausible beliefs' and 'an unusually dramatic suspension of critical powers' (p. 179). Like al-Faruqi, he believes that faith needs to be, and can be, justified in rational terms: 'the burden of "proof" . . . is on the believer's shoulders; he must, in the face of secular reservation, justify his faith in the language of reason'; he therefore feels that the best way forward for Christians and Muslims alike is the development of a natural theology (p. 37).[75] Akhtar is impatient with those Christian theologians who seem to positively celebrate paradox and irrationality, but also observes that these qualities lie at the very heart of the Christian faith, which suffers from 'fatal logical infirmities' (pp. 34, 156). The Incarnation in particular is found to be incoherent: 'the paradoxical notion of God becoming man while simultaneously remaining God is not easily intelligible'. Notwithstanding the Christian insistence that it is a question of God 'condescending' towards man, this appears to non-Christians as a Feuerbachian projection of the human onto the divine (p. 179). For his own part, Akhtar considers that this 'is actually not a step that a person – including God – can take'.[76]

On the positive side, Akhtar concedes that Christian doctrine is a response to 'the riddle of God's moral involvement with a human nature that is so strikingly recalcitrant to divine guidance', and a result of taking seriously the questions of sin and suffering. He recognizes that for the Christian, the Incarnation and Crucifixion represent 'a supreme gesture of humility' on the part of God (p. 175). Furthermore, '*if* the doctrine of the Incarnation were free from certain apparently fatal logical infirmities, *then* it could provide useful theological resources, lacking in Judaism and Islam' (his italics, p. 180).[77] He does not always feel compelled to express the difference between Islam and Christianity in terms detrimental to the latter; while Islam's 'inner religious genius' consists in its maintaining a 'moral distance between man and God in the larger attempt to frustrate the will to tragedy', in Christianity it consists of 'the gesture that closes the gap between the Creator and the creation . . . the radically tragic episode in which a merciful God pitched his tent among a sinful generation and graciously disclosed himself as self-sacrificial love' (p. 174).

Akhtar feels that in addressing humanity's inherent tendency to wrongdoing it is inappropriate to look for an 'external rescue'.[78] He rejects the possibility of redemption on metaphysical grounds, in that 'there is no mechanism that can bleach out sin from the human cloth. At best, it can be opposed, subdued, and occasionally forgiven.' Moreover, 'there are forms of evil which no morally constrained sovereignty can fully redeem', and this remains as 'an irreducible residue of history'.[79] Although he often stresses the human capacity for evil, particularly when arguing for the necessity of religious (i.e. Islamic) government, he describes the doctrine of original sin as an 'indirect condemnation of God's handicraft' (p. 161).

Like al-Faruqi, Akhtar defends the transcendence of God in Islam, where humans are not 'children of God' but 'servants of a just master; they cannot, in orthodox Islam, typically attain any greater degree of intimacy with their creator'; unlike Christians, Muslims are not encouraged by the Qur'an (which, he agrees with al-Faruqi, is concerned with God's will rather than his character) to speculate on God's essence and are therefore 'not entitled to claim that "Allah *is* love"', or anything else for that matter (pp. 180–1).

A frequent theme in Akhtar's critique of Christianity is that of its characteristic ethos, which he sees in terms of pathos, tragedy and sentimentality, in contrast to Islam's robust practicality and rationalism. Arguing that a 'sense of pathos . . . cannot atone for the poverty of logic', he invites Christians to 'suspend temporarily their deep emotional attachment to the "gesture" of the Incarnation', and suggests that they may be 'bewitched by a picture: that of a sinless God crucified by sinful men' (pp. 179–80). He feels that the belief in the Incarnation is the result of 'a particularly tempting variety of sentiment that somehow overpowers the purely rational impulse to seek theological truth', and adds that 'the impulse to pathos has most to feed on when a religion is practically and doctrinally in eclipse' (p. 180). By contrast, the God of Islam is 'neither a tragedian nor a sentimentalist', Muhammad 'was not a man cut out for tragedy', and the tragic is 'totally foreign to the authentically Muslim sensibility' (pp. 159-60).[80] Furthermore, 'Islam has always been . . . a faith that is clear, unambiguous, positive, assertive, dogmatic, defined, self-assured' (p. 159).

The Social and Political Dimensions of Religion

The social and political dimensions of religion are often seen as a key area of contrast between Islam and Christianity; this has already been observed in al-Faruqi's theory that the Christian ethic was not concerned with practical consequences and Izetbegovic's portrayal of Christianity's idealism and otherworldliness. Their approach implies that these dimensions were missing at the point of origin, whereas the more common Muslim view that Jesus did not abolish the law would imply that the de-emphasis of the legal (and by implication socio-political) dimension was a later distortion.

In *The Final Imperative*, Shabbir Akhtar deals with the relationship between religion and power in Islam and Christianity, in reponse to Kenneth Cragg's writings on the subject. He rejects the view that the Hijra represented a betrayal of Muhammad's prophetic vocation and a turning point at which Islam became politicized, insisting that the political dimension was intrinsic from the beginning (pp. 17–21). In common with most other Muslims, he asserts that Islam 'recognizes no distinction between the religious and the political', and explains that it 'seeks to absorb political community in the larger desire to sanctify it' (pp. 33, 30).

On the whole, Akhtar avoids presenting a stereotypical Christian stance on political power, and is aware of some of the nuances and diversity in Christian thought. Liberation theology, for example, with its incorporation of the political dimension, is tentatively suggested to represent an 'Islamization of Christianity' (p. 11). He nevertheless believes that 'there is a distinctively Christian perspective on power and polity . . . which categorically rejects the style of political religion which Islam adopts' (p. 83). One can infer that Akhtar finds this rejection aberrant from those instances where he hints that Jesus' fundamental orientation to political power may not have been very different from Muhammad's (pp. 12, 23, 32).

Akhtar's critique focuses mainly on the historical and contemporary record of Christianity's involvement with power, which is portrayed in fairly bleak terms. The tolerance of Muslim society is contrasted with 'the genocidal instinct which broke surface with such frequency in Christian lands', and the examples of the Conquistadors in South America and the Reconquista of Andalusia are contrasted with the comportment of 'Umar at Jerusalem and 'Amr in Egypt (pp. 69–71). Although his account is apologetic and oversimplified, he advances an interesting theoretical explanation for the contrast: 'creeds with non-violent commitments have, when eventually empowered, often prostituted power precisely because, unlike the adherents of political religion, their votaries have had no previous or regular doctrinal guidance for regulating belligerent impulses' (p. 84).

In response to the Christian critique of Islam and power, he stresses that 'the Christian faith has in the past regularly sought authority over the powers temporal', and comments that 'no religion whose votaries have conquered much of the globe in the hope of saving others . . . can be entitled to claim the privilege of a fundamental indifference to power' (pp. 66, 65). On the other hand, Christianity and Buddhism are described as 'essentially religions of private salvation calling for humble postures of powerlessness within and against worldly structures', in contrast to Islam's incorporation of 'morally constrained political action' (p. 95). Citing South Africa as an example of a country where Christianity has been used to support injustice, he comments that 'the Christian stance on power readily lends itself to such misuse', and that Muslims 'cannot endorse the Christian attitude of effective passivity in the face of gross injustice' (pp. 66, 67).

Akhtar criticizes Christians for acknowledging the reality of structural evil while only addressing evil at the individual level, in contast to Islam which opposes it institutionally (p. 38). Observing that the Marxist critique of religion has much to teach Christianity but nothing to teach Islam (p. 95), he occasionally expresses himself in startlingly Marxian terms: 'in a just society, private virtues (such as individual generosity to the poor) become virtually superfluous. At any rate, no amount of personal generosity can resolve the structural problems of society based on unjust distributions of power and wealth' (p. 72). He states forthrightly that 'a pure individual heart is no bulwark against an unjust order', and that 'if men are to do good effectively, they must act in association' (pp. 61, 44).

Akhtar believes that it is essential for any religion to engage with political power, not just for reasons of moral responsibility but for reasons of survival. His view that 'all ideologies survive by courtesy of power' may be relatively uncontroversial, but the implication here and elsewhere that Islam and Christianity are in fact 'ideologies' would be unacceptable to almost all Christians, and would not meet the approval of all Muslims (p. 85). His argument that the political realm should ideally be 'governed by ethical controls grounded in the religion itself' (p. 55), is not necessarily a point of contrast with Christianity, but many of the points he makes seem intended to amplify points of difference. Although he concedes that 'law does not change the heart' (p. 62), he sometimes implies that force is in fact the most effective means to further the cause of righteousness: 'all the peaceful instruments of prophecy – namely, persuasion, tact, endurance, patience, persistence – are of limited assistance in a world whose enmity to truth is neither casual nor intermittent' (p. 42). In Akhtar's view, faith alone 'can do little without the power that can protect its heritage and ensure its future'; he describes Islam as 'the piety which welcomes power as the effective instrument for the enactment of religious conviction' (pp. 59, 81). He refers to Christianity and Islam as 'religious rivals',[81] and sometimes characterizes Islam as the antithesis of Christianity. Islam's 'almost miraculous durability as a political variable' is contrasted with post-Enlightenment Christianity, which is described as a 'largely spent religious force'.[82] Akhtar expresses admiration for the vigour and virility of Islam, a 'religion of action', which is said to inspire 'the highest rate of martyrdom of any living faith'. Furthermore, 'in the field of political militancy, "applied Islam" is undeniably the star performer'.[83] It 'remains on the Middle Eastern landscape as proudly and as naturally as any natural feature', and its 'temper of constructive yet militant wrath' is seen as essential to its survival.[84]

Like Akhtar, al-Faruqi contrasts Islam's record of tolerance with Christianity's historical intolerance in unequivocal terms.[85] In *Christian Ethics*, modern Western civilization, in particular, is seen as illustrating the perversion of the religious impulse: 'ever since he became a Christian, Western man has lived a split life and suffered from a split personality', for Christianity dominated his consciousness but not his actions (p. 280). Western man has 'committed aggression, invaded, colonized, and imperialized. His Christian missions carried the cross only side by side with the national flag and often raised the latter higher than the former'. Torn between the Christian ideal of renunciation and the Western rapacity for power and domination, he had to resort to self-deception in order to disguise the ugliness of his deeds to his own conscience (p. 281).

For al-Faruqi, the fact that Jesus' message was addressed to the individual, as opposed to Islam's appeal to the societal level, was due to the specific circumstances which Jesus faced, and does not necessarily represent a categorical or definitive difference. Although 'Jesus was not a "*mujāhid*" [defined by al-Faruqi as holy warrior] . . . [and] did not conceive of his mission as one fulfillable in the realm of worldly action',[86] al-Faruqi believes that if Christians were to rediscover the original pristine Christianity, they could evolve from it a social ethic, enabling them to implement the religious precepts at the social and political level. He rather superfluously reassures contemporary Christians that Jesus' emphasis on the transformation of the individual does not imply that the Christian 'need not . . . exert himself to relieve the sufferings and miseries of his fellows' (p. 249), or that 'he ought to withdraw himself from the world'. This is because the enactment of God's will in the individual naturally spills over into that person's relationship with others and the outside world (p. 250). There seems to be a tension here with the argument that al-Faruqi uses to justify and explain Islam's abrogation of Christianity, namely that the new ethic of 'societism' as opposed to 'personalism' was required by changed circumstances (p. 251).

Al-Faruqi observes with approval that the majority of Christian thinkers today do in fact advocate some kind of 'societist ethic' (p. 254). However, he believes that all such developments in Christian thought are in practice hopelessly marred, since they arose purely in response to circumstantial need rather than as a spontaneous development within the religion. The fact that it is events that have 'compelled and propelled the Christian mind to think out a theological basis' gives contemporary Christian thought a piecemeal character, and the use of symbols such as 'the Kingdom of God' or Jesus' healing ministry to justify such new emphases is seen as wholly arbitrary (p. 255).

Although al-Faruqi hypothetically accepts that Christianity need not be incompatible with a social or political ethic, he appears to reject all actual Christian initiatives in this direction. The attempts of individual thinkers such as Albert Schweitzer, Joseph McLelland, William Temple and Ernest Troeltsch to reconcile the Christian teachings with a more positive view of social and political responsibility (or 'world affirmation') are seen as diametrically opposed to the teaching of Jesus as exemplified in the saying: 'My Kingdom is not of this world' (p. 283). On the other hand, Christian thinkers such as Karl Barth and Reinhold Niebuhr who are seen as promoting 'a-societism' or secularity are equally condemned (pp. 263ff., 289ff.). This is probably to be accounted for by al-Faruqi's desire to close all avenues except that of complete reconstruction, owing to his conviction that 'Christianism . . . is incongruent with societism', hopelessly paralysed by paradox and irrationality as it is (p. 283). Elaborating on this, he asks: 'how can the societist will to space-time . . . ever be reconciled with the peccatist condemnation? How could societist activism be reconciled with the saviourist contention that all that needs to be done has been done once and for all? How can . . . the will to a future, that is not yet but is actualizable by man's effort alone, be reconciled with the sudden coming of the Kingdom of power?' (p. 294).

Al-Faruqi and Akhtar reflect a general Muslim ambivalence concerning the present state and desired direction of Christian thought. While both would theoretically welcome greater political responsibility on the part of Christians, in al-Faruqi's view this could only be achieved by a radical overhaul of essential beliefs, while Akhtar gives the impression that Christianity is destined to gravitate towards one of two extremes: intolerance and coercion on the one hand and irresponsible passivity on the other. Neither they nor other Muslims advocate that Christians should follow the Islamic model and consider the possibility of a 'Christian state'; to that extent Muslims and Christians may be in agreement that Christianity, unlike Islam, is not at its best or most representative when actually holding the reins of political power.

Irenical Views of Christianity

Muslims who express the most positive appreciation of Christianity are frequently those who have participated in interfaith dialogue. In addition to Askari, Arkoun, Merad and Nasr who were mentioned earlier, those who have been active on the international level include Muhammad Talbi, Hasan Sa'ab, Mahmoud Ayoub, Khalid Duran, Riffat Hassan and Fathi Osman.[87] Of the small number of Muslim-authored non-polemical articles on comparative themes in Islam and Christianity, a disproportionate number are written by Muslims who have taken part in dialogue.[88] However, it would be premature to conclude that it is the dialogue process itself which has led to an enhanced religious openness; apart from those dialogue events that are mainly official or diplomatic, it tends to be Muslims who are already of modernist or liberal persuasion who choose to participate.

The written output of the scholars listed above, for several of whom Sufism has been a formative influence, expresses an attitude of openness towards Christianity as well as other religions, but they have not necessarily written anything substantial on Christianity specifically. This may be for a variety of reasons: because they are more concerned with socio-political issues than with religious or theological matters;[89] because their area of expertise lies elsewhere; or because of social or political constraints on presenting a view of Christianity that is 'extra-Qur'anic' (but not, it might be argued, anti-Qur'anic). It takes a certain boldness to defy such constraints, and it is no accident that several of these advocates of religious pluralism have also challenged mainstream assumptions on the relationship between religion and politics in Islam, and have either explicitly denied the necessity for an Islamic state or have argued for some form of separation between religion and politics.[90] Several also stress the priority of 'faith' over 'religion' or 'belief'.[91]

One sustained dialogue project which operates mainly on an intellectual and theological level is that of the Groupe de Recherches Islamo-Chrétien (GRIC), an independent group of Muslim and Christian scholars founded in 1977.[92] On the Muslim side the contributors come mainly from Tunisia, Morocco and France, and include Arkoun, Talbi, and fellow-Tunisians Abdulmajid Charfi and Sa'ad Ghrab. Its publications, *The Challenge of the Scriptures* (1989 – originally published in French as *Ces Ecritures qui nous questionnent: Le Bible et le Coran*, 1987), and *Foi et justice* (*Un défi pour le*

Christianisme et l'Islam) (1993) are in each case the outcome of several years of multilateral collaboration.

A section of *The Challenge of the Scriptures* written by the Muslim contributors on the subject of Muslim perceptions of the Bible is of particular interest. The authors reserve the right to depart from Muslim consensus on certain matters since 'Islam has no magisterium to legitimate one opinion or another' (p. 76). They question the traditional or majority Muslim opinion in several areas. The preferred interpretation of *taḥrīf*, for example, is 'the deviation suffered by the divine ray when it passes through the deforming prism of our imperfect humanity', and it is denied that there was any question of conscious or deliberate falsification (pp. 78, 84). It is suggested that the Muslim theory of *taḥrīf* could involve the sort of issues which have, in fact, been addressed in Christian textual criticism of the Bible, and it is held that Muslim misunderstandings have arisen from 'a false analogy between the ideas of revelation and inspiration' (p. 83). The Qur'an is taken to deny only the literal, physical understanding of the term 'son of God', as understood by seventh-century Arab Christians, and the authors express the conviction that 'Islam could tolerate any metaphorical interpretation that distanced itself from this basic sense' (p. 80). Furthermore, the Qur'anic verse which is normally understood as denying the Crucifixion, which describes the Jews as claiming to have killed Jesus 'when they neither killed nor crucified him, but it only appeared so to them' (4:157), is not interpreted as a categorical denial, but as a 'vehement retort' against the Jews, signifying that 'even if they killed and crucified him, they could never overcome the ideals he preached'. Attention is drawn to those Qur'anic passages which seem to refer to Jesus' physical death, which could be harmonized with the belief that he was in fact killed by crucifixion, although it is felt that an element of mystery surrounds the end of his earthly life (pp. 81–2). The hope is expressed that Muslims will read and reflect on the Christian scripture, since they can find therein an emphasis on certain values which, although not absent from the Qur'an, are 'insufficiently cultivated in Muslim circles, like love, forgiveness, the rejection of pharisaism, and the concern with the spirit rather than the letter of the law'. Muslims should therefore 'learn to ponder what the bible says about the source of life, which can nourish the believer's hope and spirituality' (p. 85).

In the Islamic as in the Christian context, theological pluralism can take a variety of forms, from the simple assertion that salvation is available to non-Muslims to varying degrees of relativism on the question of religious truth. While all of the above express the view that salvation is attainable by non-Muslims, it is Askari who has gone furthest in the direction of religious pluralism and who has developed his thought most fully. Drawing his inspiration partly from Neoplatonism, he is interested in evolving not only a theology of religious diversity but also, like Wilfred Cantwell Smith, an inter-religious theology which treats all the different religions within a single framework.[93] He believes that all religions are 'relative to the Absolute Truth', and that one should not make the mistake of 'equating one's own religious doctrine with the Transcendent'.[94] He compares the various spiritual teachers, including Buddha, Lao-tse, and Socrates in addition to Jesus and Muhammad, to different mirrors reflecting the image of a single candle.[95] The claims to finality within each tradition have had a divisive effect, and should be interpreted metaphorically, for to take the metaphor as equal to the transcendent is 'to suffer an inexcusable error of judgement'.[96]

Askari affirms religious diversity as an opportunity for 'creative conflict',[97] and as providential. He believes that Christianity and Islam 'constitute one complex of faith . . . their separateness does not denote two areas of conflicting truths, but a dialogical necessity'.[98] The different religions stand in need of each other and are corrective of each other. By rejecting the Qur'an, Christians reject Jesus, since the acceptance of him as the Word of God implies the acceptance of all revelation in all times and places; similarly, by rejecting the authenticity of the New Testament, Muslims compromise their own response to God.[99] Furthermore, Muslims 'require a Christian presence amidst them' to counter the danger of falling into Pharisaic legalism, and to give greater force to certain elements which are less prominent in Judaism and Islam, namely the dimensions of 'the tragic, or suffering, of submission in silence without resistance, of confronting self-righteousness, of upholding the value of humility and poverty, of going inward, of partaking of the burdens, seen and unseen, of the other'.[100]

Askari feels that the boundaries that separate the different religions are neither ultimate nor permanent, and that the important thing is the inner spiritual quest of the individual seeker.[101] He stresses the experiential nature of truth and the fact that all religious experience represents a contact with the transcendent.[102] Religious symbolism is an area of particular interest for Askari, as he believes that symbols can provide a key to unity between the religions, and that most of the differences between them are a matter of semantics.[103] He envisages a time when there will no longer be a need for the individual religious traditions, and has expressed the opinion that Islam and Christianity will one day converge.[104]

Askari not infrequently draws on biblical illustrations in his writings, and he is one of a very few Muslims who have made some attempt at biblical interpretation.[105] In a brief lecture which is reproduced in his *Spiritual Quest: An Inter-religious Dimension*, Askari singles out for special attention the Sermon on the Mount. He sees it as a 'universal message', containing mystical and ethical values which are common to Christians and Muslims; since the Qur'an includes Jewish prophetic history, the message of Jesus is in any case 'within the Islamic testimony' (pp. 90, 92). His style of exegesis closely resembles the strand within the Sufi exegetical tradition known as *ishārī* (intuitive or allusive), which more orthodox Muslims tend to consider acceptable but not authoritative, because of the subjective nature of many of its insights. Placing himself in the tradition of Sufis who have drawn inspiration from the figure of Jesus through the Qur'an, Askari sees the teachings of the Sermon as incorporating a 'mystical system', the elements of which include the mystical goal, the mystical Way, the mystical state of mind, the preparation to enter the Way, and the mystical transformation (pp. 93–6). The 'preparation to enter the Way' incorporates secret piety, the suspension of judgement, and forgiving others; the 'mystical state of mind' is when individuals abandon themselves to God, living as the birds of the air and the lilies of the field; and the 'mystical transformation' is a description of the resultant behaviour of those who have changed, who love their enemies and do not resist evil. The threefold: 'Ask, and it will be given to you; seek and you will find; knock and the door will be opened to you' (Matt. 7:7) is said to represent three progressive stages on the mystical Way (pp. 93–5). Most Christians are likely to feel that the foregoing introduces divisions which detract from the original simplicity of the message, but some of Askari's other ideas are more in harmony with mainstream Christian views. He emphasizes that in the case of Jesus 'the message and the message-giver constitute a unity' (p. 91 – this is also said to be true of Husayn, who gave his life in the fight against oppression), and that 'the ethical content of the message of Jesus is a part of the spiritual whole of his life and teachings'. Therefore, 'those who talk of the Christian ethics without realizing that it is a branch and not a root may . . .

ultimately falsify the message itself, for the branch independent of the root is a dead branch' (p. 96).

Like several contemporary Christian thinkers, Askari challenges the boundaries of religious identity and de-emphasizes propositional truth in a way that is likely to make many believers uncomfortable. The overwhelming majority of Muslims, including comparatively liberal thinkers, would recoil from any hint of religious syncretism.[106] Askari feels that religious labels can reinforce the barriers between people, and he is aware of his own marginality in Islamic terms.[107] It is important to emphasize, however, that he draws much of his inspiration from the Islamic tradition and frequently refers to the Qur'an in support of his views.

Mohammed Arkoun is another Muslim scholar whose views have the effect of blurring the distinctions between the religious traditions, although his approach is very different. He is an original and innovative thinker, and his contribution to the study of religions has been widely acknowledged.[108] His writings are not very accessible to those uninitiated into postmodernist thought and discourse or the disciplines upon which he draws, which include anthropology, sociology and semiotics. He has not written a great deal on Christianity, but he proposes the application of a thoroughgoing historicism, not just to the Islamic tradition but to the three Abrahamic religions in relation to each other. He does not believe that such an approach needs to undermine Islamic truths, and he is himself committed to an Islamic religious and spiritual identity.

Arkoun is more interested in the parallels between religions than the differences, and observes that in today's world situation 'it seems totally romantic, irrelevant, and useless to engage in debates between religions about traditional faiths, values, or dogmas'.[109] He warns of the dangers of 'reciprocal exclusion' in theological as well as political systems, which has in the past resulted in religiously motivated wars.[110] Like Askari, he believes that the apparent theological differences are often attributable to semantic differences, describing the question of the Trinity, for example, as 'linguistic more than it is theological'; he believes that 'a theory of metaphor and symbol' could enable believers to transcend 'the arbitrariness of traditional theological definitions'.[11] Differing attitudes to political power in Islam and Christianity are attributed to historical conditions at the point of origin and are therefore seen as accidental rather than intrinsic differences; while Roman hegemony constrained Jesus to confine his teachings to the spiritual and religious, the power vacuum in seventh-century Arabia meant that Muhammad was 'obliged to introduce a new political system'.[112]

Arkoun's proposed comparative method of studying the Abrahamic faiths sometimes involves using the same model to study all three, in a way which, some may feel, fails to do justice to the differences between them. His treatment of the question of revelation, for example, does not seem to take into account the very different views of revelation and canonical formation in Islam and Christianity. His suggestion that a distinction be made between three levels of revelation, namely the Archetypal Book, the earthly revelation and the final scriptural canon (Closed Official Corpus),[113] would be problematic both for Christians and Muslims, in that the concept of an 'Archetypal Book' would not be meaningful to Christians, and the distinction between the original earthly revelation and the final text would be a very difficult one for Muslims to make. Arkoun's model of revelation is nevertheless essentially Islamic, in that it assumes that the original revelation consists of God's pure and unadulterated word, as where he talks of 'the delivery of the Word of God by Jesus . . . using the Aramaic language' as comparable to the delivery of the Qur'an by Muhammad, and he lists the languages of revelation as Hebrew, Aramaic and Arabic, omitting the New Testament Greek. Similarly his suggestion that the Torah, Canon Law and the Sharīʿa have fulfilled similar functions as 'divine law' in all three religions is questionable.[114]

In some respects Arkoun's approach to the religions appears to be more an example of the levelling effect of postmodernist thought than a specifically Islamic response. Few Muslims are likely to want to follow his lead, and postmodernism has, for obvious reasons, not had a very wide appeal in the Islamic context, but his work provides one example of an attempt to join an Islamic commitment to a conscious and sophisticated use of intellectual tools that have been developed in a non-Muslim context.

Those Muslims who emphasize the inner truth or essence which is contained in each religion tend to see historical Christianity as a valid and autonomous ongoing tradition with its own distinctive religious genius. Nasr, like Askari, believes that the existence of a plurality of religions is a phenomenon willed by God, and he aligns himself with a small number of modernist Muslims who have denied that Islam abrogated or wholly superseded Christianity when he sees the separation between them not as an aberration arising from Christians' failure to perceive the truth, but as something desirable.[115] He suggests that the Qur'anic denial of the Crucifixion, described as 'the one irreducible "fact" separating Christianity and Islam', was 'placed there providentially to prevent a mingling of the two religions'.[116] While firmly rejecting any Christian criticism of the Qur'anic Christology, which is 'in perfect agreement with the total theology of Islam', Nasr states that 'neither the Islamic nor the Christian view exhausts the possibilities of the "Christic" reality'.[117] Other views bring Nasr more securely within the range of Islamic orthodoxy: among Jesus' main functions are those of preserving the Torah and announcing the coming of Muhammad (he comments that 'for Muslims it is inconceivable that such a major religious manifestation as Islam should have been passed in silence by Christ').[118] Islam is still seen as representing the culmination of the former religions; Nasr sees Muhammad as synthesizing the elements of faith, law, and the spiritual way as represented by Abraham, Moses and Jesus respectively.[119] Even where truth is deemed to be found in all religious traditions, the Islamic revelation is nevertheless believed to embody truth in its purest form.[120]

Several Muslims have offered interpretations of Jesus which go further than most in acknowledging the uniqueness of his mission. In his article 'Christ according to the Qur'an', Merad expresses the view that the classical commentaries 'do not shed light on the figure of Christ in the way he deserves' (p. 2). He feels that 'everything in the Qur'an points to the fact that Christ is seen as an exceptional event in the history of the world, an event pregnant with exceptional meanings', and furthermore 'Christ witnesses to an exceptional divine concern' (p. 7). He stresses the aura of mystery surrounding the person of Jesus in the Qur'an, the use of terminology such as 'spirit' and 'word (of God)' which is used of no one else, and the uniqueness of the miracles attributed to him, in particular those of creation and healing (pp. 11–12). He accepts that the Qur'an denies Christ's divinity, but finds it significant that 'at no time is the term *bashar* [human being] applied to Christ', although 'this would have been the best argument to weaken the notion of Christ's divinity' (p. 11). The Qur'anic denial of the Crucifixion, however, is seen as safeguarding both God's honour and man's dignity (p. 15). In Merad's view it could not, in any case, have been accommodated in the Qur'an, in which the believers always triumph over the forces of evil (pp. 13–14). God 'does not abandon His own', and, in the absence of a doctrine of redemption, in the Qur'an the Crucifixion would imply that God had failed. He does, however, acknowledge that the Resurrection is in fact the ground of

Christian hope, a hope which is not nullified by the Crucifixion (p. 15). Ending on an open note, Merad states that the Qur'an aims 'to provoke reflection rather than to furnish final answers', and feels that 'it would be presumptuous of a Muslim to believe that he possesses the whole truth with regard to Jesus and to refuse to take the road opened to him by the Qur'an of seeking other testimonies' (pp. 16–17).

Syed Vahiduddin expresses his views in a short piece entitled 'What Christ Means to Me'.[121] Like Merad, he emphasizes the mystery surrounding Christ's person, but, unlike him, he draws on the biblical as well as the Qur'anic account in his view of Christ, seeming to accept the Crucifixion as 'the consummation of his passion' and 'a prelude to his resurrection' (p. 182). Regretting that both Christian and Muslim apologetics tend to minimize the supernatural aspects of Christ's life and reduce him to a 'social revolutionary or . . . a moral preacher', he believes that Christ 'represents a spiritual force which breaks through the order of mechanical causation'; furthermore, his healing power 'is given special prominence in the Qur'an. He radiates *shifā*' [healing] both at the physical and the spiritual level' (p. 183). The spiritual power which emanates from Christ continues to be effective; he is, for Vahiduddin, a 'supreme "comforter" . . . bringing solace to souls in distress' (pp. 183–4).[122] His 'Gospel abounds with the love that overflows itself', and 'he is the embodiment of that tender aspect of the divine which the Quran calls *rahma* [mercy]'. All this, Vahiduddin believes, is borne witness to by the Qur'an. He dwells at some length on the suffering of Christ, drawing on the Gospel account of his humiliation prior to the Crucifixion (p. 184). Through his 'perfect surrender to God's will', bearing his suffering without complaint, Christ was able to conquer death itself and 'appear in all His glory'. Vahiduddin concludes that it is 'devotion to Christ and His Holy Mother' which binds Muslims and Christians together (p. 185).

Askari also believes that the person of Christ has a positive religious value for Muslims. In his article 'The Dialogical Relationship between Christianity and Islam', he maintains that Jesus represents 'the revelation as a Person' as opposed to 'the revelation in words', i.e. the Qur'an, and so guards against idolatry of the Book, just as the Qur'an, by rejecting the Incarnation, guards against 'the idolatry of the Person' (pp. 44–5). Christ is a 'sign' for both Christians and Muslims in 'the realm of the deep relation between God and man' (p. 42) and a symbol of unity, for 'once having known Christ is to belong together', and 'those who know Christ as Love do not dispute about his Being. They are silent. They are humble. They love one another' (p. 45). Like Vahiduddin, Askari exhorts Christians not to dilute or abandon their beliefs under the onslaught of modern thought; he warns against the danger of Christians 'secularizing and demythologizing the Cross', and even suggests that the Muslim could 'remind his Christian brother that there is no Cross but the Cross of Jesus' (p. 47).

Conclusions

There appears to be an increasing diversity in Muslim interpretation of Christianity, arising partly from the cross-fertilization between Islamic tradition and modern Western scholarship. While Islam is usually seen by Muslim writers as combining the best of Judaism and Christianity, in a sort of thesis–antithesis–synthesis progression, or more simply as the mean between two extremes, the thesis–antithesis poles of Judaism and Christianity may be articulated in different ways, for example in terms of legalism/love, communalism/individualism, exotericism/esotericism, or severity/lenience. Paradoxically, this involves an acknowledgement that Christianity does have distinctive qualities rather than just being a paler version of Islam. Among the mainstream Muslim intellectuals this comes out most clearly in the work of al-Faruqi, notwithstanding his claim that Islam absorbed and preserved the original Christian teachings. It has been suggested that he comes closest to his expressed aim of exercising 'epoché' and suspending his own beliefs in his sympathetic portrayal of Jesus, which sometimes sits uneasily with his Muslim beliefs.[123] This is especially true on the subject of religious law, which was supposedly rendered superfluous by the inner transformation experienced by the followers of Jesus. This involves al-Faruqi in the difficulty of providing a rationale for the reintroduction of the Sharī'a under Islam and an explanation of the distinction between the Pharisaic and Islamic understanding of law, neither of which is particularly convincing.

As was indicated earlier, Muslim scholars who acknowledge the desirability of a sympathetic treatment of other religions may find it difficult to put some of their stated ideals into practice when they perceive an irreconcilable contradiction between Islamic and Christian belief. Even sophisticated scholars are sometimes tempted to distort or oversimplify Christian belief in a way that may render it unrecognizable to Christians themselves, notwithstanding the fact that they may be identifying genuine differences of emphasis between the two faiths. The highly developed tradition of Christian ethics bears witness to the fact that Christians have not generally understood the doctrine of redemption as negating morality, *contra* the view of many Muslims, and most Christians would find it difficult to relate to the idea that the influence of their faith is restricted to the private inner life of the individual. Original sin is often presented in more uncompromising terms by Muslims than by Christians themselves.[124] Although Akhtar is aware of the diversity of modern Christian thought, he portrays the difference between Christian and Islamic political thought somewhat simplistically in terms of a polarity between passivism and activism,[125] and represents Christianity as vacillating between the two extremes of theoretical non-involvement in politics and actual abuse of power, thereby ignoring significant areas of Christian thought on the relationship between faith and politics, which are almost never seen as wholly irrelevant to each other.[126] He includes no reference either to the 'just war' tradition in Christian thought or to ideologies of nonviolent resistance, although Martin Luther King is mentioned at one point.

The principle of reciprocity in the study of religions is not necessarily acknowledged or applied; al-Faruqi, for example, applies his own (Islamic) criteria to the study of Christianity while condemning orientalists who do the same with Islam.[127] In the face of the kind of modifications to, or rather deconstruction of, Christian belief proposed by al-Faruqi, Christians are likely to feel that their faith has been altered beyond recognition and that his effective 'Islamization' of Christianity is reminiscent of some of the 'Christianizing' interpretations of the Qur'an that most Muslims find offensive.

Different criteria are sometimes employed for studying Christianity than for Islam. The temptation to compare one's own ideals with the other's realities is most apparent in the area of the historical record on political involvement and religious tolerance. Akhtar's citation of the historical events of the Conquistadors, the Spanish Inquisition, and the contemporary examples of South Africa and the Lutheran bishops who failed to oppose Hitler are matched on the Islamic side with anecdotes about the restraint of individual Muslim rulers, such as the story about 'Ali staying his hand in battle when his opponent spat at him, for fear of killing with the wrong motive.[128] Where Muslim corruption is acknowledged, Akhtar draws a distinction between ideals and realities which is not made for Christianity: while there are many contemporary Muslims who 'prostitute Islam in the service of purely personal or national interests', for example, and no contemporary Muslim state deserves to be called 'Islamic' with the possible exception of Iran,[129] he argues against Christian attempts to 'get off the hook' by disavowing certain chapters of their history, including colonialism, as an aberration of Christianity.[130]

Where use is made of historical-critical methods, these may be unevenly applied. Al-Faruqi's view that Christian orthodoxy came about by means of suppression, while Islamic orthodoxy came about by a process of consensus,[131] reflects the fact that with any religious tradition, in the often complex process which gives rise to 'orthodoxy', what appears to the insider as the providential vindication of the truth appears to the outsider as the arbitrary emergence of one school of thought among many. His historical analysis is largely subordinated to a position that has already been arrived at on dogmatic and philosophical grounds. A historian would find al-Faruqi's account of the history of Christian thought suspiciously neat; an obvious example is his identification of the opposing 'Arab' and 'Western' strands of early Christianity on the basis of how far they accord or conflict with his own Islamic ideals. Similarly, his acceptance or rejection of particular passages of the New Testament is on the basis of his own hypothesis as to the nature of Jesus' original mission; no attempt is made to apply any of the normally accepted principles of textual criticism. In both cases al-Faruqi's method is circular, and although he sees himself as participating in critical scholarship on Christianity, many of his premises and assumptions are unexamined and he does not live up to his avowed aim of undertaking an impartial study.

The rejection of the entire historical evolution of Christianity which is implicit or explicit in the writings of many Muslims implies a radical dissociation of the historical community of believers from the person of the founder, which would no doubt be unacceptable to most Christians as to any other religious group. In Christianity, as in Islam, the role of the early community in particular is intrinsic to the formation of the very basics of the faith. In the case of Christianity, such a disjunction would have the effect of aborting in one fell swoop ecclesiology and the scriptural canon, and in the case of Islam, both the scripture (since its collection was undertaken after Muhammad's death) and the Hadith and Sira would be undermined.

The most outspoken critics of Christianity are not always the best ambassadors for Islam. Not all Muslims appreciate Akhtar's abrasive style (which has been directed against the Islamic as well as the Christian tradition, notwithstanding a strongly avowed orthodoxy), or his rather militaristic interpretations of Islamic teachings.[132] Al-Faruqi's treatment of some of the traditional areas of tension in Islam, such as the relationship between God's grace and human deeds, between God's justice and His mercy, or between God's determining of history and human free will, is superficial and somewhat dismissive of the rich legacy of Islamic thought in these areas. The differences between the two faiths are sometimes exaggerated in order to safeguard and strengthen a distinctive sense of Islamic identity: al-Faruqi, for example, is strongly critical of Christians' attempts at reinterpretation of their faith, even when these seem to represent a *rapprochement* with Islamic beliefs.[133] This process can result in distortions of Islam as well as of Christianity, as where a strongly rationalist or utilitarian interpretation of Islam is brought into play to counter Christianity's perceived irrationalism and idealism.

The study of Christianity by modern Muslims does not, on the whole, compare favourably with that of the medieval Muslim scholars. The intellectual tools derived from Aristotelian philosophy have been exchanged for those of modern Western critical scholarship, which, whatever their intrinsic merits, are applied in a far less sustained and rigorous way. These Muslims show less awareness than did the medieval scholars that some of the philosophical problems arising in Christian theology, concerning, for example, the Incarnation and the Trinity, have their counterparts in Islam in the areas of the attributes of God, the eternality and Uncreatedness of the Qur'an, and the need to reconcile the fact of God's absolute transcendence with His commmunication with humankind.[134]

Muslims educated in the West find themselves in an ambivalent position. On the one hand is the almost irresistable temptation to draw on the vast legacy of biblical and historical criticism, which in some cases provides a powerful ally to Muslim beliefs; on the other is the feeling that the greater threat (now that Christianity in the West is seen as being on the decline) is represented by the forces of atheism, secularism and materialism, resulting in a desire to join ranks and co-operate constructively with Christians as fellow theists.[135] Conversely, it is in the process of refuting Christianity that Muslims often appear in the guise of heirs of the Enlightenment rather than of the legacy of classical Islamic thought. The complex triangular relationship between Islam, Christianity and secular humanism gives rise to many ironies and ambiguities, arising partly from the fact that it is Christianity, and not Islam, which has been most thoroughly subjected to the scrutiny of modern humanist scholarship. Both al-Faruqi and Akhtar express approval of selected strands of Christian liberal thought, and sometimes conscript them in their critique of Christianity,[136] but would not countenance any comparable liberalism in the Islamic context.[137]

In the case of the Muslim scholars described above, enhanced knowledge of Christianity has not necessarily led to a more empathetic approach to Christian beliefs. A Western academic training may supply the necessary technical expertise, but otherwise may be just as likely to compound as to attenuate Muslim–Christian or Muslim–Western confrontationalism. It is probably not just coincidental that Christianity is sometimes portrayed in the very same terms that have been used of Islam in both earlier orientalist scholarship and the contemporary media: as power-seeking and warmongering on the one hand, and irrational, obscurantist, backward-looking, and in need of reformation on the other. Some of the more conciliatory material comes from India, where Muslims have long accepted the need for co-existence and where Sufi influences are prevalent. One can expect to see an increase in the numbers of competent Western Muslim commentators on Christianity (whether irenic or polemical) as new generations have access to the expertise needed to tackle Christianity on its own ground rather than on purely Islamic ground, although the latter will, of course, continue to hold an important place in internal Muslim apologetic. The relatively small number of non-polemical, though rather brief, articles on comparative themes in Islam and Christianity, such as redemption and martyrdom, which were alluded to earlier, are likely to be supplemented by more substantial studies in the future.[138]

The views on Jesus expressed by Merad, Vahiduddin and Askari are unusual, but not without precedent in Muslim thought. The belief in Jesus' ongoing spiritual efficacy is not so surprising when one considers the widespread Muslim belief that Jesus did not die but still lives with God in heaven, awaiting the time for his return at the end of the world. Their approach is reminiscent of the Sufi tradition in which Jesus is usually seen as embodying the ideals of poverty, detachment, sacrificial love, and spirituality. Although later Sufis drew on the Gospels as well as the Qur'an for inspiration, they were eclectic. They were interested in a 'cosmic Christ' whose nature was often only loosely based on the scriptural accounts, rather than the 'historical Jesus'.[139] Like many Sufis, these writers are not primarily interested in questions of historical veracity,[140] but seek rather to draw spiritual sustenance from the teachings about Christ, whether Qur'anic or biblical.[141]

The Muslims who advocate some form of religious pluralism, whether they draw their inspiration from the Sufi tradition or from contemporary philosophies or epistemologies, seem to stand apart from the others. For the most part they are either participants in Muslim–Christian dialogue, or strongly influenced by Sufism, or both; they are people who seem able to accommodate uncertainty and diversity of opinion without feeling threatened in their own religious identity, and they not infrequently use terms such as 'mystery', 'ambiguity', 'tension', and even 'paradox'. Like Christian pluralists, they emphasize 'subjective' spiritual or religious experience rather than 'objective' propositional truth. It is probably not accidental that the most sympathetic Muslim scholars of Christianity have not embarked on any in-depth or systematic study, which would inevitably raise the type of confrontational theological issues which they desire to avoid.

The seemingly wide gulf between these and other Muslims raises the question of representation; it is doubtless true that 'pioneers seeking open relationships across traditional borders may often be found affirming a strongly personal version of the faith', but at the same time it may be deemed important that these pioneers 'should not part company too radically with the Islam broadly understood as normative among Muslims'.[142] Even the relatively brief section of this chapter which was devoted to irenical writings is disproportionately large in relation to their representativeness. In spite of some of al-Faruqi's slightly eccentric views (from an Islamic standpoint), he has been aptly described as 'vigorously representative of Islam'.[143]

Although many Muslims argue that religious tolerance is an Islamic obligation, this obligation is not usually understood as extending to the non-judgemental study of others' religious traditions, and in practice few are willing to explore or show an understanding of what makes Christianity attractive to Christians.[144] The majority of Muslims, like the majority of Christians, hold an exclusivist view of truth, in that they believe that their religion is true to a degree that others are not. However, there is a closer correlation between openness to other faiths and marginality in one's own tradition in Islam than in Christianity. For the time being, it is by and large in literature, poetry and mystical writings that Christians may expect to encounter the greatest degree of imaginative sympathy.[145]

Notes

1. Malik, *God and Man in Contemporary Islamic Thought*, pp. 88–9.
2. Sharpe, *Comparative Religion*, p. 11.
3. See Aasi, 'Muslim Contributions to the History of Religions', p. 419; Waardenburg, 'Types of Judgment', pp. 137–8.
4. See, e.g., the account of the refutation of Christian doctrine by al-Kindī and Yaḥyā ibn 'Adī's reply in Wolfson, *The Philosophy of the Kalam*, pp. 318–36.
5. Thomas, *Anti-Christian Polemic in Early Islam*, p. 34.
6. Ibid., ch. 3: 'Early Islamic Refutations of Christianity'.
7. Wolfson, *The Philosophy of the Kalam*, p. 314.
8. Waardenburg, 'World Religions as Seen in the Light of Islam', p. 263.
9. For example, the study of individual Christian theologians by Shabbir Akhtar, especially in *The Light in the Enlightenment*, and the treatment of the Jewish background to Christianity by al-Faruqi, in *On Arabism*, chapter 2, and *Christian Ethics*, chapter 1.
10. Esposito, 'Isma'il R. al-Faruqi: Muslim Scholar-Activist', pp. 71–2.
11. See, e.g., his suggested 'fields of cooperative endeavour' for Muslims and Christians in 'The Muslim–Christian Dialogue', pp. 11ff.
12. See, e.g., his *Christianity/Islam: Essays on Esoteric Ecumenism* (Bloomington: World Wisdom, 1985), and *The Essential Writings*.
13. The institutional base for this initiative was the International Institute of Islamic Thought in Washington (with branches worldwide), founded in 1981; it publishes the *American Journal of Islamic Social Sciences* jointly with the Association of Muslim Social Scientists. The Islamization of Knowledge movement seeks to establish an Islamic epistemological foundation for the social sciences and to apply this in the first instance in the field of higher education.
14. For further details see Kimball, 'Striving Together in the Way of God', chapter 4; Cragg, *The Pen and the Faith*, pp. 109–25.
15. *Islamic Horizons*, August and September 1986, p. 26, cited in Marshall, 'Isma'il al-Faruqi and Christianity', pp. 2–3.
16. Al-Faruqi, 'Meta-Religion', pp. 39–40.
17. Schuon, *The Essential Writings*, p. 19.
18. See, e.g., Al-Faruqi, *Christian Ethics*, p. 164; *On Arabism*, pp. 102ff.
19. Al-Attas, *Islam, Secularism and the Philosophy of the Future*, p. 18.
20. Al-Faruqi, 'Islam and Other Faiths', pp. 93–4.
21. *Christian Ethics*, p. 33. Al-Faruqi coins the term 'meta-religion' to describe this archetypal religion, of which Islam is the only true representative ('Meta-Religion', p. 57).
22. Al-Faruqi, 'Islam and Christianity', p. 5.
23. Ibid., pp. 12–14.
24. Al-Faruqi, *On Arabism*, p. 58.
25. Ibid., p. 62.
26. *Christian Ethics*, pp. 98ff.; a similar though less straightforward interpretation is given of Jesus' teaching on divorce, pp. 101–9.
27. *On Arabism*, p. 64; *Christian Ethics*, p. 93.

28. *On Arabism*, p. 65.
29. Ibid., p. 66; *Christian Ethics*, p. 117.
30. *Christian Ethics*, p. 282. However, in a later publication al-Faruqi describes world denial, asceticism and monasticism, among other things, as misguided according to Islam: 'On the Nature of Islamic Da'wah', p. 41.
31. *On Arabism*, pp. 66, 69.
32. Ibid., p. 68. Al-Faruqi's ascription of all such retributive sayings to 'decrepit Jewish conservatism' is surprising in the light of Islam's confirmation of the law of talion (*qiṣāṣ*).
33. *Christian Ethics*, p. 88.
34. *On Arabism*, p. 72.
35. Ibid., p. 73.
36. Ibid., p. 85.
37. Ibid., p. 87. Interestingly he traces a parallel development in Islam, attributing the Shi'ite 'misunderstanding' of Islam to a lack of expertise in Arabic.
38. This was a theological concept developed by the Catholic theologian Karl Rahner (d. 1984) in order to accommodate the possibility of salvation without explicit Christian faith.
39. Izetbegovic gives a rather free-ranging account of the historical development of Christian institutions, claiming that the appearance of the clergy came after the proclamation of Christianity as the state religion in 435, and that baptism and the Eucharist were introduced at a similarly late stage (*Islam Between East and West*, pp. 255–6).
40. *Christian Ethics*, p. 251. Cf. 'Divine Transcendence', p. 18, where he refers to this effective elimination of hermeneutical problems as a '"miracle" of the history of ideas'.
41. Al-Faruqi, *Christian Ethics*, pp. 3–8; see also Akhtar, *A Faith for all Seasons*, p. 182.
42. *On Arabism*, p. 69.
43. *Christian Ethics*, p. 294.
44. *On Arabism*, p. 59; *Christian Ethics*, p. 312.
45. *On Arabism*, p. 108.
46. Ibid., p. 101.
47. In the Qur'anic account, which has many similarities with the biblical account, the tree is not named, although Satan refers to it as 'the Tree of Eternity' (20:120). Al-Faruqi infers from the Judaeo-Christian nomenclature that Christianity thus 'transformed man's noblest endowments, viz. his knowledge and will to know . . . into an instrument of utter doom' (*Christian Ethics*, p. 202).
48. *On Arabism*, p. 75.
49. *Christian Ethics*, p. 199.
50. *On Arabism*, p. 75.
51. *Christian Ethics*, p. 236.
52. Ibid., p. 230. Elsewhere he refers to 'the superciliousness and complacency which the carrying around of one's title to paradise generates' ('Islam and Christianity', p. 26).
53. 'Islam and Christianity', p. 26. Smith's original quotation is to be found in *Islam in Modern History*, p. 21.

54. *On Arabism*, p. 68.
55. *Christian Ethics*, p. 226.
56. Ibid., p. 227. British Muslim academic Jamil Qureshi similarly contrasts Islam's constructive energy, as exemplified in the Hijra, with the Christian 'staying put . . . and feeling crucified' (' "Alongsidedness – In Good Faith?" ', p. 242).
57. *On Arabism*, p. 67.
58. *Christian Ethics*, p. 206.
59. Al-Faruqi, 'On the Nature of Islamic Da'wah', p. 41, and *Christian Ethics*, p. 158.
60. 'On the Nature of Islamic Da'wah', p. 39.
61. Ibid., pp. 47–8. Cf. al-Faruqi, 'A Comparison of the Islamic and Christian Approaches', p. 286.
62. Castro et al. (eds), *Christian Mission and Islamic Da'wah*, pp. 49–51. Khurshid Ahmad, a fellow-participant in the same discussion, also stresses God's impassibility, stating that 'God is in no way dependent on or in need of man's worship' (ibid., p. 49).
63. Al-Faruqi, 'A Comparison of the Islamic and Christian Approaches', p. 291.
64. Ibid., p. 292. Qureshi similarly maintains that 'no Muslim could desire to exchange the status of "servant" for that of "fellow" ' (' "Alongsidedness – In Good Faith?"', p. 236).
65. Christian Ethics, p. 231. In fact, Christians usually view the Crucifixion as the unique event in which God's mercy and justice are reconciled and therefore, by definition, not in contradiction with each other.
66. Ibid., p. 230.
67. 'Islam and Christianity', p. 19, fn. 10.
68. *On Arabism*, p. 98.
69. 'A Comparison of the Islamic and Christian Approaches', p. 286.
70. *On Arabism*, p. 67.
71. E.g. 'Islam and Christianity', pp. 17, 19, 20, 23.
72. *Christian Ethics*, p. 232.
73. *On Arabism*, p. 67.
74. *Christian Ethics*, p. 233.
75. See also Akhtar, *The Light in the Enlightenment*, p. 8.
76. Akhtar, *The Final Imperative*, p. 103.
77. Muhammad Hamidullah, a Muslim academic resident in France, similarly acknowledges the potential value of such a doctrine: 'there are several ways of establishing contact or communication between man and God. The best would have been incarnation; but Islam has rejected it' (*Introduction to Islam*, p. 47).
78. *The Final Imperative*, p. 106.
79. Ibid., p. 47.
80. See also ibid., p. 108.
81. Akhtar, *A Faith for all Seasons*, p. 187.
82. *The Final Imperative*, p. 116.
83. Ibid., p. 96.
84. Ibid., p. 110. Some of Akhtar's Muslim reviewers do not appreciate his tendency to collaborate with Western stereotypes of an aggressive and resurgent Islam

(notwithstanding his own condemnation of the same in *The Final Imperative*, p. 79). See P. Manzoor's review of *The Final Imperative* (*MWBR*, 13, 1, 1992), p. 7.

85. See, e.g., 'Islam and Christianity', pp. 1–3.

86. *On Arabism*, p. 64.

87. Most of these have articles in Swidler (ed.), *Muslims in Dialogue*. On Talbi and Sa'ab, who are respectively Tunisian and Lebanese, both having spent time in the West, see Kimball, 'Striving Together in the Way of God'. The rest are all resident in the USA.

88. E.g., H. Askari, 'Limits to Comparison: New Testament and Qur'an' (*Newsletter of the Centre for the Study of Islam and Christian–Muslim Relations*, 5, May 1982); M. Ayoub, 'Martyrdom in Christianity and Islam', in *Religious Resurgence: Contemporary Cases in Islam, Christianity and Judaism*, ed. R. Antoun and E. Hegland (New York: Syracuse University Press, 1987); M. H. Siddiqi, 'The Doctrine of Redemption: A Critical Study', in *Islamic Perspectives: Studies in Honour of Mawlānā Sayyid Abul A'lā Mawdūdī*, ed. K. Ahmed and Z. Ansari (Leicester: The Islamic Foundation, 1979).

89. See Duran, 'Interreligious Dialogue and the Islamic "Original Sin"', pp. 50–1.

90. See, e.g., Askari, 'Religion and State', in *Islam in a World of Diverse Faiths*, ed. D. Cohn-Sherbok (London: Macmillan, 1991); Ayoub, 'The Islamic Context of Muslim–Christian Relations', pp. 471, 473; Duran, 'Muslims and Non-Muslims', pp. 104ff.; Kimball, 'Striving Together in the Way of God', pp. 307–8 (on Sa'ab); Talbi, 'A Community of Communities', p. 71.

91. See, e.g., Ayoub, 'Islam and Christianity between Tolerance and Acceptance', pp. 173–4; Kimball, 'Striving Together in the Way of God', pp. 204–5 (on Askari); Talbi, 'A Community of Communities', p. 78. Askari and Ayoub have both been directly influenced by the thought of Wilfred Cantwell Smith, particularly as expressed in *The Meaning and End of Religion* and *Faith and Belief*.

92. See on the formation and aims of the group, R. Caspar, 'The Muslim–Christian Research Group' (*Encounter*, 58, October 1979).

93. See for this his book *Inter-Religion* (Aligarh: Printwell Publications, 1977).

94. Askari, 'Within and Beyond the Experience of Religious Diversity', pp. 191, 196.

95. Ibid., p. 210.

96. Ibid., pp. 208–9.

97. Ibid., p. 194.

98. Askari, 'The Dialogical Relationship between Christianity and Islam', p. 45.

99. Kimball, 'Striving Together in the Way of God', p. 197, quoting Askari's article, 'Le Complexe islamo-chrétien de foi et d'engagement', in *Les Musulmans: Consultation islamo-chrétienne*, ed. Y. Moubarac (Paris: Beauchesne, 1971).

100. 'Within and Beyond the Experience of Religious Diversity', pp. 205–6.

101. Kimball, 'Striving Together in the Way of God', pp. 217ff.

102. 'Within and Beyond the Experience of Religious Diversity', p. 209.

103. Kimball, 'Striving Together in the Way of God', pp. 221, 250.

104. Ibid., pp. 222–3, 180, 230.

105. A notable precursor in the field of Muslim biblical exegesis was the Indian reformer and modernist Sayyid Ahmad Khan (d. 1898), whose *Tabyīn al-Kalām:*

The Muhammadan Commentary on the Holy Bible (Ghazeepore: privately published, 1862–5), incorporates a commentary on the first parts of Genesis and Matthew.

106. See, e.g., Talbi, 'A Community of Communities', p. 81, and Akhtar on Askari in *A Faith for all Seasons*, pp. 242–3.

107. Kimball, 'Striving Together in the Way of God', p. 246.

108. See, e.g., J. Waardenburg, 'Some North African Intellectuals' Presentations of Islam', in *Christian–Muslim Encounters*, ed. Haddad and Haddad.

109. Arkoun, 'New Perspectives for a Jewish–Christian–Muslim Dialogue', p. 348.

110. Arkoun, 'Is Islam Threatened by Christianity?', p. 50.

111. Arkoun, *Rethinking Islam*, p. 32.

112. Ibid., pp. 18–20.

113. Ibid., p. 38, and 'New Perspectives for a Jewish–Christian–Muslim Dialogue', pp. 349–50; see also his article 'The Notion of Revelation: From Ahl al-Kitab to the Societies of the Book' (*Die Welt Des Islams*, 28, 1988).

114. For the foregoing points see Arkoun, *Rethinking Islam Today*, pp. 15–16, and *Rethinking Islam*, p. 32.

115. For the denial of supersessionism see, e.g., Ayoub, 'The Islamic Context of Muslim–Christian Relations', p. 462; A. Sachedina, 'Is Islamic Revelation an Abrogation of Judaeo-Christian Revelation? Islamic Self-identification in the Classical and Modern Age', in *Islam: A Challenge for Christianity*, ed. H. Küng and J. Moltmann (London: SCM Press, 1994). They do not, however, elaborate on the broader implications of this denial for a new Muslim understanding of Christianity.

116. Nasr, *Islamic Life and Thought*, p. 209.

117. Nasr, 'Response to Hans Küng's Paper on Christian–Muslim Dialogue', p. 101.

118. *Islamic Life and Thought*, p. 210. The third main function of Jesus is described less Islamically (and more enigmatically) as 'celebrating and perpetuating the Eucharist'.

119. Ibid.

120. Nasr, 'Islam and the Encounter of Religions', p. 53.

121. See Goddard's comments on this piece in 'Modern Pakistani and Indian Muslim Perceptions', pp. 173–7.

122. Similarly, Ayoub maintains that Jesus' power 'may still be felt if we are gentle enough to feel it', and that he 'can be our savior from our evil selves' ('The Word of God and the Voices of Humanity', p. 61).

123. Marshall, 'Isma'il al-Faruqi and Christianity', pp. 48–9.

124. Cragg, for example, implies that there is no great divide between the Qur'anic and Christian view of sin, since both acknowledge to some extent an inherent human tendency to wrongdoing: 'Isma'il al-Faruqi', in *Troubled by Truth*, pp. 138–40.

125. Herbert, 'Shabbir Akhtar on Muslims, Christians and British Society', p. 112.

126. Seminal works in this area include Richard H. Niebuhr's *Christ and Culture* (London: Faber, 1951), and J. Moltmann's *Theology of Hope* (London: SCM Press, 1967).

127. Al-Faruqi, 'The Muslim–Christian Dialogue', p. 18.

128. *The Final Imperative*, p. 63.

129. Ibid., pp. 57, 77.

130. Ibid., pp. 65–6.

131. 'Islam and Christianity', p. 13.

132. In addition to Manzoor's review of *The Final Imperative* cited in note 84 see, e.g., J. Qureshi's review of *A Faith for all Seasons* (*MWBR*, 12, 3, 1992), pp. 11–17.

133. See, e.g., al-Faruqi's refutation of Christian attempts to interpret original sin in less categorical terms than did Augustine or Luther (*Christian Ethics*, pp. 217ff).

134. On the parallelism between the doctrine of Incarnation and that of 'inlibration', see Wolfson, *The Philosophy of the Kalam*, pp. 724–5.

135. Sardar's article, 'The Ethical Connection', provides an illustration of this ambivalence: the rise of secularism, characterized as hegemonic and intolerant of diversity, is attributed to Christianity's capitulation, and Sardar calls for a joint ethical endeavour by Muslims and Christians; however, he simultaneously maintains that Christianity, with its view that salvation is attained through Jesus, 'cannot cast aside the imperialistic character that is intrinsic to any cult' (p. 61).

136. Citing Geza Vermes' work on the Jewish character of Jesus, Akhtar observes with approval the way in which recent historical scholarship has not only Judaized but 'Islamicized' Jesus, who emerges as 'a charismatic reformer concerned to pose an active challenge to those institutions and individuals who degrade the powerless and dispossessed' (*The Final Imperative*, p. 12).

137. Akhtar has strong liberal impulses, but they are selectively indulged and there are, necessarily perhaps, certain areas in which they are not allowed to impinge. Compare his eloquent plea for religious freedom on the grounds that 'heresy and even apostasy are morally more acceptable than any hypocritical attachment to orthodox opinion out of the fear of public sanctions' (*A Faith for all Seasons*, p. 21) with his vigorous *a priori* defence of the absolute and verbatim integrity of the Qur'anic text and the traditional Muslim view of revelation: *A Faith for all Seasons*, pp. 68, 74; 'An Islamic Model of Revelation' (*ICMR*, 2, 1991).

138. In addition to the articles by Askari, Ayoub, and Siddiqi listed in the section on religious pluralism, one could mention A. R. Doi, 'The African and Christian View of "Dying Saviour" and the Islamic Concept of Sacrifice' (*Islam and the Modern Age*, 7, 1976), and M. Abdel Haleem, 'The Story of Joseph in the Qur'an and the Old Testament' (*ICMR*, 1, 1990).

139. See generally, R. Arnaldez, *Jésus fils de Marie prophète de l'Islam* (Paris: Desclée, 1980), chapter 10; Cragg, *Jesus and the Muslim*, chapter 3; J. Nurbakhsh, *Jesus in the Eyes of the Sufis* (London: Khaniqahi–Nimatullahi Publications, 1983).

140. Cf. Vahiduddin's remark that 'our focus ought not to be on the question of the historical authenticity of the events, but rather on the mystery that haunts the life of Christ from beginning to end' ('What Christ Means to Me', p. 183), and Merad's statement that 'revelation teaches matters of faith, which are not necessarily objective and formal data' ('Revelation, Truth and Obedience', p. 61).

141. A small number of Egyptian Muslims have drawn on the Gospel accounts in their writings about Jesus, which are often semi-fictional. For a review of four Egyptian authors – 'Abbās Maḥmūd al-'Aqqād, Kāmil Ḥusain, Khālid Muḥammad Khālid,

and 'Abdul Hamīd al-Saḥḥār – see 'Christ Seen by Contemporary Muslim Writers' (*Encounter*, 87, 1982).

142. Cragg, *The Pen and the Faith*, pp. 113–14.

143. Ibid., p. 127. Swidler observes that it was partly al-Faruqi's orthodoxy which made him such a valuable Muslim participant in dialogue, rendering it more acceptable to Muslims of the mainstream ('The Evolution of a Dialogue', p. v).

144. Al-Faruqi, in particular, is found wanting in this respect – see Marshall, 'Isma'il al-Faruqi and Christianity', p. 51, and J. Ford, 'Isma'il al-Faruqi on Muslim–Christian Dialogue', p. 278.

145. Most often cited in this regard is the Egyptian Kāmil Ḥusain's novel, *City of Wrong*, which explores the events of Good Friday: see Cragg, *The Pen and the Faith*, chapter 8. See also Goddard on modern Urdu poetry in 'Modern Pakistani and Indian Muslim Perceptions of Christianity'; on Egyptian poetry in *Muslim Perceptions of Christianity*; and Cragg on the theme of the Cross in Palestinian poetry in 'Christian–Muslim Dialogue', pp. 119–20.

five

APPROACHES TO ISLAM BY CHRISTIAN ISLAMICISTS AND THEOLOGIANS

C hristian scholarship and theological reflection on Islam represents a large and growing body of literature to which it would probably not be possible to do justice within the confines of a single volume, let alone a chapter. For an overview of the Christian study of Islam, or of the evolution of thought within the various Christian traditions, the reader will have to look elsewhere.[1] The aim here can be no more than to present a sample of some of the main lines of thought and issues of debate, and to give some idea of the extent of diversity of opinion. Many Christian scholars who have written on Islamic history, civilization or mysticism, such as Louis Gardet, Georges Anawati and Hamilton Gibb, have been omitted in favour of those who have focused more specifically on the central religious and theological issues.

The Christian study of Islam in the modern period has been undertaken both from the standpoint of the study of religion and from a theological point of view. Notwithstanding the difficulty of acquiring expertise in both Islamic studies and Christian theology within the span of a single lifetime, most of the authors reviewed in this chapter combine the two in varying degrees, and it is the combination which is of interest here. To write about Islam as a Christian (for the concern here is not with those whose writings are indistinguishable from those of non-Christians) already implies a certain theological input. All who are still living are of a fairly advanced age; most of the Catholics and several of the Protestants have been ordained as priests or clergymen, and have received theological training prior to embarking on Islamic studies. These facts, together with the absence of female contributors, are perhaps further indications that to be proficient in both traditions requires a lifetime of single-minded study.

There is an institutional dimension to the Christian study of Islam which is lacking in the Muslim study of Christianity. Quite apart from the faculties of theology and religious studies in universities, there are numerous Christian study centres, some of which are based in Muslim countries. These often see themselves as having more than just an intellectual role, and many involve Muslims on their teaching and research staff as well as Christians from various denominations. On the Catholic side, these include the Pontifical Institute for Arabic and Islamic Studies (PISAI) in Rome; the Institut Dominicain d'Etudes Orientales (IDEO) in Cairo; the Centre d'Etudes Diocésain in Algiers; and the recently established Center for Muslim–Christian Understanding at Georgetown University, Washington, DC. Protestant centres include the Duncan Black Macdonald Center at Hartford Seminary in Connecticut; the Centre for the Study of Islam and Christian–Muslim Relations (CSIC) at Selly Oak Colleges in Birmingham, England; the Christian Study Centre in Rawalpindi; and the Henry Martyn Institute of Islamic Studies in Hyderabad.[2] Most of the specialist journals on Muslim–Christian relations, including *Islamochristiana*, *The Muslim World*, *Islam and Christian–Muslim Relations*, and *Mélanges de l'Institut Dominicain d'Etudes Orientales*, are produced by these centres.

Over the last century it is probably true to say that Catholics have engaged more extensively with the Islamic tradition than have Protestants.[3] This has not only been on an intellectual level; some, such as Charles de Foucauld, Henri Sanson and others in the traditions of presence theology and desert spirituality, have spent prolonged periods living and interacting with Muslims. The writings which have been produced in such traditions usually reflect a spiritual or mystical approach to Islam rather than a theological or scholarly approach. Since Vatican II, official Catholic statements have tended to highlight commonalities rather than differences between the two faiths, and individual Catholics have felt freer to express their own views, sometimes expressing a desire to go beyond Vatican II which stopped short of explicitly recognizing Islam as an objective part of the Abrahamic legacy, or Muhammad as a prophet.

The most influential figure in recent Catholic thinking about Islam is, by general consensus, Louis Massignon (d. 1962); one commentator describes him in that context as 'a headlamp which sweeps the whole field'.[4] His legacy, together with that of Vatican II, which was itself indebted to his thought in the sections relating to Muslims, has been a unifying factor in Catholic approaches to Islam. Although Massignon's writings are from an earlier period, this chapter describes his ideas in so far as they are seminal to later Catholic thinking. Massignon called for a 'Copernican revolution' in the Christian understanding of Islam, whereby Christians would attempt to place themselves at the centre of Islam rather than viewing it from the outside, as they had done in the past. Like many Christian Islamicists before and since, he had a special interest in Sufism, which he saw as an authentically Islamic development. His interest in Islam was far from being merely academic; he felt that he owed his conversion to Christianity in Baghdad in 1908 partly to an experience of Islamic hospitality, and he founded the Badaliyya (from the Arabic for 'substitution'), an association of Christians who lived among Muslims and, rather than proselytizing, expressed their Christian presence or witness by offering prayers of intercession and fasting on their behalf. Among those who were profoundly influenced by Massignon and who popularized some of his ideas are two of the authors whose writings are discussed below: the Maronite priest Youakim Moubarac (d. 1994), and Giulio Basetti-Sani, an Italian Franciscan.

Robert Caspar, a Père Blanc, has been a professor of theology and Islamic mysticism at PISAI and at a sister institution in Monastir, Tunisia; he was officially involved in the formulation of the texts relating to Islam in Vatican II, and was co-founder of the Groupe de Recherches Islamo-Chrétien (GRIC) in 1977. The publication of this group entitled *The Challenge of the Scriptures* is discussed in this chapter as it was in chapter 4; the Christian contributors, in addition to Caspar himself, include Joseph Cuoq, Jean-Paul Gabus, Claude Geffré, Georges Khodr, Michel Lelong, Jacques Levrat, Marston Speight, and John Taylor. Of these, all are Catholic except Speight and Taylor, both Protestants, and Khodr, the Metropolitan of Mount Lebanon and the only Orthodox contributor. The Orthodox study of Islam is at not at present highly developed, although there are individuals who are actively involved in the sphere of Muslim–Christian relations, including Khodr himself and Olivier Clément, a French lecturer in theology.

Hans Küng (b. 1928) is a prominent Swiss Catholic theologian and Professor of Ecumenical Theology at Tübingen University. After studying philosophy and theology, he was ordained in 1954, and like

Caspar was an official adviser to the Second Vatican Council in the early 1960s. During the 1970s he was involved in controversy over the issues of papal and ecclesiastical infallibility, and his authorization to teach officially as a Catholic theologian was revoked in 1979. Of the authors under review, Küng is at one and the same time the most eminent theologian and possibly the least qualified as an Islamicist. Roger Arnaldez has recently retired as Professor of Islamic Philosophy at the Sorbonne, and Jacques Jomier is a Dominican who was based for many years at IDEO in Cairo. Robert Zaehner (d. 1974) was an English convert to Catholicism and an eminent scholar in the field of comparative religion, specializing in Zoroastrianism.

Among Protestants, there has been much new thinking on relations with followers of other faiths, but this has not as yet been applied on a wide scale to the Islamic tradition. This means that there is a greater variety of individual views, notwithstanding a general trend in the direction of greater recognition and appreciation of the religious or spiritual dimensions of Islam. The single most influential figure in contemporary Protestantism is arguably Kenneth Cragg. Born in 1913, he had an evangelical Christian upbringing, read modern history at Oxford and later acquired theological training and competence in philosophy, as well as in Arabic and Islamic studies. He was ordained as a priest in the Anglican Church in 1937. Throughout his career he has combined ministerial duties and missionary concerns with academic life; he lived for many years in the Middle East (he was Assistant Bishop of Jerusalem in the early 1970s), and spent several years as Professor of Arabic and Islamic Studies at Hartford Seminary in the 1950s. He is now retired Assistant Bishop of Oxford, although still active in scholarly pursuits. When he began writing in the 1950s, his approach was quite revolutionary in the context of the Christian study of other religions in general and Islam in particular. The title of an early work, *Sandals at the Mosque* (1959), illustrates his conviction that in studying another's faith one is 'walking on holy ground' and one should therefore, metaphorically, take off one's shoes (cf. Exod. 3:5). He maintained that in order to understand and enter into Islam it is 'better to go to the mosque than to reach for the dictionary', and in 1970 published an anthology of Muslim and Christian prayers intended to be used by members of both traditions, to encourage them to pray together.[5]

Wilfred Cantwell Smith is a distinguished Canadian historian of religions who was born into a Presbyterian family in 1916 and trained in oriental languages and history, then in theology. In the early 1940s he taught for a few years at the Henry Martyn Institute of Islamic Studies which was then in Lahore, in British India; during that time he was ordained as a minister. He founded the Graduate Institute for Islamic Studies at McGill University, Montreal, and subsequently became Professor of World Religions at Harvard. The well-known orientalist scholar and Islamic historian William Montgomery Watt (b. 1909) received a broad academic training which included the study of theology and philosophy. He became a minister of the Episcopalian Church of Scotland in 1939, and spent most of his academic career at the University of Edinburgh, where he held the post of Professor of Arabic and Islamic Studies until his retirement in 1979. Willem Bijlefeld is a member of the Dutch Reformed Church and the founding director of the Duncan Black Macdonald Center; he edited *The Muslim World* from 1967–92.

These brief biographical sketches hint at but do not fully show the extent to which the paths of these scholars have crossed; all of them have an interest in interfaith dialogue and many have participated in various dialogue forums (together with some of the Muslims discussed in chapter 4); virtually all have practical concerns alongside their academic interests. The majority have lived in Muslim countries for at least part of their academic or pastoral careers. Küng is an ecumenist, active in the World Parliament of Religions; he feels that religions have an important role to play in attaining future world peace, and in helping humanity to arrive at an agreement on a 'global ethic'. Smith holds similar views, and both he and Watt have suggested that there might be a single unified world religion in the future, while both he and Küng aim at formulating a global theology as a co-operative endeavour between members of the different faiths.

The topics treated in this chapter are closely related to one another. There is an integral relationship between the questions of whether Islam can be seen as having a positive role in salvation history; whether Muhammad can be seen as a prophet; and whether the Qur'an can be seen as the Word of God. However, in all cases the answer is far from being a simple question of affirmation or negation; there are many intermediate areas of inquiry and questions of definition to be explored. The authors in this chapter are almost unanimous in seeking to give some kind of affirmative answer to all three of the above questions, but their grounds for doing so, and the way in which they do so, vary considerably.

Islam in Salvation History

Christians have viewed Islam in a variety of ways: as a Christian heresy; as a harbinger of the end of the world; as diabolical; as a natural or man-made religion; as a punishment for Christian infidelity (just as Muslims later explained their subjugation by the European imperial powers with reference to their own infidelity to Islam); as a *praeparatio evangelica* (preparation for the gospel); or as an independent way of salvation. On the other hand, many Christians, particularly in the modern period, have been hesitant to categorize Islam in such ways, either because this would be speculating on matters which can be known only to God, or because they do not see Islam as a reified or monolithic entity but rather in more fluid and undefined terms which would preclude making such generalizations.

Among contemporary Christians who write about Islam on an academic level, the views at the more negative end of the spectrum have largely disappeared; no one appears to be advocating the idea that Islam was inspired by the devil. Caspar finds such a view to be not only repugnant in the case of such a major world religion but also based on a mistaken theology; he argues that Satan is incapable of creating anything, let alone anything good, and that evil is only good turned away from its goal. In fact the greater the good, the greater the resulting evil when it is perverted. Although this reasoning is not in itself incompatible with the view of Islam as a 'perversion' of Christianity, Caspar definitely excludes such a view since he believes there is much that is good in Islam. He further argues that evil is in any case operative in all spheres of human activity, and that the history of Christianity has been no more immune to it than the history of Islam.[6]

Bijlefeld, in his 1959 thesis 'Islam as a Post-Christian Religion',[7] has urged caution against any hasty classification of Islam. He argues that the fact that Islam is a post-Christian religion does not imply that it is anti- or semi-Christian. This is because it is not possible to know how far Muhammad refused or understood the gospel, and therefore 'whether Islam has consciously repudiated or unintentionally misconceived the Biblical Message; whether it has been scandalized by the Cross or by a caricature of Christianity' (p. 324). He does not exclude the possibility that scholarly research will give an answer to these questions in the future. In his view, premature rationalizations of the relationship between Islam and Christianity also include the view of Islam as a *praeparatio evangelica*; a too-easy identification of common ground between the two religions; and an unquestioning assumption that Muslims and Christians worship the same God. Bijlefeld's view of Islam as a post-Christian religion is not just to do with chronology, but is a recognition of the overlap between the Islamic and Judaeo-Christian traditions, both because Islam has been influenced by the latter and because Muslims see their own faith as a continuation of the Judaeo-Christian tradition and believe that the Jewish and Christian revelations originally contained essentially the same message as the Qur'an (pp. 322–4). In his later writings Bijlefeld has preferred to avoid theological evaluations and has approached Islam from the point of view of the phenomenological school of the study of religions.

To see Islam as the religion of nature is not necessarily to see it in negative terms. Some of the philosophers of the Enlightenment, such as the Comte de Boulainvilliers, used this approach to view Islam in a favourable light; several saw in the God of Islam the 'God of the philosophers', and found less to offend human reason in Islam than in Christianity. The view of Islam as a natural religion can dovetail with the distinction between 'general' or 'natural' revelation on the one hand, and 'special' or 'supernatural' revelation on the other, a distinction which facilitates the recognition of God's activity in and through Islam. Some point out that Muslims themselves see Islam as 'the religion of nature' (*dīn al-fiṭrah*), in the sense that it is the true religion which humankind is innately disposed to recognize, and that it is ideally suited to human nature. Moubarac feels that this facilitates the Christian recognition of Islam as a natural revelation;[8] Arnaldez, however, feels that this is quite a different concept from the Christian view of Islam as a natural religion. He argues that Muslim theology does not recognize the concept of natural religion – on the contrary it has traditionally elevated revelation above reason and sees the will of God as the sole justification for ethical and legal commands.[9] Caspar points out that there is no agreed or satisfactory definition of the term 'natural religion' and that it can therefore be confusing when applied to Islam. He rejects the idea that Islam is natural as opposed to supernatural, or human as opposed to divine, since any human impulse towards God has a supernatural element, and it is unthinkable that the human impulse would not be taken up by divine grace immediately. He feels that Islam is also supernatural in the sense that it calls people to believe in truths which are not knowable by reason alone.[10]

The view of Islam as a Christian heresy is also ambiguous. Although this idea has often been mooted in the context of a negative view of Islam, since it draws attention to ways in which it 'deviates' from true Christianity, in a positive sense it implicitly acknowledges a certain common ground and even kinship between the two. Of the authors studied, only Jomier, in his *How to Understand Islam*, seems to give partial support to such a view, although he does not appear to distinguish between a heresy and a reform movement. Referring to the corrupt state of Christianity at the time of the coming of Islam, he points out that the emergence of reform movements has generally coincided with specific failures of the Church (p. 147). He quotes Toynbee, apparently with approval, as saying that 'Islam, like communism, succeeded to the degree that it claimed to be reforming abuses which had crept into the Christianity of the time. And the success of Islam from the beginning shows the power that a heresy can have when it claims to be reforming an orthodoxy which does not seem inclined to reform itself' (p. 146). He further compares Islam to the Reformation or to Marxism, in the sense that it formed a separate movement, and comments in this connection that 'rebels who are not saints re-read the message of the Bible in their own way, in their own cultural context'. Such a rereading may illuminate certain points while rejecting others (p. 147). Caspar argues against the view of Islam as a Christian heresy on the grounds that in order to be a heretic one would first have to be a Christian, whereas Muhammad, although he knew something of the biblical heritage and accepted some of its ideas and rejected others, only related to Christianity from outside the tradition. He feels it would be more appropriate to view Islam as a 'para-Christian' religion, on a par with certain Gnostic sects which borrowed from Christianity without adhering to it.[11]

Smith suggests that one should take seriously the view of John of Damascus and others who saw Islam as a Christian heresy in one particular respect, namely that it casts doubt on the view that Islam and Christianity were always seen as separate religions. He suggests that in the Middle Ages conversion from Christianity to Islam may not have been perceived as a change of religious allegiance, especially in view of the Qur'anic veneration of Jesus. If this was the case, to become a Muslim would have been no different from opting for a different Christian position, given the divisions between Christians at that time.[12] He prefers not to think of religions as having origins with a particular founder at a particular point in time (the 'big bang' theory, as he refers to it), preferring instead the image of rivers in constant flux. All religions are to be thought of as a divine–human complex, the ratio between the divine and the human varying with time and place.[13] In line with his views on the concept of religion, described below, Smith increasingly feels 'Islam' to be an unhelpful abstraction; as far as he is concerned, there is God, and there is Islamic history, i.e. the activities of Muslims throughout the ages, and he sees no 'intermediary fixed system' between them. 'Islam' is for him a dynamic concept: 'Something that people do . . . in relation to God'.[14]

Islam has also sometimes been seen by Western scholars, such as the Belgian Jesuit orientalist Henri Lammens (d. 1937), as a Jewish rather than Christian heresy. Jomier, after drawing attention to several positive aspects and historic achievements of Islam, such as its capacity to adapt to local customs, and the fact that it has brought peace and security and an awareness of God to large numbers of people, expresses the view that 'the religious level of Islam is comparable to that of the Old Testament, with some simplifications . . . Islam is an Old Testament, reread and simplified, and does not have any New Testament'.[15] The theme of Judaeo-Islamic continuity is also taken up by those who draw attention to similarities between Muhammad and some of the Old Testament prophets in order to offer some kind of affirmation of Muhammad's prophetic status, as described in the next section. Alternatively, the link between Islam and Jewish Christianity may be seen as a fruitful avenue of enquiry. While in some writings this has led to the view of Islam as a Christian heresy, it can also be used to suggest that Islam has preserved certain elements of the Christian heritage which were lost in the process of Hellenization. Küng refers to the work of von Harnack, Adolf Schlatter, Claus Schedl and others in this area; he believes that there is a direct historical link between the early Jewish strand of Christianity and Islam, and that 'Muhammad's "Christology" was not too far removed from that of the Judaeo-Christian church'; he thinks it probable that this Christology was handed down by scattered Jewish Christian communities until Muhammad actually encountered it centuries later in Arabia. He sees in this shared legacy, although one which was historically marginalized in the Church, a possibility for future dialogue between Muslims and Christians, and expresses the hope that the Jewish Christian Christology will have a greater appeal and be more culturally relevant for Muslims than the Christology of the ecumenical councils.[16]

One possible means of effecting a *rapprochement* between the two religions is to focus on the shared Abrahamic legacy. For Massignon and several Catholic thinkers who followed him, this takes the form of seeing Muslims as the heirs to God's promise (in response to Abraham's prayer) to bless Ishmael and make of his descendents a 'great nation' (Gen. 17:18–20).[17] This view usually assumes the physical descent of the Arabs from Ishmael. Massignon saw Islam as the ingathering of those who had been excluded from previous covenants, which had embraced first Jews and then Christians, an ingathering that was necessitated in part by the exclusivism and other failings of Jews and Christians themselves. In the events and symbols of Muhammad's life he found evidence of a reclaiming of the Abrahamic legacy. Thus he drew attention to, among other things, the parallel between the expulsion of Hagar and Ishmael and Muhammad's expulsion from Mecca; the use in the Qur'an of the Abrahamic heritage to criticize Jewish and Christian infidelity to their own traditions; and Muhammad's return to Mecca and the institution of the pilgrimage, with its strong historical links with the Abrahamic story in the Qur'an. However, Massignon also refers to Muhammad's denial of certain Christian truths, and sees him as the representative of an 'intransigent monotheism', stopping at the threshold of the divine mysteries and forbidding his followers from proceeding any further.[18]

Others who have taken up this theme with varying approaches and emphases include Moubarac, Basetti-Sani, Charles Ledit and Michel Hayek.[19] In his earlier writings Moubarac followed Massignon in believing that there were two parallel lines of salvation: one via Isaac, the Jewish people, and the Church, the other via Ishmael, the Arabs, and Islam.[20] However, in his later writings he is more critical of 'Ishmaelitism' in its various forms. He rejects the view of those orientalists who see in Islam a kind of Judaized Arabism; Lammens, for example, saw a disjunction between the Meccan and Medinan portions of the Qur'an and believed that in the early Medinan period Muhammad deliberately rejected Christianity and opted to Judaize his own message, the Ishmaelite link being used to strengthen Arab nationalist feeling. Moubarac also expresses reservations about literalist readings of Genesis, urging against an 'abusive ethnicism' which grants privileges on the basis of descent, or a narrow reading of salvation history which is categorically distinguished from secular history. Such considerations, he feels, should relativize 'Ishmaelitism', as well as Jewish exclusivism and Christian élitism. The important point is that 'all are excluded by sin and redeemed by grace'.[21]

Caspar also has strong reservations about the use of the Ishmaelite theme. He argues that the genealogical link between Ishmael and the Arabs is somewhat doubtful, and, in any case, the New Testament denies that mere physical descent from Abraham has salvific value. Furthermore, according to the Bible it is with Isaac and not Ishmael that the Covenant is established, and the use of this argument would therefore tend to exclude rather than include Islam. This is especially so, he argues, if one follows Paul's reasoning in Galatians 4, which sees Ishmael and Hagar as the type of slavish, legalistic religion, surpassed by the new Covenant in Christ which makes people no longer slaves but sons and heirs. Caspar points out that the Ishmaelite link was in fact used for the purpose of exclusion in early Christian thinking about Islam, as in John of Damascus' disparaging references to Muslims as 'Hagarenes'. He concludes that the disadvantages of such an approach outweigh the advantages, and that if one wishes to find common ground it is more fruitful to focus on the essential religious values of Islam, such as monotheism, adoration and submission.[22]

On this issue, Bijlefeld expresses the view that the use of 'biblical insights' in the interpretation of the Qur'an is highly questionable; he would rather see Abraham as 'the father of the faithful' and a figure of unity for Jews, Christians and Muslims.[23] Karl-Josef Kuschel, a lecturer in theology at the University of Tübingen, explores the theme of Abraham as a possible figure of unity for the three religions at some length, in his book *Abraham: A Symbol of Hope for Jews, Christians and Muslims* (London: SCM Press, 1995). He argues that the three traditions have each in turn tried to domesticate and particularize Abraham, whereas the scriptures themselves do not warrant this, allowing for a more inclusivist view. His work is based on a detailed scriptural analysis which demonstrates that both the Bible and the Qur'an see Abraham as primarily a figure of faith, and his true descendents as those who follow his example of faith rather than his physical progeny. He hopes that this might prompt the followers of the three faiths to accept each other as 'children of Abraham', and co-operate in the causes of peace, spirituality and human rights.

A question which is interwoven with all of the above is that of the salvation of Muslims. Vatican II stated quite specifically that it is possible for Muslims to attain salvation, and none of the authors considered here, of whatever Christian affiliation, deny this possibility. However, not all feel it appropriate to pronounce on such matters, which may be considered to be among the mysteries of God, and the belief that Muslims can be saved leaves open the question of whether Islam as such plays a role in that salvation.

Some argue for the legitimacy of Islam as a way of salvation on an empirical basis, referring to the criterion of 'fruits', from the famous saying of Jesus on the subject of distinguishing true and false prophets: 'By their fruits you shall know them' (Matt. 7:16, 20). Watt points out that as a result of the Islamic revelation 'a religious community developed, claiming to serve God . . . The quality of life in this community has been on the whole satisfactory for the members. Many men and women in the community have attained to saintliness of life, and countless ordinary people have been enabled to live decent and moderately happy lives in difficult cirumstances'. He concludes from this that 'the Qur'ān is true and from God, and that . . . Muhammad is a genuine prophet'. Watt believes that this is true not just of Islam but of all the major religions.[24]

Smith, like Watt, adheres to a pluralist position in questions of truth and soteriology. In his *The Meaning and End of Religion* he advances the view that the category of 'religion' is an abstract and unhelpful reification, and that it is more helpful to talk of personal faith on the one hand, and culmulative tradition on the other. While cumulative traditions are dynamic and evolving, and display the diversity between religions, he believes there is a fundamental unity at the level of faith, defined as a quality of openness to the divine, or an innate capacity to apprehend the transcendent. In Smith's view, human faith is itself salvific, regardless of the particular tradition to which the individual belongs; however, he bases this view on a Christian conception of God which emphasizes His grace, His saving will and His all-embracing love as demonstrated in the life and death of Jesus.[25]

Caspar feels it is inconceivable that such a 'powerful movement of faith towards God' could count for nothing in the history of salvation, and asks whether Divine Providence could have simply remained passive in the face of such a movement.[26] He argues that the issue is not whether Islam contains sufficient truth for salvation, for if the salvation of Christians depended on doctrinal correctitude, few of them would be saved. Even if the Qur'an denies Christian truths, he feels this does not affect the purity of the movement of faith towards God and of submission to His will, a concept which is also central to Christianity. As evidence of Muhammad's (and by extension Muslims') willingness to submit to God and worship Him however He wishes to be worshipped, Caspar quotes the Qur'anic verse (43:81) in which Muhammad is told to say: 'If God had a son, I'd be the first to worship him'.[27]

Moubarac feels that is unacceptable to envisage a way of salvation independent of Christ. However, if one starts from the premise that all salvation takes place through the mediation of Christ, one is then at liberty to seek to enlarge the sphere of operation of this way of salvation, rather than conceiving it as a narrow thread in history incorporating a relatively small number of human beings.[28] Caspar, influenced like many Catholics by Karl Rahner, similarly believes that Christ plays a role in the salvation of Muslims and other non-Christians.[29] He points out that according to Christian belief, the Resurrection liberated Christ from the limits of time and place so that he is now present to every human being; although aware that such a view might sound like spiritual imperialism to non-Christians, he insists that this is the logical outcome of the belief in the Resurrection. Other religions, including Islam, are therefore salvific to the extent that they help people to open themselves to God and His grace.[30]

Khodr, in his article 'Christianity in a Pluralistic World: The Economy of the Holy Spirit', agrees with Moubarac and Caspar that it is not possible to circumscribe the activity of Christ in the world to Christians or Christianity; he writes that 'it is Christ alone who is received as light when grace visits a Brahmin, a Buddhist or a Muhammadan reading his own scriptures'. He stresses that not all have been able to see in the Church an effective Christian witness, and that God may therefore send other witnesses to 'those who have not been able to see the uplifting manifestation of Christ in the face which we have made bloody with our sins or in the seamless robe which we have torn by our divisions' (p. 125). Khodr's inclusivism draws on pneumatology no less than Christology; the idea of the activity of the Holy Spirit outside the historic structures of Christianity (and therefore potentially or actually in Islam) can be found in all three Christian traditions, and Massignon and Cragg have both referred to this possibility. Khodr calls on Christians studying other religions to 'seek to discern the truth in them according to the breath of the Holy Spirit' (p. 127).

Muhammad as Prophet

In a concluding section of *Muhammad at Medina* entitled 'The Alleged Moral Failures', Watt states that 'of all the world's great men none has been so much maligned as Muhammad' (p. 324). He proceeds to offer a defence of certain aspects of Muhammad's life or mission which have been criticized by orientalists in the past: the opening of hostilities during the sacred month in the early Medinan period; the orders or encouragement to assassination; the execution of the men of Banu Qurayzah; the number of his marriages and his marriage to Zaynab in particular. He points out that most of these events, far from arising from some whim or personal desire on the part of Muhammad, were aimed at strengthening the Muslims' position or at breaking with tribal tradition in some way, and that in nearly all cases his conduct did not scandalize his contempories. Watt ends his piece by explaining that he is viewing Muhammad 'only in relation to the moral standards of his time', and that he wishes to refrain from judging Muhammad by a 'universal moral standard' (p. 333).

Watt's proviso illustrates the point that even among those who allow that Muhammad is in some sense a prophet, as he does, the relationship between Muhammad the man and Muhammad the prophet is rather different for Muslims than it is for non-Muslims. For Muslims, Muhammad's impeccable moral character (according to a universal standard) is inextricably bound up with his prophethood. Whether his unique moral probity is seen as the cause of God's choosing him as a prophet or the result, it is essential to the view of him as an exemplar and is presupposed by the almost universally accepted doctrine of *'ismah* (protection from error). Christians may refer to Muhammad's human or religious 'genius', but neither this nor prophethood are seen as excluding moral fallibility. Zaehner, for example, expresses himself in a characteristically Christian manner when he argues that 'Muslims should see in the very imperfections of Muhammad the sign of God's sovereign power to use what vessel He will, however imperfect, for the furtherance of his own inscrutable purpose.' He compares Muslim idealization of Muhammad to that of Luther by Protestants and that of an 'amazing cavalcade of abominable Popes' by Catholics.[31]

Addressing another perennial orientalist theme, Watt feels that it is essential to believe in Muhammad's sincerity, and gives as reasons for this 'his readiness to undergo persecution for his beliefs, the high moral character of the men who believed in him and looked up to him as leader, and the greatness of his ultimate achievement'.[32] Caspar, acknowledging that the possible 'use of revelation for personal ends' causes qualms for some Christians, supports Muhammad's sincerity, arguing that a belief in his own prophethood on Muhammad's part would not be incompatible with the belief that prophets are granted certain privileges; he also draws attention to Muhammad's constant and unwavering conviction both at Mecca and Medina that he was chosen by God to convey the revelation.[33] Arnaldez, in his *Mahomet*, bases his argument for Muhammad's sincerity on certain empirical observations, mostly connected with the scrupulous distinction which was upheld by Muhammad (and by Muslims after his death) between his own words and the revelation. He argues that there is no evidence of any confusion on Muhammad's part between God's words or thoughts and his own, and the relationship between Muhammad the man and Muhammad the prophet remained constant even when Muhammad increasingly gained the authority to speak in his own name (pp. 20–2).

One common theme in Christian or Western writings on Muhammad has been the progression from Muhammad as preacher in Mecca to Muhammad as not only preacher but also diplomat, soldier and politician in Medina. Over against earlier orientalist scholarship, for example that of Snouck-Hurgronje, Becker, and Lammens, recent scholars have tended to deny any strong discontinuity and to locate the change in external circumstances rather than in Muhammad's character. Caspar argues that despite the additional temporal concerns in the Medinan revelations, the religious ethos is not diluted, and he draws attention to Muhammad's uninterrupted consciousness of his own religious mission and to the doctrinal continuity of the Meccan and Medinan revelations.[34] Moubarac and Bijlefeld have upheld this continuity particularly with regard to the Qur'anic material relating to Abraham, in response to the view of certain orientalists that the greater emphasis on Abraham in the Medinan, as opposed to the Meccan, period was a direct result of Muhammad's increasing knowledge of the biblical stories on the one hand, and deteriorating relations with Jews and Christians (necessitating the consolidation of Islam as a distinct religion) on the other.[35]

In his first published monograph on Islam, *The Call of the Minaret*, Cragg sees the Hijra as a significant turning point, marking a transition in the Prophet's function which is 'implicit in the emergence of the preacher into the ruler, the "warner" into the warrior' (p. 72). He contrasts the 'unmistakable elements of greatness in the suffering preacher-prophet [i.e. at Mecca], bearing obloquy and calumny with tenacious fidelity to the truth he had been given to see', with what he terms 'the mingled magnanimity and opportunism' of the Medinan period (p. 83). The fate of the Banu Qurayzah is seen as representing 'the darkest depth of Muslim policy', which took place at a time when Muhammad 'could hardly yet afford to be magnanimous' (p. 87). However, he does not see the transition as a simple case of deterioration in Muhammad's character, but rather as an inevitable outcome of Muhammad's fateful decision, seen as 'formative of all else in Islam': 'a decision for community, for resistance, for external victory, for pacification and rule'. He compares this with an equally fateful decision on the part of Jesus: 'The decision for the Cross – no less conscious, no less formative, no less inclusive – was the contrary decision' (p. 93).

In his later writings Cragg is more inclined to view the Meccan and Medinan periods of Muhammad's mission as a continuum, and attempts to assess the methods used in the Medinan period in the light of the message of the Meccan period. He acknowledges that the resort to power was 'not a crude power-lust but a means devised to enforce a revelation about humanity under God', and wishes to explore the issue of 'how well the meaning [i.e. the Qur'anic message] and the means agree'.[36] He is somewhat ambivalent as to whether the Medinan developments were in fact consistent with the Meccan message. On the one hand, he seems to acknowledge that the seeds of the former are contained in the latter, and that there is an internal Islamic logic whereby if success 'was manifestly *not* attained by preaching, then the very loyalty that preached must pass beyond its verbal task into an active accomplishment of "victory"'. According to this criteria 'the Hijra is not rightly seen as a lapse away from prophethood, but as its due sequence of obedience. There was the impulse of dire necessity, if Prophet and prophethood were even to survive.'[37] He further acknowledges that the Hijra involved sacrifice and commitment, and that it represented the Islamic rejection of tribalism, vested interests and the 'idolatrous hegemony'.[38] On the other hand, Cragg finds in the Meccan portions of the Qur'an 'an implicit critique of the subsequent equation between the task of faith and the force of arms', with its emphasis on the inner dimensions of faith and its acknowledgement of the impossibility of compelling it.[39]

Cragg does not conceal his reservations about a religion which has 'firmly espoused the power equation' in its confidence that 'state and law can effectuate genuine religion'.[40] He questions whether using external means of imposing conformity are compatible with a free and voluntary response to God on the part of the individual, and suggests that when faith is too closely associated with the ruling power it loses the independence necessary to curb the excesses of that power.[41] Acknowledging that historically Christianity has fallen short of its ideals, he nevertheless wishes to uphold the distinction between ideals and realities, stating that 'to the Christian mind, it will always be a burden and a tragedy that force has been so uncomplicatedly enshrined in the very canons of Islam via the pattern of the *Sīrah*', concluding with respect to Christianity and Islam that 'in their origins in Jesus and Muḥammad an abiding, and irreducible, disparity persists'.[42] Cragg is unapologetic about what might be viewed as his subjective response to this dimension of Muhammad's mission; while wishing to alert fellow Christians to mitigating environmental factors, he feels that 'the military dimensions of original Islam and its uninhibited embrace of the political arm are . . . crucial factors in deterring the Christian from a positive response to Muhammad'. In his opinion there is ultimately 'no escape from the burden of the actual events', for an 'appeal to benevolent oversight, or tactful goodwill, would be disloyal both to Islamic criteria and to religious integrity'.[43]

Coming more specifically to the question of Muhammad's prophethood, Massignon's thinking on this subject is again pertinent, given his considerable influence on subsequent Catholic thinking. He defended Muhammad against the charge of being a false prophet, and drew a distinction between 'positive' and 'negative' prophecy, both of which could be used to describe Muhammad's role.[44] Massignon's style of writing is neither straightforward nor systematic, and as a result his many commentators are not always agreed as to precisely what he meant by these terms, but it seems that Muhammad's negative prophecy consisted largely of the fact that he bore witness to the eschatological truths of the second coming of Jesus and the final judgement. A further aspect was the tendency to define God in negative terms, that is to say in terms of what he was *not*, as in the apophatic tradition. His positive prophecy consisted in the fact that there was a radical element to his teaching: he challenged prevailing human values and introduced social reforms. In Massignon's thinking the common objection to considering Muhammad a prophet on chronological grounds, namely that he could not be a precursor to Christ, was transcended by the consideration that he bore witness to Christ's *second* coming. Nevertheless, he felt that there were limitations to Muhammad's prophetic role, since he did not preach the central Christian truths of Incarnation and redemption, and that he was 'enlightened on certain points, but not on others'.[45]

Other Catholics have used slightly differing categories or terms; some thinkers have sought to locate Muhammad within the framework of Thomist theology, and have spoken in terms of 'directive prophecy'[46] or a 'prophetic charism', both of which can be extra-biblical. A directive prophet is one who does not bring new truths, but who provides guidance and direction suited to the needs of his community, and confirms the truth of that which has previously been revealed. A charism is defined as a special grace given by God for the benefit not of the recipient but of those around him. The prophet in this sense would throw light on certain religious truths while leaving others – including the Christian mysteries – in obscurity.[47] The main religious truth illuminated by Muhammad is generally considered to be that of monotheism (as opposed to the prevailing polytheism) or aspects of monotheism, such as the transcendence and majesty of God. Caspar initially held to the idea that Muhammad enjoyed a 'partial prophetic charism' while in Mecca, i.e. prior to establishing Islam as a religion separate from Christianity and Judaism; however, he later revoked this idea, feeling it inappropriate to divide Muhammad's mission into two distinct phases, or indeed to subsume everything under narrowly defined theological categories.[48]

Jomier and Arnaldez believe that it is better to avoid using the term 'prophet' when speaking of Muhammad, given that Christians could not mean the same by it as Muslims, and would not see obedience to Muhammad as a corollary of his prophethood. Neither feels that this precludes acknowledging the value of his religious teachings; Jomier suggests that it would be better for Christians 'to recognize the truths that the Muslim message contains, to respect the spiritual journey of sincere Muslims, and to see Muhammad as a religious and political genius'. Arnaldez similarly recognizes Muhammad's 'religious genius', and feels that it is important that Christians show some kind of positive appreciation of Muhammad, since to fail to do so would be to cause pain to Muslims in view of their strong attachment to him. He suggests that for them it is as if one had a close friend but was unable to persuade one's other friends to like him or her.[49]

Watt is prepared to say unequivocally: 'I consider Muhammad was truly a prophet';[50] his suggested criterion for such recognition, namely that of 'fruits', has already been referred to. However, his acknowledgement of Muhammad as a prophet is not without reservations and he expresses himself somewhat tentatively at times, as where he claims that the Christian rejection of negative medieval images of

Muhammad 'involves accepting Muhammad as a religious leader through whom God has worked, and that is tantamount to holding that he is in some sense a prophet'. He goes on to say that 'such a view does not contradict any central Christian belief. It has, however, to be made clear to Muslims that Christians do not believe that all Muhammad's revelations from God were infallible, even though they allow that much of divine truth was revealed to him.'[51] While keen to respect Muslim sensibilities on the issue of Muhammad's prophethood, Watt's definition of prophecy, elaborated more fully in the next section, differs markedly from the Muslim view. In one place he describes a prophet as being 'an intellectual because he is the bearer and transmitter, and indeed the originator, of the directive ideas on which a religious movement is based'.[52] In effect, although willing to use the term 'prophet', Watt is saying no more in terms of Muhammad's religious contribution to humanity than do Jomier and Arnaldez, who refrain from using the term; to put it more positively, they are saying no less than he is.

In *Muhammad and the Christian*, Cragg aims to facilitate a Christian appreciation of Muhammad. He does not take issue with the fact of Muhammad's 'prophethood', the function of prophecy being understood as 'forthtelling the divine word', and a prophet as one 'through whom that divine education of humanity proceeds . . . which enlightens, informs, guides, exhorts, warns, disciplines, prohibits and enjoins' (p. 125). Characteristically, though, he argues from the Muslim understanding of prophethood, as exemplified in Muhammad, to the conclusion that humankind requires 'more than a prophet'; he asks: 'Is "education" man's total need? Should there, on prophecy's own showing, be something more than prophecy? Does law, by prohibition and injuction, make good its own intention?' (p. 126). He finds the Qur'an to be realistic about the human capacity for recalcitrance and perversity, and therefore asks 'whether the persistence and pathos of human evil do not argue a more resourceful divine initiative of grace' (p. 130).

Küng deals with the issue of Muhammad's prophethood in a section of *Christianity and the World Religions* entitled: 'Muhammad: A Prophet?'. He regrets Vatican II's silence on Muhammad, and calls on Christians to respect 'the man whose name is omitted from the declaration out of embarrassment' (p. 27). Like Watt, Küng draws attention to the empirically observable 'fruits' of Muhammad's mission – that the Arabs 'were lifted to the heights of monotheism from the very this-worldly polytheism of the old Arabian tribal religion'; that Muslims 'received from Muhammad, or rather from the Qur'an, a boundless supply of inspiration, courage, and strength to make a new departure in religion, toward greater truth and knowledge'; that Muslims today enjoy a 'feeling for the fundamental equality of all human beings before God, and an international brotherhood that has managed to overcome barriers between the races'; and that 'nearly 800 million men and women . . . are all marked by the exacting power of a faith that, more than practically any other, has shaped its followers into a uniform type' (pp. 26–7).

Küng points out that the New Testament does not rule out the possibility of future prophets (p. 28), and draws attention to the similarities between Muhammad and the prophets of Israel in order to raise the question of how Christians could accord the title of prophet to the latter and not to the former. These include his special relationship with God, which provided the basis of his authority vis-à-vis the community; the modesty of his claim to be only the mouthpiece of God; his strong sense of calling and commitment; the fact that he spoke to a social and religious crisis and challenged the privileged classes; his ceaseless proclamation of the One God and his denunciation of idols; his emphasis on obedience and submission to God; and his general teachings on faith, moral accountability and the final judgement (pp. 25–6). Küng describes Muhammad as a 'prophetic corrective' for Christians, primarily in the sense of restoring some of the original Judaeo-Christian emphases in Christology, as previously mentioned, but also in the sense that he was to a certain extent a witness for Jesus to those who had not been incorporated into the Christian fold, and he reminded the Jews that 'Jesus fits into the continuity of *Jewish salvation history*' (his italics, p. 126). Küng hopes that a Christian re-evaluation of Muhammad on the basis of Islamic sources will encourage Muslims to re-evaluate Jesus on the basis of historical sources, 'namely the Gospels' (p. 111).

The Qur'an as the Word of God

In an article entitled 'Is the Qur'an the Word of God?', Smith points out that in the past neither Muslims nor non-Muslims have ever asked this question; for Muslims, to ask such a question would be verging on blasphemy, while non-Muslims have always assumed a negative answer. With characteristic optimism, he believes that in the future, the intellectual understanding of Muslims and Christians on this question will converge (p. 299). Smith argues elsewhere, in his article 'The True

Meaning of Scripture: An Empirical Historian's Non-reductionist Interpretation of the Qur'an' (1980), that the important thing is to know and discover what the Qur'an means or has meant for Muslims, and that the significance of the Qur'an lies in its 'prodigious and continuing force in the lives of men and women' (p. 498). He understands scripture primarily as a human category, since it is mediated through and interpreted by human beings in all ages, and he asserts that 'meaning is first and last a human fact' (pp. 489, 503). From this it follows that 'the real meaning of the Qur'an is not any one meaning but is a dynamic process of meanings . . . the solid historical reality of the continuum of actual meanings over the centuries to actual people' (p. 504). In short, the true meaning of the Qur'an as scripture lies 'not in the text, but in the minds and hearts of Muslims' (p. 505). Smith believes that this need not necessarily be in contradiction to the Muslim belief that 'the true meaning of the Qur'an is what God means by it', since God 'presumably is more aware than are any of us of the complexities and the fluidity of human history' (p. 504).

Bijlefeld shares with Smith a phenomenological approach to the Qur'anic text, and rejects the idea put forward by Rodinson, among others, that the Qur'an should be classified as either the work of God or the work of a man; he believes this impasse can be avoided by seeing the Qur'an as the sacred scripture of Muslims, which is all the more appropriate given that the Qur'an reached a non-Muslim audience only through Muslims, and it is only because of its significance for Muslims that it is now an object of study and interest among the wider academic community. In Bijlefeld's view, those who wish to understand the Qur'an as a religious document would do better to refrain from some of the areas of study with which Westerners have hitherto been preoccupied, such as the Qur'an's relationship to prior sources and traditions, which study, however, remains the legitimate concern of historians.[53]

Caspar, in his article 'Parole de dieu et langage humain en Christianisme et en Islam' (1980), uses a comparative approach to highlight the differences between the Christian and Muslim understandings of revelation and scripture. He points out that for Muslims, the scripture is primary and anterior to any religious tradition, while for Christians and Jews it is the events which are recounted in scripture that constitute the primary locus of revelation, and the scriptures fulfil the role of preserving the memory and the meanings of those events for future generations (p. 44). Caspar's comparison is aimed at facilitating mutual understanding rather than arriving at any judgement or evaluation; for him it explains, for example, Muslims' reluctance to subscribe to any theories of revelation or interpretation which highlight the human element in scripture (p. 46). Arnaldez, in a similarly non-evaluative comparison in his *Three Messengers for One God*, contrasts the Qur'an's asynchronicity with the Bible's diachronicity; in the Qur'an, 'the word falls vertically, so to speak, at distinct points in time, without ever unfolding within the horizontal continuity of historical immanence' (p. 11). There is an abruptness to the Qur'anic revelation, so that it 'bursts from the height of heaven like a clap of thunder', while the biblical revelation 'seeps into human history and spreads along with it' (p. 13). The will of God is 'woven into the events of human life' in the Bible, so that it 'demonstrates this will concretely as work in human affairs', while 'the Qur'an affirms it abruptly, as a theological truth in itself' (p. 16).

Despite the differences in the Christian and Islamic models of revelation, Caspar feels that philosophically the problems raised in both traditions are the same. Both have to deal with the 'scandal of the historicity of revelation', in the sense that the original revelation appealed to a specific audience and reflected a specific cultural background and specific events, and both need to avoid the opposing dangers of a literalistic reading of scripture involving a simple transposition of the categories of the original age to the present (he gives the Qur'anic penal laws as a possible example on the Islamic side), and an anachronistic reading into the original text of matters which could not have been there, such as advanced scientific knowledge.[54] Caspar points out that scholars in both traditions have tried to avoid the extremes of rationalism, on the one hand, and fideism or literalism, on the other, and in both the Word of God must be interpreted afresh by each generation, in order not to become fossilized and irrelevant. Ultimately, he believes there is a sense in which all revelation is anthropomorphic, in that an infinite God condescends to limit Himself to human language.[55]

In *The Challenge of the Scriptures*, the Christians of the GRIC emphasize that all scripture is affected by degrees of relativity and therefore no scripture, including the Christian scripture, can be considered 'the words of God in a pure state – that is, without human mediation' (p. 66). Human words, situated in time and place, are 'by definition inadequate to express the totality of the eternal Word of God', and the meaning of scripture is never completely unambiguous; the fact that the original context has changed provides a further relativizing factor. Such factors make it unnecessary to measure others' revelations by the criteria of one's own. The authors deny that their approach leads to relativism or agnosticism, but it is noteworthy that what rescues them from this is framed in specifically Christian terms: 'Across these human expressions of the mysteries of God and Christ [i.e. the scriptures], the faith of the believer truly reaches the person of Christ and, through him, God in the fulness of divinity'. They see as an integral part of Christian identity the belief that 'the Jesus Christ event cannot be surpassed' (pp. 62–3).

The Christians of the GRIC are aware of factors which may inhibit a positive view of the Qur'an on the part of Christians. These include the fact that it adds nothing new to the Bible; the mundanity or legalism of certain sections; and the fact that certain elements in the Qur'an and the Bible appear to contradict each other. They set against these factors certain countervailing considerations: that the Qur'an does not claim novelty for itself; that there is also an element of legalism in the Old Testament, for example in Leviticus, and this could play a positive role in 'reminding every believer that faith imposes requirements and that it must be carried into all of life'; and that while it is true that ultimately there are irreducible differences between the two, there are also contradictions within the scriptures themselves (p. 66). The group does not deny that Islam and Christianity embody 'two diverse and irreconcilable conceptions of monotheism' (p. 65), but the issue is partly circumvented by saying that many contradictions can be explained by the limitations of human expressions of the Word of God: 'It is not God who is self-contradictory, but those who speak in God's name'; it is further pointed out that the belief that only God is absolute relativizes both scripture and tradition (p. 62). This fits in with the view that 'the Gospels and other New Testament writings have only transmitted to us a portion of [the] words and signs of Jesus, as St. John himself has said (John 20:30; 21:31). What has been said is enough for us to "believe that Jesus is the Christ, the Son of God, and . . . believing we may have life in his name" (John 20:31)' (their ellipsis, pp. 62–3).

Although the group does not adhere to 'the Muslim idea that the whole Qur'ān, down to the minutest detail, was dictated verbatim by God to the Prophet' (p. 66), in view of the quality and fruitfulness of the Qur'anic message, they feel able to conclude that the Qur'an represents 'an authentic Word of God, but one in part essentially different from the Word in Jesus Christ' (p. 73). For them, the Qur'an, along with the

Islamic religious tradition, could be regarded as 'a repository of treasures of prayer, love and justice' (pp. 71–2).

Caspar's own writings, which include many of the above points, demonstrate the extent of his influence on the GRIC as well as the group's influence on him, which he freely acknowledges. He feels that it is no longer an option to think of the Qur'an as diabolical or even as purely human, and believes that even if one chooses not to approve of the whole content of the Qur'an, one cannot deny the high religious tone and quality of its central message.[56] Caspar is aware that the Qur'anic negation of Christian truths has always been a stumbling block to Christian recognition of a divine element in the Qur'an, and he deals with this objection in part by pointing out that it is Christian heresies, rather than orthodox Christian belief, that the Qur'an negates. These include the divinization of humankind (as opposed to the humanization of God), the belief in a triad of gods, and physical sonship. In these matters, Caspar maintains that Christians can agree with the Qur'an. He acknowledges that the absolute monotheism which is the central message of the Qur'an is 'profoundly different' to the Christian vision of God in Jesus Christ, but maintains that the Qur'an could be seen as emphasizing one true dimension of the mystery of God, which finds its fuller expression in the New Testament. A parallel is drawn here between the Qur'an and the Old Testament, which has a different emphasis to the New Testament but, properly interpreted, does not contradict it.[57] Caspar abjures relativism in matters of truth and maintains that he would cease to be a Christian if he were to deny that 'the Word of God in Jesus Christ is, in the eyes of faith but also in reality, unsurpassable and the deepest Word of God'.[58]

Although Cragg and Watt come from very different perspectives, they share an interest in the triangular relationship between the Qur'an, its original environment, and Muhammad's mind, and they both put forward their own understanding of the actual revelatory process.[59] Both are aware that this is a delicate area and make a conscious attempt to avoid unnecessarily offending Muslim sensibilities. Watt, for example, wishes to avoid causing affront to Muslims by stating or implying that Muhammad is the author of the Qur'an.[60] When discussing the influence of the Judaeo-Christian heritage on the Qur'an, he feels it is better to approach this from the point of view of what the contemporary Arabs believed, given that the Qur'an, in order to be received and understood by them, must have addressed them at the level of their understanding and awareness; it is therefore relevant to observe what kind of ideas were 'in the air', and the extent of the pre-Islamic Arabs' knowledge of biblical matters.[61] Furthermore, the Qur'an must also bear a relationship to Muhammad's own thinking and can be taken as evidence for his outlook, as well as that of the contemporary Arabs; this is because 'even if he did not originate the Qur'ānic ideas, they were the ideas that dominated and moulded his thoughts'.[62] Watt finds it untenable to say that there is no human element in revelation, since all human language is culturally conditioned, and open to more than one interpretation.[63] He not infrequently avers that 'the Qur'ān contains what Western historical criticism can only regard as palpable errors', giving as examples the alleged confusion of Mary the mother of Jesus with Miriam the daughter of Imran (19:28), the denial of the Crucifixion (4:157), and the assertion that Christians worship three gods (4:171 etc.). He feels that such errors can be accommodated within the Muslim view of the divine origin of the Qur'an by taking the view that God 'adapted the wording of the Qur'ān to the outlook of the people of Mecca, among whom these erroneous opinions were current, and that it was not part of the purpose of the revealed message to correct such errors'.[64]

As far as the actual revelatory process is concerned, Watt holds 'the Qur'ān to be in some sense the product of a divine initiative and therefore revelation'.[65] In order to explain the phenomenon of the revelations received by Muhammad, he resorts to several paradigms and concepts, such as the Jungian concept of the individual or collective unconscious, or L. S. Thornton's views on modes of revelation and inspiration in the latter's *Revelation and the Modern World* (London: Dacre Press, 1950).[66] He refers to the possibility that revelations might come from a prophet's unconscious while the prophet genuinely experiences the revelation as coming from outside himself, 'since the unconscious is beyond the self in the sense of being beyond the conscious mind'; this is not seen as invalidating the revelations since God may, in Watt's view, work through a prophet's unconscious, and this view would allow for both a divine element and a human, therefore fallible, element in scripture.[67] A prophet also participates in the collective unconscious of his community, and 'most religious ideas emerge from the collective unconscious into consciousness'.[68] Watt refers as well to the concept of 'creative imagination' in which artists, poets and writers participate; he observes that 'great works of the creative imagination have . . . a certain universality, in that they give expression to the feeling and attitudes of a whole generation'. He feels that prophets also have a share in this, in that 'they proclaim ideas connected with what is deepest and most central in human experience, with special reference to the particular needs of their day and generation'. According to Watt, 'in Muhammad . . . there was a welling up of the creative imagination, and the ideas thus produced are to a great extent true and sound'. However, he adds that they are not exclusively so, and believes that it is a mistake to regard such revelation as an independent source of historical fact; to use the Qur'an, for example, as a source for denying the historicity of the Crucifixion is 'an exaggeration of the role of "revelation"'.[69]

Cragg grapples with the same issues as Watt, but with rather more reference to Muslim tradition. His most thorough treatment of the issue of revelation is to be found in *Muhammad and the Christian*. Here and elsewhere he questions the Muslim view that 'the more a thing is God's the less it is man's, that divine employment of prophetic messengership means an abeyance of personal powers and qualities' (p. 6). On the contrary, he believes that 'God's employment of human agency might in fact enhance, harness and fulfil the human potential so honoured' (p. 84). He is aware that 'it has always been crucial for Muslims to insist that the will and personality of Muhammad do not consciously participate' (p. 83), and that for them this is a necessary guarantee of the divine status of scripture; he sees this attitude as arising from 'the yearning for religious certitude' (p. 85). However, he personally denies that 'celestial dictation, rather than inward travail, verifies the Qur'an as the divine Word' (p. 6). Cragg finds evidence of the close link between Muhammad's psyche and the revelation in the Qur'an itself, which speaks of the revelation as descending on Muhammad's heart (26:193–4, 2:97; p. 84). Always alert to developments within Muslim thought, he observes elsewhere that this same argument has been used by the eminent Muslim scholar Fazlur Rahman.[70]

Pursuing this theme, Cragg draws attention to the relationship between the content of the revelations and Muhammad's own situation, for example the stories of opposition experienced by former prophets, revealed at a time when Muhammad himself was experiencing similar opposition; these revelations both encouraged him and provided a warning to his opponents (p. 88). Cragg also refers to the Qur'anic concern with the Prophet's private domestic affairs (e.g. in Suras 33 and 66; p. 89), and finds reflected in the Qur'an the very human emotions of Muhammad – his perplexities, yearnings, and prophetic despair. For him, to see the Prophet as fully human is to fully appreciate his human greatness. He concludes that 'one cannot intelligently suppose a momentary suspension of personal participation, while *Waḥy* [revelation] supervenes, between the lively personal engagement of Muhammad in the before and after', and argues that the alternative view would allow Muhammad to be seen as 'a personality *wholly* occupied in and with prophethood, rather than negated at its most critical' (p. 89). Cragg refers to the strand of Islamic thought that has emphasized Muhammad's exceptional qualities of intellect and feels that it would be anomalous for these to be wholly irrelevant to the crucial process of revelation itself (p. 98).

Certain elements within the Islamic tradition are seen by Cragg as providing further evidence of the significance of the Qur'an's relationship to its original environment. These include the gradualism of the revelation (referred to in 17:106), and the importance for the classical scholars of establishing the chronology of the revelations and the 'occasions of revelation' (*asbāb al-nuzūl*, i.e. the situation in which a revelation came), which were sometimes considered essential for understanding the actual import of a particular passage (p. 88).

Cragg argues that the acknowledgement of a human element, a positive relation between the revelation and Muhammad's own thoughts and feelings, need not detract from the status of the Qur'an but would entail positive advantages, most notably in the field of exegesis. He feels that the traditional view of revelation has led to 'a less than lively approach to the sense of the text and to an excessive preoccupation with grammar, parsing and syntax'; an emphasis on the physical arts devoted to the text, such as recitation and calligraphy, although not undesirable in themselves, may exclude the reflection (*tadabbur*) on the actual content and meaning of the text which the Qur'an itself prescribes (p. 95). Cragg acknowledges the fear that 'any emphasis on the Qur'an's having a timed context will lead to the notion that it has only a timed significance' (p. 96), but argues the contrary view: 'If we can understand the revelation as proceeding within a full engagement of mental and spiritual capacity, responsive to living situations, we can more readily require alert reception of it . . . in the present context of the reader's world' (p. 97). In this way the ongoing relevance of the scripture will be ensured rather than diminished.

In *The Event of the Qur'an*, Cragg inclines towards a view of revelation based on literary inspiration. Acknowledging that the Qur'an distances itself from the poetry of the pre-Islamic poets, he nevertheless observes that, paradoxically, the Qur'an is 'a thing of surpassing poetic worth' (p. 41). He finds this confirmed by the Qur'an's references to its own literary worth and the traditional Muslim view of its superior if not unique literary quality. Cragg himself expresses the belief that 'where prophecy is most authentic, there is poetry . . . a poetry which is more than an artistry of words because its quality as language is enthused with a purpose and a power that require what they create' (p. 45). This amounts to 'an inwrought mystery of content and form, or meaning and word . . . The Qur'an is understood to say *what* it says in an inseparable identity with *how* it says it' (his italics, p. 46). Cragg refers to the experience of the English poet Blake of receiving 'a sort of dictation from beyond, without straining, or study, or conscious effort'; such inspiration cannot be contrived but only waited on (pp. 46–7). Cragg denies that such a view of the revelation detracts from the Qur'an's uniqueness, for all inspiration is unique, and believes that it is 'simply to acknowledge and study the implications of the literary status Muslim faith has always attributed to its Scripture' (p. 48). He further believes that Muhammad's periods of self-doubt in the early phase and the physical symptoms he experienced in the receiving of revelation become more intelligible in the light of this view (p. 49).

Some believe that the Qur'an could be a 'word of God' not only for the Muslim but also for the Christian. The Christians of the GRIC hold that the Qur'an 'reveals a deep experience of God to the Christian who approaches the task without prejudice' (p. 64), and may have the effect of leading Christians to look afresh at their own scripture and find their own faith 'cleansed, renewed, and enriched by a different religious experience' (p. 70); Islamic monotheism, furthermore, constitutes 'an exhortation to purify one's theological outlook and the forms of one's religious life' (p. 72). Caspar gives as an example of this the Qur'anic insistence on God's transcendence as a reminder to Christians that their faith has to end with the Father, while Jesus is the way.[71] Küng sees Muhammad's message as a reminder to Christians of the centrality of God and of the relevance of faith to all areas of life.[72] Some feel that Islam helps them to appreciate the uniqueness of their Christian faith in a dialectical way, by providing a contrast in certain essential respects.[73]

Several Christians have used the Qur'an in worship or meditation; the GRIC Christians state that some Christians 'reach the point of actually praying with the Qur'ān, for their own spiritual nurture and in union with their Muslim friends' (p. 49). F. Peter Ford, a Christian academic who was based at Temple University, refers to Christians who are 'reading the Qur'an for their own spiritual benefit', and goes on to say that 'many are finding that the Qur'an . . . can be read with profit, and even that God can be found speaking there despite a divergence at times with central themes of their belief'. He suggests that the Qur'an could be given a status 'somewhere between biblical canonicity and mere devotional literature'; it could be regarded as sacred yet non-canonical, and be used as 'a kind of scriptural supplement for spiritual and theological reflection'.[74]

Christian Interpretation of the Qur'an

This is an area of considerable importance and debate because it is closely related to the broader issue of the implications of studying one religious tradition from within another. There is a wide variety of opinion on the matter among Christians themselves as to the legitimacy of a Christian interpretation of the Qur'an; many have expressed reservations about 'reading Christian meanings into the Qur'an', and yet most would agree that complete objectivity and suspension of one's own beliefs is an impossibility. An observation of two examples of Christian attempts to interpret the Qur'an – those of Basetti-Sani and Cragg – will illuminate some of the issues involved.

Basetti-Sani provides what is generally regarded by other Christians as an extreme example of a Christian interpretation of the Qur'an, which is almost universally decried, albeit with an acknowledgement of his good intentions. In his *The Koran in the Light of Christ: A Christian Interpretation of the Sacred Book of Islam*, he describes his spiritual journey from a hostile position which regarded Islam and the Qur'an as inspired by the devil, to a much more positive approach which resulted from personal contact with Muslims and the influence of Massignon. He subscribes to the view expressed by Pope Pius XII in 1952: 'Whatever is just and good in other religions finds its deepest meaning and final perfection in Christ' (p. 24); he is by no means unusual in regarding other religions, including Islam, as a preparation for the gospel, but he takes the potential implications of this for the interpretation of the Qur'an further than anyone else. He wishes to depart from the centuries-old Christian tradition of assuming that the Qur'an could not be a revealed book, and to accommodate the Muslim belief in its divine origin. He does this by advocating the use of a 'Christian key' to interpret the Qur'an (pp. 38–9); this key must be derived from the New Testament, and is the same key which Christians use when they interpret the Old Testament (pp. 101–2). Basetti-Sani claims that it is this 'Christian reading' of the Qur'an which makes possible a Christian recognition of Muhammad as a prophet and the Qur'an as an authentic revelation, particularly in the light of the Christian belief in 'the possibility of private, special, and relative revelations' (p. 102, 105). He believes that the real meaning of the Qur'an has been hidden from Muslims by a veil, and that the Muslim exegetical tradition has failed to understand it aright (p. 103); he feels that Muslim exegesis rests on a literalist attitude to the text, which arises from a literal understanding of the idea of a 'heavenly archetype' of the Qur'an and a 'material conception of *Tanzīl* [revelation]', and he calls for a 'dematerialization' of the interpretation of the Qur'an (pp. 115–6). According to him, only Christians can perceive the 'fullest meaning' of the Qur'an, which they can then 'fraternally point out to Muslims' (p. 104).

In expounding the Qur'anic meanings, Basetti-Sani refers to the Muslim exegetical concept of *bāṭin* – the inner meanings of the Qur'an – echoing the view common among Muslim mystics that the Qur'an contains esoteric meanings which are not immediately apparent but can be discovered by those who are spiritually equipped to do so.[75] His interpretations resemble many Sufi interpretations, in that they often appear somewhat arbitrary, as the fruits of subjective meditation rather than resting on any particular evidence. Thus, he sees the Qur'an as abounding with 'Christian symbols', including many of the biblical symbols for Christ or the Messiah, such as the morning star, the dawn, the fig, the olive, the fish, the pen, the serpent, the rock and water.[76] He applies a typological methodology which mirrors the Christian perception of 'types' or prefigurements of Jesus in the Old Testament, for example in God's command to Abraham to sacrifice his son. Many of the stories which are seen as prefiguring Jesus in the Old Testament are shared by the Qur'an, and Basetti-Sani sees them as pointing to Christ in the Qur'an no less than they do in the Old Testament. Parts of the Qur'an which have been understood by Muslims as referring to the Qur'an or to Mecca are not infrequently understood by Basetti-Sani as referring to the Bible or Jerusalem; he further suggests that the 'Night of Power' referred to in Sura 97 could refer to Christmas night, that the use of the first person plural for God could hint at the Trinity, and so on.[77] Like many Sufis, he advances interpretations of the 'mysterious letters' at the beginning of certain Suras without any supporting evidence; he puts forward the opinion that they too are symbols of Christ, and makes suggestions as to what they stand for.[78] There are many other elements to Basetti-Sani's Qur'anic interpretation which might be discussed, but what has been said will suffice to show how far removed his approach is from that of those who believe that priority must be given to the believers' own interpretation of their scriptures. Basetti-Sani is aware that his views are difficult not only for Muslims but also for Christians to accept (p. 102).

Cragg has been accused by more than one scholar of reading Christian meanings into the Qur'an. Charles Adams has characterized Cragg's position as implying that 'the Islamic religious tradition means not what Muslims have always thought it to mean, but something else that Christians are in a better position to understand'. By 'deliberately seeking and finding Christian meaning in Islamic experiences and doctrines', he feels that Cragg is infringing the integrity and autonomy of the Muslim religious tradition.[79] Cragg himself explicitly denies this charge, claiming to read into the Qur'an only what is potentially already there,[80] rather a fine distinction, and ultimately a moot point. The only arguably authoritative point of reference, namely what was in the author's mind, is not accessible in any objective sense; in any case many Muslims (especially but not exclusively Sufis) have expressed the view that one cannot exhaust the meanings of God's word, and therefore one cannot exclude the possibility of new interpretations which may not have been uncovered by classical scholarship. The related question of whether it is legimate or acceptable for a non-Muslim to uncover such meanings is one which Cragg addresses at some length.

Cragg's defence in principle of the legitimacy of a Christian – or other non-Muslim – interpretation of the Qur'an should be seen in the context of his whole endeavour to enter into a relationship with Islam and Muslims as a Christian. He addresses this question in *Muhammad and the Christian*, where he claims that 'there are liabilities to mutual reckoning in every religion', adding that to deny this would be to 'effectively terminate all relationship. Each would then be left in impenetrable self-congratulation or delusion' (p. 13). His avowed respect for the autonomy of the Islamic religious tradition is tempered by a 'refusal to allow that the autonomies of religion have other than one humanity' (p. 123). He is aware that 'no reading can be without presupposition', but states that 'what matters is that presupposition should not be prejudice, or, if it be prejudice, be prejudice in the right direction. For too long, a wrong Christian prejudice has virtually sealed off the Qur'ān from attentive encounter or doomed it to barren neglect' (p. 119). He does not claim to speak for Christians and is aware that 'all a single writer can do is to undertake a personal venture' (p. 13).

Cragg defends the right of the non-Muslim to seek to interpret the Qur'an, on Qur'anic grounds – namely the claim to universality. The Qur'an is, in its own words, 'a reminder to the worlds', therefore none can be considered 'outsiders', beyond its purview.[81] He believes that 'the Qur'an is truly open to more than its formal community of institutional allegiance' and furthermore suggests that 'there may well be a capacity of penetration that is the better for its being the outsider's search'. This is to some extent because 'Muslim possessiveness of the book has developed attitudes and skills which have in part obscured and impeded its fullest relevance'.[82] He points out that the Qur'an itself calls on non-Muslims to engage in 'penetrating reflection' (*tadabbur*) on its contents (e.g. 47:24), and concludes: 'So we are only following the Qur'ān's own desire when we give ourselves, with full intelligence and unclosed mind, to its contents'.[83] More pointedly, he remarks that 'an Islam that has no mind to privatize its relevance has no warrant to immunize its claims', and 'no legitimate exemption from considerations belonging to Christian humanity, providing these are rightly pressed'.[84] Cragg notes the Qur'an's 'deep relevance to contemporary man' and feels that 'the domestic role of the Qur'ān in the direction of its immediate community does not exhaust its relevance'.[85]

Cragg concedes the need for a deliberate effort to suspend judgement, while observing that 'such openness of heart often goes against the grain of religious conviction'. He acknowledges that any non-Muslim interpretation of Islam should be 'subject to the correctives of the proper custodians', and that 'the Qur'ān can never be authentically known in neglect of the sensitivities, the emotions, the spiritual property in it, of Muslims'.[86] He believes that he can in part avoid the 'vexed question of authority' in Qur'anic interpretation by 'taking the Qur'ān in its own seriousness and with respect for, and yet independence of, its own faith-system'. He does not call for a dry or detached academic response to the Qur'an, for it 'did not, and does not exist in order to be "interesting". It was, and is, a living summons asking a personal response.'[87] Nevertheless, Cragg never disavows the view he expressed in an early publication that 'it may happen that the Christian endeavour to understand Islam to the full will result in Christian expositions of Islam that many actual Muslims would not recognize as familiar . . . But there is nothing surprising in this possibility, nor inappropriate. To see anything through Christian eyes is to see it in the light of Christ.'[88]

In many of his publications, and especially in *The Event of the Qur'ān* and *The Mind of the Qur'ān* (London: George Allen & Unwin, 1973), Cragg explores Qur'anic themes with a depth and sensitivity which is not infrequently appreciated by Muslim reviewers. Aspects of the Qur'an that he finds particularly attractive are its vigorous rejection of idolatry; its strong and insistent call to obedience; its 'sacramental' view of nature, described in the Qur'an as containing 'signs' which call for a response of wonder and reverence; the sense of God's mercy and majesty; and the frequent exhortations to prayer and praise of God. There are, not surprisingly, occasions when his interpretations drift rather far away from traditional Muslim interpretations. Perhaps most controversial of all is Cragg's propensity for identifying Qur'anic themes common to Islam and Christianity, and seeking to show that, taken to their logical conclusions, they lead to essentially Christian truths. For example, he argues that the act of Creation, so fully treated in the Qur'an, already implies a divine self-limiting and self-emptying (*kenosis*) which hints at the Incarnation, and there is a 'sense in which all prophecy and revelation are incarnational in that they locate what God is saying in what men are and do'.[89] The following quotation succinctly illustrates the way in which Cragg uses Islamic premises to arrive at Christian truth: 'Does not the whole possibility and actuality of *shirk*, of idolatry, of human "exclusion" of God from all that is humanly his due, require in some sense a divine "vulnerability" to humankind of which the cross, for Christians, is the supreme and ultimate measure?'[90]

On this issue, and in his writings as a whole, Cragg provokes opposing reactions which are not polarized along Muslim–Christian lines. Christian critics, for example, include not just those who have reservations about a 'Christian' interpretation of the Qur'an but also those who feel that his reading of Islam is too sympathetic and neglects differences between the two faiths, detracting from the integrity or uniqueness of Christian truth.[91] Cragg has been aptly described as 'anthologizing' Islam, in that he tends to concentrate on areas with which he feels the keenest sympathy while neglecting some of the more prosaic aspects of the Qur'an, such as its legislation.[92]

Several of the Christian scholars treated in this chapter seem to lend a degree of support to Cragg's approach; Bijlefeld, for example, while critical of any attempts to imbue the Qur'an with biblical meaning, agrees with Cragg that 'a living interaction of theologies is not only highly desirable, but absolutely necessary'. He accepts that Christians inevitably see all 'in the light of Christ', but denies that this necessarily leads to an exclusively 'Christian' interpretation of the Qur'an; he believes that 'every man – Muslim and Christian – has the absolute right to testify to his belief that God has opened his eyes to a new and unexpected dimension of the Qur'ān and that God has "revealed" to him a hitherto hidden meaning of some Qur'ānic passages, an interpretation quite different from the traditional one'.[93] The delicate distinction which Bijlefeld wishes to uphold here may be the same one to which Moubarac refers when he argues for the acceptability of a 'Christian reading' as opposed to a 'Christian interpretation' of the Qur'an. He feels that just as there are differences between a Christian and a Jewish reading of the Old Testament, so too Christian readings of the Qur'an are likely to differ from Muslim readings, but this does not of itself invalidate the former.[94]

An issue which has often drawn Christians into the sphere of Qur'anic interpretation is the Qur'anic view of Christ and Christianity. The majority, including Bijlefeld, Küng, Jomier and Cragg, express reservations about Christian interpretations of the Qur'an which, for example, understand the Qur'anic description of Jesus as 'a word of God' in a Christian sense and without reference to Muslim understandings through the centuries. Küng remarks that 'it does not promote dialogue when well-meaning Christians find more theological implications in the Qur'an than it actually yields'.[95]

The Qur'anic verse pertaining to the Crucifixion is one to which Christians have responded in different ways. This is partly because the verse itself (4:157) is not grammatically straightforward or entirely free from ambiguity, and could therefore be seen to invite divergent interpretations; Muslim exegesis of it has in fact differed in important details.[96] Nevertheless, it could fairly be said that the most obvious meaning of the verse is that it denies that Jesus was crucified. Yusuf Ali's translation of the verse (bearing in mind that any translation is already an interpretation) renders it thus: 'They [i.e. the Jews] said (in boast), "We killed Christ Jesus the son of Mary, the messenger of Allah"; but they killed him not, nor crucified him. Only a likeness of that was shown to them. And those who differ therein are full of doubts, with no (certain) knowledge. But only conjecture to follow [i.e. they only follow their own conjecture], for of a surety they killed him not [or: they did not kill him for certain].' The following verse begins: 'Nay, Allah raised him up unto Himself.'

Most of the Christian scholars reviewed here do not approve of what they see as a forced interpretation of this verse in order to show that it does not deny the Crucifixion. Caspar points out that even if the Qur'an is interpreted as *not* denying the Crucifixion, the *meaning* of the Crucifixion, as embodied in the doctrine of redemption, is definitely absent, and probably excluded by central Qur'anic tenets.[97] Cragg agrees that the underlying logic of Islam with regard to the Crucifixion is that 'it did not, historically, it need not redemptively, and it should not morally, happen to Jesus'. However, he does attempt to retrieve from the Qur'an as much as possible of the Christian understanding of the event, pointing out, for example, that the Qur'an denies neither the will of human beings to crucify nor Jesus' readiness to be crucified, even if it maintains that that will was thwarted and Jesus rescued.[98] Basetti-Sani is one of a minority who seek to reinterpret the verse; for him, the view that the Qur'an is divine revelation means that 'it is not possible for it to contain such a clear contradiction of historical data and Christian revelation'; he therefore understands the verse as signifying that the Crucifixion was brought about not by the Jews but rather by the will of God, and because of Jesus' willingness to give up his own life.[99] Zaehner supports the view that the verse is referring to divine rather than human instrumentality by drawing a parallel with another Qur'anic verse which, referring to the victory over the enemy at the Battle of Badr, states: 'You did not kill them but God killed them' (8:17).[100] Geoffrey Parrinder, a Christian comparative religionist and author of the monograph *Jesus in the Qur'an*, feels that the Qur'anic material pertaining to the end of Jesus' life weighs in favour of an actual earthly death, as opposed to the belief that Jesus was saved from the Cross and miraculously raptured up to heaven; he suggests that the Crucifixion verse may have been abrogated by the verses which contain apparent references to his earthly death (p. 121).

Several Christians suggest, as have some Muslims, that the Qur'an is in fact not as hostile to Christianity as Muslim interpretation of it generally has been. This may be argued in various ways, and generally presupposes that the Christianity envisaged by the Qur'an is more or less unorthodox, whether it be Arianism, Docetism, Nestorianism, Ebionitism, Elkaisitism, or any other of a range of possibilities. Zaehner, who believes that the Qur'anic Christology is Nestorian, claims that orthodox Muslim beliefs about Jesus and Christianity do not arise from an impartial study of the Qur'an but rather from historical conflicts with Christians which began during Muhammad's lifetime.[101] Jomier describes the way in which, in the light of such conflicts, the doctrine of *taḥrīf* increasingly hardened into an orthodoxy which posited the corruption, as opposed to the misinterpretation, of the scriptures, despite the fact that the Qur'an appears on several occasions to accord a degree of legitimacy to the extant Christian and Jewish scriptures when it criticizes people for neglecting those scriptures, or exhorts them to abide by them.[102] Caspar says that although the Qur'an did not directly address itself to mainstream Christianity, Muslims naturally applied the Qur'anic negations of heterodox Christian beliefs to the actual orthodox Christian beliefs that they encountered with the expansion of the Islamic empire. He also points out that in negating certain assertions about Jesus, the Qur'an was seeking to defend Jesus from blasphemy, bearing in mind, among other things, the pagan associations of the idea of God having offspring.[103] In an article entitled 'The Christianity Criticized in the Qur'an', Watt rehearses some of the above arguments and also draws attention to the fact that the Crucifixion verse is primarily directed against Jews rather than Christians, specifically attacking 'the Jewish contention that the crucifixion had been a victory for them'. He concludes that 'there is no primary attack on Christianity in the Qur'ān', and sees in this profound implications for Muslim–Christian relations (pp. 200-1).

Christian attitudes to the Qur'anic view of Jesus illustrate the difficulty of applying abstract hermeneutical principles when the issue at stake is one which is central to one's own faith. Several Christians who express admiration for many aspects of the Qur'an cannot refrain from pronouncing it 'inadequate' in this respect. Küng, for example, complains that 'the portrait of Jesus in the Qur'ān is all too one-sided, too monotone, and for the most part lacking in content . . . it is very different from the Jesus of history, who . . . counters all legalism with radical love which even extends to his enemies. That is why he was executed, though the Qur'ān fails to recognize this.' Küng feels that just as Christians should not seek to make 'anonymous Christians' out of Muslims, so Muslims ought not to turn Jesus into an 'anonymous Muslim'.[104] Cragg also laments the missing dimensions of Christ, or as he puts it 'the emasculated Jesus of the Qur'ān', and writes: 'Where are the words from the Cross . . . ? Where the triumph of the Resurrection from a grave which was not occupied? We have in the Qur'ān neither Galilee, nor Gethsemane; neither Nazareth nor Olivet . . . Is the Sermon on the Mount to be left to silence in the Muslim's world? Must the story of the Good Samaritan never be told there? The simple, human narrative of the prodigal son never mirror there the essence of waywardness and forgiveness?' With regard to the Qur'anic Jesus, he fears that 'the partial truth . . . forestalls its own completion'.[105]

Many Christian scholars express the view that for Muslims to apply some sort of higher criticism to the Qur'an is highly desirable; Watt states forthrightly that 'the methods of historical and literary criticism must be accepted'.[106] Küng feels that this will inevitably happen, and he refers to the fact that in Christianity and Judaism, too, there was at first considerable resistance to higher criticism which had to be overcome by a number of bold pioneering spirits, his assumption being that Muslim scholarship will follow the same trajectory.[107] He links the process of historical criticism of the Qur'an with that of secularization, which he sees as an inevitable result of the functional differentiation of modern society and a phenomenon to which Muslims are by no means immune. Islam's resistance to the legacy of the Enlightenment in terms of critical thought is compared to the former resistance of Catholicism, which in the end could not avoid absorbing the paradigm changes of both the Reformation and the Enlightenment.[108] Although Küng denies that historical criticism would necessarily lead to a weakening of faith,[109] it is clear that he envisages far-reaching consequences for it. In common with a number of other Christians, including Watt and Cragg, he feels that the Qur'anic penal laws, among other things, constitute part of the medieval legacy which is simply impracticable or unacceptable in the present day, and suggests: 'Instead of interpreting the Qur'ān as a collection of fixed maxims, rigid doctrines, and immutable statements of law which . . . must be slavishly reproduced and literally interpreted in all points . . . why not perceive the Qur'ān as a great prophetic witness to the one and only powerful and merciful God . . . ?'[110]

Several Christian thinkers acknowledge that there are strong reasons for Muslim reluctance to embark on higher criticism. Smith, drawing a parallel between Christ and the Qur'an, suggests that the Muslim equivalent of biblical criticism is not Qur'anic but Hadith criticism, and 'to look for historical criticism of the Qur'ān is rather like looking for a psychoanalysis of Jesus'.[111] Caspar's observance of the way in which the Muslim denial of a human element in revelation accounts for their reluctance to apply certain critical methods to their scripture was described above. With regard to the Muslim belief that the Qur'an represents the verbatim Word of God, Ford comments that Christians should not 'expect Muslims to forfeit a concept which, in the absence of a doctrine of Incarnation, provides for them a direct link to God'.[112]

Conclusions

Any Christian who chooses to study Islam as a Christian, relating it in some way to his or her own faith, and who wishes to do so with a measure of sympathy, has to maintain a delicate balance between acknowledging Muslims as fellow believers and recognizing and respecting their 'otherness'. To go too far in either direction is to entail opposing risks: the temptation to harmonize Muslim and Christian beliefs may lead to an undue Christianizing of the Islamic, while laying emphasis on the otherness of Islam may lead to alienation.

Much of the discussion described above is an intra-Christian phenomenon, i.e. Christians trying to relate to Islam from within their own conceptual framework, although some represents a deliberate attempt at *rapprochement* with Muslims. It is now no longer possible for Christians or others to write only for a non-Muslim readership; Charles Adams speaks of the 'moral responsibility' this lays on contemporary Islamicists, who must 'learn to speak in two realms of discourse at the same time', being sensitive in matters which are precious to others while at the same time satisfying the conditions of critical scholarship. Given that the application of critical methods to Islamic origins may itself be seen or experienced as an attack on the Qur'an or Muhammad, this poses 'extraordinarily intractable dilemmas'.[113]

Muslims are increasingly publishing their responses to the Christian study of Islam, and particular attention has been paid to two of the most prolific and well-known Christian Islamicists, Watt and Cragg; reactions to both are rather more negative than positive, and there is considerable distrust of their motives. A few brief quotations will have to suffice as examples, but it should be noted that the reviewers in question are highly educated individuals and most of them hold, or have held, academic posts. One reviewer says of Watt that his 'recent writings . . . show that his much-acclaimed courtesy and sympathy were part of a studied effort, more in the nature of a tactical compromise than any renunciation of the ultimate strategic aims of the Christian approach to Islam'; another finds some aspects of his scholarship to be 'reminiscent of the bigotry and hatred shown by Christian polemicists in the medieval period'.[114] Similarly, Cragg's more sympathetic treatment of Islam vis-à-vis some of his Christian predecessors is seen as 'evidence rather of changed tactics than of changed objectives'.[115] An extended review article on Cragg by Jamil Qureshi, a Muslim academic based in the UK, sees him as 'open to the charge of attempting not conversion but "subversion"'. He sees Cragg's approach as being in line with colonialist disregard for the opinions and values of the 'natives', and attributes his views on revelation to a Western bias, thus politicizing what others might see as a religious difference: 'For a European, man is the measure of *all* things: thus, a man made the Muslims' Book'.[116] Many Muslims (and some non-Muslims) would prefer it if Christians did not study Islam *as Christians* at all; the late Palestinian scholar A. L. Tibawi has said quite frankly that non-Muslims should 'leave matters of faith alone'.[117]

The issue of revelation highlights the difficulties inherent in any attempt at Muslim–Christian *rapprochement*, and illustrates the way in which attempts at conciliation on the part of Christians tend to be a rather unsatisfactory 'halfway house' from a Muslim point of view. To see the Qur'an as a unique piece of inspiration is not to see it as the final and complete revelation, and to see Muhammad as in some sense a prophet is not to see him as the seal of the prophets. The vast majority of Muslims are not prepared to compromise on the categorical distinction between that which originates with Muhammad and that which originates with God, i.e. the Qur'an in its entirety. A close observation of the Qur'anic use of the terms *waḥy* and *tanzīl* reveals a fairly consistent dissociation of the Prophet from the process of revelation, notwithstanding the verses which speak of the Qur'an as descending on his heart.[118] Reacting primarily to Cragg, Qureshi writes: 'A Christian would prefer it if the Qur'ān were a part of the *sīrah*, contained within human experience . . . The silence of the Prophet in the receipt of God's word, his non-participation in it, is essential to its universality'.[119]

All the thinkers reviewed in this section see Christian scripture or revelation as a combination of human and divine elements, and all go some way towards considering the Qur'an in the same light. However, since they do not subscribe to the Muslim theory of revelation – either for the Qur'an or for their own scriptures – their approaches, however well-meaning, are often seen by Muslims as potentially or actually subversive. Several thinkers draw attention to factors which relativize the human understanding of scripture, if not scripture itself; they are ready to apply such considerations to both the Bible and the Qur'an, but it remains the case that this is easier for Christians, for whom the absolute can still somehow be located in the contingent realm in the person of Jesus Christ.

Those who draw attention to parallels between the Qur'anic view of Christ or Christianity and certain strands of the Christian tradition, in particular the Nestorian, Ebionite, Gnostic and Jewish Christian elements, sometimes do so for irenical reasons. For Küng, for example, the possibility of Judaeo-Christian influence on Muhammad or the Qur'an lessens the divide between Christianity and Islam. Often, however, there are implications of 'influences' on the Qur'an which Muslims find offensive. Similarly those who offer positive affirmation of Muhammad sometimes stress his human greatness at the expense of his prophetic role according to Muslim understanding. Cragg, for example, sees the Muslim view of revelation as detracting from 'the personal genius of Muhammad'; Qureshi responds to this: 'Nothing could be more horrifying to a Muslim than hoisting the Prophet onto a Christian pedestal by making him the author of Islam'.[120]

It will already be apparent with reference to some of the Muslim opinions cited in chapter 4 that there is an overlap between some Christian views and some Muslim views at the modernist end of the Islamic spectrum. Christian Islamicists often refer to the work of liberal or modernist Muslim scholars such as Fazlur Rahman or Mahmoud Ayoub in support of their opinions; the need to find kindred voices within Muslim ranks leads to an 'intelligent neglect' of the issue of representativeness. A number of Muslims have called for a reading of the Qur'an which relates it more fully to its historical context in order to facilitate a more flexible interpretation which they, like Cragg, see as enhancing rather than detracting from its contemporary relevance.[121] Even the most extreme example of Christian interpretation, that of Basetti-Sani, has something like a counterpart in the Muslim world: the idea of a true and full interpretation of the Qur'an which can only now be uncovered, and the accompanying detachment of the Qur'an from Muslim tradition, resembles the thinking of Muhammad Mahmud Taha (d. 1985), founder of the Republican Brothers of the Sudan. Because of their radical discontinuity with mainstream Muslim understanding, Taha's ideas have gained very little acceptance beyond a small circle of followers; the possibility of Basetti-Sani's ideas gaining any acceptance at all among Muslims, even if mediated by sympathetic Christians as he envisaged, seems extremely remote. As far as future trends in Muslim interpretation are concerned, Seyyed Hossein Nasr represents mainstream Muslim thinking when he responds to Küng on this subject, strongly denying that Muslims will take the same path that Christians have taken.[122] For him it is a cause for regret that 'the application of rationalistic and empirical methods of research and so-called higher criticism have removed the sense of the sacred from the Bible', and he deplores the desacralization of the Qur'an through the application of 'Western methods irrelevant to Islam'.[123]

It is sometimes the attempts with the best intentions which lead Christians furthest from Muslims' own self-definition. Paradoxically, liberal Christians are generally those who are at one and the same time most eager to accommodate Islam and offer it recognition, and furthest from the mentality and approaches to religion of most Muslims. Smith is one of the most insistent that 'Islam is what Muslims say it is', and yet his own conception of Islam, as a non-reified and fluid entity, not entirely distinct from other religions but rather part of the flux of a wider religious tradition in history, is far removed from mainstream Muslim views and definitions of Islam. His prioritizing of the believer's account of his or her own faith ends in a subjectivism and a humanism to which few Muslims would subscribe; his assertion that meaning resides in the individual sit very uneasily with the fact that, as he himself is aware, Muslims have a strong and growing sense of the existence of an ideal, normative Islam. The phenomenological approach could thus be considered a two-edged sword from a Muslim point of view. Similarly, Watt's theological pluralism means that he is among the most forthright in considering Islam as an alternative path of salvation, but it also entails a de-emphasis of questions of truth and doctrine which is not welcomed by most Muslims. In his search for areas of commonality and desire for religious *rapprochement*, Watt applies his religious ideas equally to Christianity and Islam, rejecting, for example, many of the supernatural elements in both traditions and emphasizing the symbolic nature of religious language. One of his concerns is to defend religion in a secular world (as well as to defend Islam to a Western readership), and his apologia for religion is somewhat rationalistic, based on an implicit faith in the values of modern Western civilization in general and scientism in particular. Liberal by Christian standards, and applying his Christian liberalism to Islam, his understanding is far removed from the way in which the average Muslim views his or her own faith. Those who have been most ready to apply critical methods to their own tradition may too easily assume that the same must and will happen in Islam, or that religious law is a moribund entity. Küng is one who tends to underestimate the strong attachment that Muslims feel to the ideal of the comprehensiveness of the Sharī'a.

Some of the changes taking place in the Christian study of Islam are a result of increased contact with Muslims. Caspar describes his evolution from the application of fairly rigid neo-Thomistic theological categories to a much more flexible, albeit still self-consciously Catholic, approach; he says this change was largely due to profound friendships with Muslims, through which he was able to appreciate, or as he puts it, to touch with his finger 'the density and compactness of their faith . . . their trust in God in suffering as well as joy'. He comments on the chasm between such experiences and 'theological reasoning devised in an office, far from living realities', and he feels that there is an element of risk involved in such profound human encounters – that it is not just one's theology that is at stake, but one's faith.[124] Cragg does not wish to indulge in 'a scholarship that exempts itself from the patient toils of due relationships'; for him, 'a positive relation to Muhammad' is 'precisely in the name and in the pursuit of a positive relation with Muslims'.[125] Arnaldez feels that it is not possible to be close to Muslims unless one recognizes the religious value of their teachings.[126]

One should not overlook the possibility that friendships with Muslims might have not just an emotional but also a philosophical and epistemological impact.[127] Questions about the nature of truth may be raised – if expressing what one believes to be true is hurtful to others, this may lead to the search for a way in which truth and love can be reconciled. It is partly in order to avoid this seeming impasse (but also for academic reasons) that some Christian scholars, including Smith and Bijlefeld, prefer to pursue a phenomenological approach to the Qur'an that refrains from attempting to make sense of Islamic phenomenona outside an Islamic framework, and therefore observes certain self-imposed limitations.

In the discussion of Christian interpretation of the Qur'an, the language and phrases used are often emotive if not prejudicial: the phrase 'Christianizing the Islamic' for example, first used by Adams of Cragg, has somewhat imperialistic overtones. Few stop to unpack the hermeneutical issues in sufficient detail. One who attempts to do so is Christopher Lamb, in the context of his study on Cragg;[128] he believes that recent developments in hermeneutical thinking, particularly by Gadamer in his *Truth and Method* (London: Sheed & Ward, 1979), tend to legitimate the bringing of Christian questions to Islamic material.[129] One reason for this is the impossibility of distinguishing between understanding, on the one hand, and interpretation or evaluation, on the other – incidentally the very distinction which phenomenologists of religion attempt to uphold. The act of understanding is not a passive one but involves simultaneous interpretation, inasmuch as readers understand the text in the light of their previous experience and knowledge. This implies that any reader, whether Christian, Muslim or other, cannot avoid consciously or unconsciously bringing his or her own tradition (or a personal version of it) to bear on any text. Given that no text can be perfectly restored, as it were, to its original environment nor restricted to a hypothetical 'original' sense, Gadamer suggests that historical distance from the text can be an asset rather than a hindrance. Lamb observes that in the case of Cragg, cultural and communal distance might be analogous to historical distance. Among Lamb's conclusions from the foregoing are the observations that if an analogy is drawn with literary criticism (although Muslims may wish to question the analogy), the only prerequisite for an interpreter would be a serious engagement with the text; and that if one disallows Cragg's approach to the Qur'an on the grounds that he does not belong to the Muslim community, one would have to disallow virtually the whole Western scholarly venture in the study of non-Christian religious traditions.

Notes

1.   The most substantial of these are Bijlefeld's published doctoral thesis, *De Islam als Na-Christelijke Religie: een Onderzoek naar de Theologische Beoordeling van de Islam, in het Bijzonder in de Twintigste Eeuw* (Islam as a post-Christian religion: an inquiry into the theological evaluation of Islam, mainly in the twentieth century), and Moubarac, *Recherches sur la pensée chrétienne et l'Islam dans les temps modernes et à l'époque contemporaine.*

2.   For a more exhaustive list see Kraan, 'Muslim–Christian relations and Christian Study Centres', pp. 173ff.

3.   In preparing this chapter I benefited from reading a forthcoming article by C. Troll, 'Changing Catholic Views of Islam', to be published in J. Waardenburg (ed.), *Christianity and Islam: Mutual Perceptions since the Mid-20th Century* (Kampen: Kok Agora, 1997).

4.   Moubarac, *Recherches*, p. 361.

5.   Cragg, *The House of Islam*, p. 5; the anthology is called *Alive to God: Muslim and Christian Prayer* (London: Oxford University Press).

6.   Caspar, *Traité de théologie musulmane*, p. 96.

7.   Bijlefeld, *De Islam als Na-Christelijke Religie*: this is only available in Dutch but it contains a summary in English.

8.   Moubarac, 'La Pensée chrétienne et l'Islam', p. 47.

9.   Arnaldez, *Three Messengers for One God*, p. 2.

10. *Traité de théologie musulmane*, vol.1, pp. 96–7.

11. Ibid.

12. Smith, 'Muslim–Christian Relations', p. 20; see also *On Understanding Islam*, pp. 248ff.

13. Ipema, 'The Islam Interpretations of Duncan B. McDonald, Samuel M. Zwemer, A. Kenneth Cragg and Wilfred C. Smith', p. 58.

14. The last two quotations are cited in ibid., p. 60.

15. Jomier, *How to Understand Islam*, p. 160.

16. Küng, *Christianity and the World Religions*, p. 127; see also his 'Christianity and World Religions', pp. 91–4.

17. The nineteenth-century English scholar Charles Forster also used this approach (see Bennett, *Victorian Images of Islam*, chapter 2), although Massignon was unaware of this.

18. *Traité de théologie musulmane*, pp. 80–1.

19. See Ledit's *Mahomet, Israël et le Christ* (Paris: La Colombe, 1956), and Hayek's *Le Mystère d'Ismael* (Paris: Mame, 1964).

20. See especially Moubarac's *Abraham dans le Coran. L'Histoire d'Abraham dans le Coran et la naissance de l'Islam* (Paris: Vrin, 1958).

21. 'La Pensée chrétienne et l'Islam', pp. 49–51.

22. *Traité de théologie musulmane*, pp. 98–100.

23. Bijlefeld, 'Controversies around the Qur'anic Ibrāhīm Narrative', pp. 90–1.

24. Watt, *Islam and Christianity Today*, pp. 60–1.

25. Jones, 'Wilfred Cantwell Smith and Kenneth Cragg on Islam as a Way of Salvation', pp. 106–7.

26. Caspar, 'Pour une vision chrétienne du coran', p. 26.

27. *Cours de théologie musulmane*, p. 17.

28. 'La Pensée chrétienne et l'Islam', p. 47.

29. *Cours de théologie musulmane*, p. 17.

30. Caspar, 'Une rencontre avec l'Islam', pp. 19–23.

31. Zaehner, *At Sundry Times*, p. 160; he actually uses the word 'whitewash' in all three cases.

32. Watt, *Muhammad at Mecca*, p. 52.

33. *Traité de théologie musulmane*, pp. 64–5.

34. Ibid., pp. 101, 64.

35. See Moubarac's *Abraham dans le Coran* and Bijlefeld's 'Controversies around the Qur'anic Ibrāhīm Narrative'.

36. Cragg, *Returning to Mount Hira*', p. 45.

37. Cragg, *Muhammad and the Christian*, p. 23.

38. Cragg, *The Event of the Qur'ān*, pp. 129–30.

39. *Returning to Mount Hira*', pp. 46–7.

40. Cragg, 'Being Christian and Being Muslim', p. 206.

41. Cragg, *Christianity in World Perspective*, p. 128.

42. *Muhammad and the Christian*, p. 51.

43. Ibid., pp. 31, 27.

44. See on this Kerr, '"He Walked in the Path of the Prophets"', pp. 429–30.

45. From Massignon's personal correspondence, quoted in Caspar, *Traité de théologie musulmane*, p. 114.

46. This is used by Ledit in his *Mahomet, Israël et le Christ*.

47. Caspar, *Traité de théologie musulmane*, p. 100.

48. Ibid., p. 101.

49. See Jomier, *How to Understand Islam*, pp. 146–7, and Arnaldez, 'Dialogue Islamo-Chrétien', p. 15.
50. Watt, *Muhammad's Mecca*, p. 1.
51. Watt, *Muslim–Christian Encounters*, p. 138.
52. Watt, *Truth in the Religions*, p. 83.
53. Bijlefeld, 'Islamic Studies within the Perspective of the History of Religions', pp. 5–6.
54. Caspar, 'Parole de dieu', pp. 54–5.
55. Ibid., pp. 34–5.
56. *Pour un regard chrétien sur l'Islam*, p. 102; *Traité de théologie musulmane*, p. 95.
57. *Pour un regard chrétien sur l'Islam*, p. 105.
58. Ibid., p. 198.
59. For a sharp critique of both Watt and Cragg with particular reference to their view of revelation, see D'Souza, 'Christian Approaches to the Study of Islam'.
60. See, e.g., *Muhammad at Mecca*, p. x.
61. Ibid., pp. 83, 29.
62. Watt, *Muhammad: Prophet and Statesman*, p. 19.
63. Watt, *Islamic Fundamentalism and Modernity,* pp. 82–3.
64. Ibid., p. 83.
65. Watt, *Islamic Revelation in the Modern World*, p. 8.
66. Watt explicitly bases himself on Thornton's ideas in *Islamic Revelation in the Modern World*.
67. *Islamic Fundamentalism and Modernity*, pp. 82–3; see also *Muhammad's Mecca*, p. 68.
68. *Islamic Revelation in the Modern World*, p. 109.
69. *Muhammad: Prophet and Statesman*, pp. 238–40.
70. *Returning to Mount Hira'*, p. 50.
71. *Pour un regard chrétien sur l'Islam*, p. 35.
72. 'Christianity and World Religions', p. 94.
73. E.g., Jomier, 'The Kingdom of God in Islam', p. 271.
74. F. P. Ford, 'The Qur'ān as Sacred Scripture', pp. 162–3.
75. Basetti-Sani, 'Christian Symbolism and Christological Typology', p. 143.
76. Ibid., pp. 115–31.
77. See respectively Basetti-Sani, *The Koran in the Light of Christ*, pp. 112–5; 'Christian Symbolism and Christological Typology', p. 121; *The Koran in the Light of Christ*, p. 75.
78. With regard to the five letters preceding Sura 19, Basetti-Sani states that 'according to the very satisfactory explanation given by Morris S. Seale' they stand respectively for the Arabic words for priest, temple, John, Jesus and Truthful ('Christian Symbolism and Christological Typology', pp. 124–5).
79. Adams, 'Islamic Religious Tradition', p. 39.
80. *Muhammad and the Christian*, p. 12.
81. Cragg, 'Tadabbur al-Qur'ān', p. 181.
82. *The Event of the Qur'ān*, p. 20.
83. *Muhammad and the Christian*, pp. 119–20.

84. Ibid., p. 13.
85. *The Event of the Qur'ān*, pp. 16, 23.
86. *Muhammad and the Christian*, p. 11; 'Taddabur al-Qur'ān', p. 182.
87. *The Event of the Qur'ān*, pp. 20–1.
88. Cragg, *Sandals at the Mosque*, p. 90.
89. *Muhammad and the Christian*, p. 136; 'Islam and Incarnation', p. 134.
90. 'Temple Gairdner's Legacy', p. 166.
91. Lamb, 'The Call to Retrieval', p. 200. At the time of writing, the book based on this dissertation, *The Call to Retrieval: The Missionary Theology of Kenneth Cragg* (London: Grey Seal, 1997), was forthcoming.
92. Ibid., pp. 222–7.
93. Bijlefeld, 'The Danger of "Christianizing" our Partners in the Dialogue', p. 177.
94. 'La Pensée chrétienne et l'Islam', p. 45.
95. *Christianity and the World Religions*, p. 110.
96. For a detailed description and analysis of Muslim interpretations of this verse see B. Lawson, 'The Crucifixion of Jesus in the Qur'ān and Qur'ānic Commentary: A Historical Survey' (*BHMIIS*, 10, 1991).
97. *Traité de théologie musulmane*, pp. 70–1.
98. *Jesus and the Muslim*, pp. 178, 167–9.
99. *The Koran in the Light of Christ*, pp. 164, 172.
100. *At Sundry Times*, p. 212.
101. Ibid., pp. 203, 209.
102. *Bible et Coran*, pp. 39–43.
103. *Traité de théologie musulmane*, pp. 71, 70.
104. 'Christianity and World Religions', p. 89.
105. Cragg, *Call of the Minaret*, pp. 262, 254.
106. *Islamic Fundamentalism and Modernity*, p. 88.
107. 'Christianity and World Religions', p. 120.
108. *Christianity and the World Religions*, pp. 52–3.
109. 'Christianity and World Religions', pp. 120–1.
110. *Christianity and the World Religions*, p. 61; 'Christianity and World Religions', p. 87.
111. *Islam in Modern History*, p. 18, fn. 13.
112. 'The Qur'ān as Sacred Scripture', p. 162.
113. Adams, 'The History of Religions', p. 189–90.
114. See, respectively, P. Manzoor's review of Watt's *Islam and Christianity Today* (*MWBR*, 6, 1, 1985), p. 7, and Buaben, *Image of the Prophet Muḥammad in the West*, p. xv, from the foreword by Muhammad Manazir Ahsan.
115. A. L. Tibawi's review of *The Dome and the Rock* (*IQ*, 12, 1968), p. 120.
116. Qureshi, ' "Alongsidedness – In Good Faith?" ', pp. 203–4, 253. Lamb reviews Muslim responses to Cragg in 'The Call to Retrieval', pp. 188ff.
117. Tibawi, 'English-Speaking Orientalists', p. 32. See also on Watt and Cragg, among others, Tibawi's 'Second Critique of English-Speaking Orientalists' (*IQ*, 23, 1979).
118. D'Souza's critique of Cragg and Watt incorporates a brief study which convincingly demonstrates this point: see 'Christian Approaches to the Study of Islam', pt. 2, pp. 56–62.

119. J. Qureshi, Review of *The Pen and the Faith* (*MWBR*, 7, 4, 1987).

120. See Cragg, *The Event of the Qur'ān*, p. 21, and Qureshi, '"Alongsidedness – In Good Faith?"', p. 253.

121. In addition to Fazlur Rahman, one could mention the Iranian scholar Abdolkarim Sorush and the Egyptians Muhammad Khalafallah and Nasr Abu Zayd. All have engendered a degree of controversy.

122. Section by Nasr in Küng, 'Christianity and World Religions', pp. 123–4.

123. Nasr, 'Comments on a Few Theological Issues in the Islamic–Christian Dialogue', p. 461.

124. 'Une rencontre avec l'Islam', pp. 20, 16.

125. *The Event of the Qur'ān*, p. 20; *Muhammad and the Christian*, p. 94.

126. Arnaldez, 'Dialogue islamo-chrétien', p. 15.

127. I am indebted to David Kerr for this insight.

128. 'The Call to Retrieval', pp. 200–8.

129. He does however distinguish between the approach of Cragg, who acknowledges the status of the Qur'an for Muslims and allows himself to be challenged by the text, and that of Basetti-Sani, who ignores 'the proper objectivity of the Quranic text' and tries to effect a premature 'fusion of horizons' (ibid., p. 211).

CONCLUSION

Throughout this study, the perceived differences between Islam and Christianity, whether polemically expressed or not, have tended to emerge as a series of inverse mirror images. To Muslims, the Christian view of humankind may seem pessimistic and lacking in dignity; Christians' view of God may seem sentimental; and their view of religion and state appears politically irresponsible. Conversely, to Christians, the Muslim view of humankind may appear over-confident in humans' own ability to follow the right path and attain salvation; Muslims' view of God may seem abstract and impersonal; and their view of religion and state may be seen as utopian, or as confusing the sacred with the secular. The list could be greatly extended. In each case there is an internal logic binding the various elements together which is difficult to break into or disturb from the outside, as it were. If one wishes to indulge in polemics, almost every accusation has a counter-accusation. Even given a sincere desire to be fair, one is likely to give greater weight to elements which are most prominent in one's own tradition, such as law or social institutions in Islam, or God's redemptive love in Christianity, and find the other wanting in comparison.

One of the reasons why Muslims and Christians often talk past each other is that in evaluating religious phenomena they apply different criteria, which arise from essentially different fundamental categories. One of the biggest obstacles to understanding is a contrasting perception of what constitutes a 'religion'. Muslims often have a highly reified view of Islam; religious institutions such as the five pillars are seen as intrinsic to the origins of Islam, whereas for Christians, certain rites and festivals developed over time and there is greater variety in their observance. Christian thinkers have sometimes drawn a contrast between religion and revelation, the latter being God's downward initiative towards humans while the former is humans' necessarily imperfect upward search for God. On this understanding, Christianity as a social and historical phenomenon is flawed, as are other religions, and to be distinguished from the gospel, or the 'good news' which God revealed in Christ. For Muslims, religion incorporates not just faith, ritual and ethics but also culture, government and law; the Qur'anic word for religion, *dīn*, is sometimes translated as 'way of life'. By Islamic standards, Christianity seems rather inadequate as a religion; by Christian standards, Islam over-prescribes for its followers, and may seem regimented.

Similarly, doctrine is seen as having different roles in Islam and Christianity. For Muslims it is something that is revealed directly by God in human language; hence the Qur'an itself is the main source of doctrine, which is relatively simple, the essential elements being *tawḥīd* and the prophethood of Muhammad. For Christians, it is more often seen as an inevitably flawed human attempt to express eternal truths in a language accessible to the intended audience; an element of cultural conditioning is taken for granted. On this understanding, doctrinal elaboration or evolution is a natural outcome of the need to present the faith in culturally meaningful terms to each generation. The influence of Greek thought on the early development of Christian theology, or even of paganism on Christian rites and festivals, can be acknowledged within a Christian framework because it is not seen as touching on the essential core of religion or faith. It is generally accepted that Paul was the pioneer of Christian systematic theology and to that extent elaborated on certain doctrines which may be seen as implicit in the Gospels, even if not all Christians would be happy to describe him as the 'founder' of Christianity.

The way in which history is viewed is also different on either side. Christians do not tend to see Christian history as any kind of an ideal, because 'history' is generally the history of government and rule, and because the Kingdom of God is only ever partially realized in this world. Muslims, for whom the Islamic state or caliphate can represent – in theory at least – an ideal system (although not a utopia), and for whom the idea of religious government is acceptable, are more likely to see Islamic history in a positive light and are more willing to identify themselves with it. The Christian argument with respect to the aberrations of Christian history, that a religion *must* be divine to have survived such vicissitudes and scandalous representatives, is probably not one that would appeal to many Muslims.

Because of these fundamentally different categories, criticism across religious boundaries often misses the mark. An example of this is the Muslim doctrine of *taḥrīf*, usually understood to mean that the Jewish and Christian scriptures have been 'altered' and 'corrupted'. It presupposes a view of revelation that Christians do not share: that it originally consisted of words spoken directly by God and channelled through a passive human mediator. The fact that the Bible is mainly in the form of human narrative and does not even purport to fit in with this view of revelation requires an explanation for Muslims, but not for Christians. Things which appear self-evidently detrimental to Muslims employing Islamic criteria, such as evolution in doctrine or ritual, diversity in theological thought or in the presentation of Jesus in the four Gospels, are not so for Christians, and may even be seen in positive terms. The same is true of many Christian criticisms of Islam, for example regarding the military role of Muhammad.

Thus far the picture is one of symmetry, or rather inverse symmetry. However, the ways in which Christians and Muslims relate to each other are not entirely reciprocal, and some of the reasons for this are intrinsic rather than incidental. While on the face of it Muslim recognition of Jesus and Christianity appears easier than the reverse, for chronological reasons, there are other considerations which weigh in the opposite direction. Christians applying their view of revelation (incorporating a human element) to the Qur'an, can accord a measure of recognition to it; Muslims applying their view of revelation (wholly divine) to the Bible, cannot easily reciprocate. Christian theological understandings of revelation and prophecy, particularly in the contemporary period, do not necessarily exclude extra-biblical or post-biblical witnesses to the truth. Muslim recognition of pre-Qur'anic revelations, on the other hand, is tempered by the consideration that they are not believed to have been preserved in their original form.

When it comes to interpretation of each other's scriptures, there is a similar imbalance; biblical interpretation is something which Muslims have always felt at liberty to engage in, even without knowledge of biblical Greek or Hebrew. This is not seen as giving any corresponding right to Christians to interpret the Qur'an, since Muslims are, according to their own beliefs, in a position to interpret the Bible (or such of the authentic text as remains) in the light of God's later, corrective dispensation – Islam and the Qur'an. Such views obviously counteract attempts on the part of Christians either to convey to Muslims their own understanding of the Bible or to establish reciprocity or equality in the sphere of scriptural interpretation.

If Christians studying Islam are faced with the twin dangers of over-harmonizing or alienation, as observed in chapter 5, for most Muslims approaches to Christianity are already polarized into the two extremes: original, true Christianity is largely subsumed under Islam, while historical Christianity is alien and other. The comparative and phenomenological approaches to the study of religion have potential implications for both Christian study of Islam and Muslim study of Christianity, but they have as yet scarcely impinged on the latter. Although several Muslim thinkers do find an Islamic basis for some kind of religious pluralism, up to the present there is little that one could describe as an explicit or developed Islamic rationale for an empathetic treatment of Christianity which might correspond to certain theological ideas that have been used, and not only by liberals, in the Christian context. These include the universality of the Logos, the ubiquitous presence of the Holy Spirit, and the ideas of 'self-emptying' (*kenosis*) and incarnational theology – God's readiness to take on human garb being echoed in humans' readiness to walk in others' shoes.[1] However, the fact that Muslims have compelling Islamic reasons for believing that their view of Christianity is the true one need not in itself preclude an empirical or sympathetic study of Christianity on its own terms, any more than the conflicting truth-claims of the two faiths bar Christians from empathetic study of Islam.

For almost all the authors reviewed in this book, there is no question of syncretism or glossing over the differences between the two faiths, and the differences are seen as concerning essentials rather than secondary matters. It is sometimes assumed that when religious and theological misunderstandings are cleared up, Muslims and Christians will automatically enjoy more cordial relations. This needs to be balanced by the realization that when all is said and done, even given a relatively sound understanding of Christian doctrine, there is a good chance that a Muslim will still be genuinely repelled and even offended by it. One sometimes encounters – not only on the part of Muslims, but especially so – a kind of aesthetic aversion to central Christian truths, particularly the Crucifixion. Muslim rejection of Christian beliefs cannot always be attributed to misunderstanding, obtuseness or polemicism. The same would have to be true, *mutatis mutandis*, of Christians who find it difficult to see in the Muhammad of history an ideal model of human conduct, or who have reservations about parts of the Qur'an. This is not necessarily as inauspicious for Muslim–Christian relations as it may seem; it may be existentially impossible wholly to suspend judgement in areas which directly impinge on one's own truth-claims, but as in life generally, one does not need to denigrate those with whom one disagrees.

This book has observed considerable variety in Muslim responses to Christianity as well as Christian responses to Islam; there is little doubt that there are other paths yet to be explored. For those who have a religious faith, there is a tension between believing that they have received a true revelation, and acknowledging that unlike God, humans can know only partially in this world – even if they anticipate a day when they will see not through a glass darkly but face to face.

Note

1.   See, e.g., Neill, *Crises of Belief*, pp. 32–3; Newbigin, 'The Gospel Among the Religions', pp. 18–19.

GLOSSARY OF ARABIC AND ISLAMIC TERMS

ahl al-kitāb	the 'People of the Book', especially Jews and Christians
da'wah	'call' or 'invitation', i.e. to Islam
Hadith	a report containing a saying or action of Muhammad; a collective term for these reports
Hijra	the migration of the Muslims in 622 from Mecca to Medina
Mahdi	Messianic figure who will appear at the end of the world to usher in a new order
Sharī'a	Islamic law
shirk	polytheism, or 'associating partners with God'
Sira	biography of Muhammad
Sunna	the model behaviour of the Prophet
taḥrīf	scriptural alteration or corruption
tanzīl	revelation
tawḥid	the Oneness or unity of God
waḥy	revelation

SELECT BIBLIOGRAPHY

Books and Theses

Abbott, W. (ed.) *The Documents of Vatican II*. London: Geoffrey Chapman, 1966.

Abdul-Haqq, A. *Sharing your Faith with a Muslim*. Minneapolis: Bethany House, 1980.

Ahmed, A. *Postmodernism and Islam: Predicament and Promise*. London: Routledge, 1992.

Ahmed, J. *Christianity: Its Appeal, Reaction and Failure*. 3rd ed. Karachi: International Islamic Publishers, 1994.

Ajijola, A. *Myth of the Cross*. Chicago: Kazi Publications, 1979.

Akhtar, S. *A Faith for all Seasons: Islam and Western Modernity*. London: Bellew, 1990.

—— *The Final Imperative: An Islamic Theology of Liberation*. London: Bellew, 1991.

—— *The Light in the Enlightenment: Christianity and the Secular Heritage*. London: Grey Seal, 1990.

Ali, A. Y. (trans.) *The Holy Qur'ān: Text, Translation and Commentary*. Leicester: The Islamic Foundation, 1975.

Anderson, G. and Stransky, T. (eds) *Mission Trends No. 5: Faith Meets Faith*. Grand Rapids: Eerdmans, 1981.

Anderson, N. *God's Law and God's Love: An Essay in Comparative Religion*. London: Collins, 1980.

—— *Islam in the Modern World: A Christian Perspective*. Rev. ed. Leicester: Apollos, 1992.

—— *The World's Religions*. 3rd ed. London: Inter-Varsity Fellowship, 1957.

Ansari, M. *Islam and Christianity in the Modern World*. 4th ed. Karachi: World Federation of Islamic Mission, 1965.

Arkoun, M. *Rethinking Islam: Common Questions, Uncommon Answers*, trans. R. Lee. Boulder: Westview Press, 1994.

—— *Rethinking Islam Today*. Washington: Georgetown University (Center for Contemporary Arab Studies), 1987.

Armstrong, K. *Muhammad: A Biography of the Prophet*. San Francisco: HarperCollins, 1992.

Arnaldez, R. *Mahomet*. Paris: Editions Séghers, 1970.

—— *Three Messengers for One God*. Notre Dame, Ind.: University of Notre Dame Press, 1994.

Asad, T. *Genealogies of Religion: Discipline and Reasons of Power in Christianity and Islam*. Baltimore: Johns Hopkins University Press, 1993.

Askari, H. *Spiritual Quest: An Interreligious Dimension*. Pudsey, W. Yorks: Seven Mirrors Publishing House, 1991.

'Ata ur-Rahim, M. J*esus, Prophet of Islam*. Elmhurst, New York: Tahrike Tarsil Qur'an, 1991.

Al-Attas, S. *Islam, Secularism and the Philosophy of the Future*. London: Mansell Publishing, 1985.

Aziz-us-Samad, U. *A Comparative Study of Christianity and Islam*. Delhi: Noor Publishing House, 1986.

Azhar, A. *Christianity in History*. Lahore: Sh. Muhammad Ashraf, 1991.

Badawi, M. A. Z. *Islam in Britain*. London: Ta-Ha Publishers, 1981.

Barelvi, M. *Islam and World Religions*. 2nd ed. Lahore: Islamic Publications, 1983.

Basetti-Sani, G. *The Koran in the Light of Christ: A Christian Interpretation of the Sacred Book of Islam*. Chicago: Franciscan Herald Press, 1977.

Bennett, C. *Victorian Images of Islam*. London: Grey Seal, 1993.

Bewley, A. *The Key to the Future*. London: Ta-Ha Publishers, 1992.

Bijlefeld, W. *De Islam als Na-Christelijke Religie: een Onderzoek naar de Theologische Beoordeling van de Islam, in het Bijzonder in de Twintigste Eeuw*. The Hague: Van Keulen, 1959.

Brown, D. *The Way of the Prophet*. London: Highway Press, 1962.

Buaben, J. *Image of the Prophet Muḥammad in the West: A Study of Muir, Margoliouth and Watt*. Leicester: The Islamic Foundation, 1996.

Bucaille, M. *The Bible, the Qur'an and Science: The Holy Scriptures Examined in the Light of Modern Knowledge*, trans. A. Pannell and M. Bucaille. Indianapolis: American Trust Publications, 1978.

al-Bukhārī, Muhammad b. Ismā'īl. *Ṣaḥīḥ al-Bukhārī*, trans. M. Khan. 9 vols. Gujranwala, Pakistan: Sethi Straw Board Mills, 1973.

Burnett, D. *Clash of Worlds*. Eastbourne: MARC, 1990.

Caspar, R. *Cours de théologie musulmane*. Rome: PISAI, 1993.

—— *Pour un regard chrétien sur l'Islam*. Paris: Centurion, 1990.

—— *Traité de théologie musulmane*. Vol. 1: *Histoire de la pensée religieuse musulmane*. Rome: PISAI, 1987.

Castro, E., Ahmad, K. and Kerr, D. (eds) *Christian Mission and Islamic Da'wah: Proceedings of the Chambésy Dialogue Consultation*. Leicester: The Islamic Foundation, 1982.

Chapman, C. *Cross and Crescent: Responding to the Challenge of Islam*. Leicester: Inter-Varsity Press, 1995.

Charfi, A. M. *Al-Fikr al-Islāmī fi'l-Radd 'ala al-Naṣārā ila Nihāyat al-Qarn al-Rābi'*. Tunis: Al-Mu'assassat al-Waṭaniyya li'l-Kitāb, 1986.

Cooper, A. (ed.) *Ishmael, My Brother: A Christian Introduction to Islam*. 2nd ed. Bromley, Kent: MARC, 1993.

Cragg, K. *The Call of the Minaret*. New York: Oxford University Press, 1965.

—— *Christianity in World Perspective*. London: Lutterworth Press, 1968.

—— *The Event of the Qur'ān: Islam in its Scripture*. Oxford: Oneworld, 1994 (first published 1971).

—— *The House of Islam*. California: Dickenson, 1969.

—— *Jesus and the Muslim: An Exploration*. London: George Allen & Unwin, 1985.

—— *Muhammad and the Christian: A Question of Response*. New York: Orbis, 1984.

—— *The Pen and the Faith: Eight Modern Muslim Writers and the Qur'ān*. London: George Allen & Unwin, 1985.

—— *Returning to Mount Hira': Islam in Contemporary Terms*. London: Bellew, 1994.

—— *Sandals at the Mosque*. London: SCM Press, 1959.

—— *Troubled by Truth: Life-Studies in Inter-Faith Concern*. Durham: Pentland Press, 1992.

Daniel, N. *Islam and the West: The Making of an Image*. Rev. ed. Oxford: Oneworld, 1993.

D'Costa, G. *Christian Uniqueness Reconsidered: The Myth of a Pluralistic Theology of Religions*. Maryknoll, NY: Orbis, 1990.

Denffer, A. von. *Some Reflections on Dialogue between Christians and Muslims*. Leicester: The Islamic Foundation, 1980.

Denffer, A. von and Siddiqui, A. *Christian Literature for Muslims*. Leicester: The Islamic Foundation, 1985.

Durrani, M. H. *The Qur'anic Facts about Jesus*. Delhi: Noor Publishing House, 1992.

Esposito, J. (ed.) *The Oxford Encyclopedia of the Modern Islamic World*. 4 vols. New York: Oxford University Press, 1995.

Al-Faruqi, I. *Christian Ethics: A Historical and Systematic Analysis of its Dominant Ideas*. Toronto: McGill University Press, 1967.

—— *Islam*. Illinois: Argus Communications, 1979.

—— *On Arabism: 'Urubah and Religion*. Amsterdam: Djambatan, 1962.

Gardet, L. and Anawati, M. *Introduction à la théologie musulmane: essai de théologie comparée*. Paris: Vrin, 1948.

Gaudeul, J. *Encounters and Clashes: Islam and Christianity in History*. 2 vols. Rome: PISAI, 1990.

Geisler, N. and Saleeb, A. *Answering Islam: The Crescent in the Light of the Cross*. Grand Rapids: Baker Books, 1994.

Gilchrist, J. *Jam' al-Qur'an: The Codification of the Qur'an Text*. Warley, West Midlands: TMFMT, 1989.

—— *Muhammad: The Prophet of Islam*. Benoni: Muslim Evangelism Resource Centre of Southern Africa, 1994.

Goddard, H. *Muslim Perceptions of Christianity*. London: Grey Seal, 1995.

Goldsmith, M. *Islam and Christian Witness*. London: Hodder and Stoughton, 1982.

Groupe de Recherches Islamo-Chrétien, *The Challenge of the Scriptures: The Bible and the Qur'an*, trans. S. Brown. New York: Orbis, 1990.

Haddad, S. *The Principles of Belief in the Qur'an and the Bible*. Pittsburgh, Pa.: Dorrance, 1992.

Haddad, Y. Y. and Haddad, W. Z. (eds) *Christian–Muslim Encounters*. Gainsville, Florida: University Press of Florida, 1995.

Hamidullah, M. *Introduction to Islam*. London: Muslim Welfare House, 1979.

Hick. J. and Askari, H. (eds) *The Experience of Religious Diversity*. London: Gower, 1985.

Hodgson, M. *The Venture of Islam: Conscience and History in a World Civilization*. 3 vols. Chicago: University of Chicago Press, 1974.

Hourani, A. *Europe and the Middle East*. London: Macmillan, 1980.

—— *Islam in European Thought*. Cambridge: Cambridge University Press, 1991.

Ipema, P. 'The Islam Interpretations of Duncan B. McDonald, Samuel M. Zwemer, A. Kenneth Cragg and Wilfred C. Smith: An Analytical Comparison and Evaluation'. Ph.D. diss., Hartford Seminary Foundation, 1971.

Izetbegovic, A. *Islam Between East and West*. Indianapolis: American Trust Publications, 1993.

Jameelah, M. *Islam Versus Ahl al-Kitab: Past and Present*. Delhi: Taj Company, 1989.

Jomier, J. *Bible et Coran*. Paris: Cerf, 1959.

—— *How to Understand Islam*, trans. J. Bowden. London: SCM Press, 1989.

Kimball, C. 'Striving Together in the Way of God: Muslim Participation in Christian–Muslim Dialogue'. Ph.D. diss., Harward Divinity School, 1987.

Kitagawa, J. *The Comparative Study of Religions*. New York: Columbia University Press, 1958.

Knitter, P. *No Other Name? A Critical Survey of Christian Attitudes Towards the Religions*. London: SCM Press, 1985.

Küng, H. et al. *Christianity and the World Religions: Paths of Dialogue with Islam, Hinduism, and Buddhism*, trans. P. Heinegg. London: Fount Paperbacks, 1987.

Lamb, C. 'The Call to Retrieval: Kenneth Cragg's Christian Vocation to Islam'. Ph.D. thesis, University of Birmingham, 1987.

Lazarus-Yafeh, H. *Intertwined Worlds: Medieval Islam and Bible Criticism*. Princeton: Princeton University Press, 1992.

Lewis, B. *Cultures in Conflict: Christians, Muslims, and Jews in the Age of Discovery*. Oxford: Oxford University Press, 1995.

—— *The Muslim Discovery of Europe*. London: Weidenfeld & Nicolson, 1982.

Lings, M. *Muhammad: His Life Based on the Earliest Sources*. London: Unwin Paperbacks, 1986.

Lochhead, D. *The Dialogical Imperative: A Christian Reflection on Interfaith Encounter*. Maryknoll, NY: Orbis, 1988.

McAuliffe, J. D. *Qur'ānic Christians: An Analysis of Classical and Modern Exegesis*. Cambridge: Cambridge Unversity Press, 1991.

McCurry, D (ed.) *The Gospel and Islam: A 1978 Compendium*. Monrovia: MARC, 1979.

Malik, C. *God and Man in Contemporary Islamic Thought*. Beirut: American University of Beirut, 1972.

Maqsood, R. *The Separated Ones: Jesus, the Pharisees and Islam*. London: SCM Press, 1991.

Marshall, D. 'Isma'il al-Faruqi and Christianity'. MA diss., University of Birmingham, 1988.

Meherally, A. *Understanding the Bible through Koranic Messages*. Burnaby, Canada: A.M. Trust, 1989.

Miller, W. *A Christian Response to Islam*. Bromley, Kent: STL Books, 1981.

Moubarac, Y. *Recherches sur la pensée chrétienne et l'Islam dans les temps modernes et à l'époque contemporaine*. Beirut: Université Libanaise, 1977.

Moucarry, C. *Islam and Christianity at the Crossroads*. Tring: Lion, 1988.

Muir, W. *The Life of Mohammed*. Edinburgh: John Grant, 1923.

Murad, K. *Da'wah Among Non-Muslims in the West: Some Conceptual and Methodological Aspects*. Leicester: The Islamic Foundation, 1986.

Musk, B. *Passionate Believing: The 'Fundamentalist' Face of Islam*. Tunbridge Wells: Monarch, 1992.

—— *Touching the Soul of Islam: Sharing the Gospel in Muslim Cultures*. Crowborough: MARC, 1995.

—— *The Unseen Face of Islam: Sharing the Gospel with Ordinary Muslims*. Eastbourne: MARC, 1989.

Muslim, b. al-Ḥajjāj. *Ṣaḥīḥ Muslim*, trans. A. Siddiqi. 4 vols. Lahore: Sh. Muhammad Ashraf, 1972–5.

Nasr, S. H. *Islamic Life and Thought*. London: George Allen & Unwin, 1981.

Nazir-Ali, M. *Frontiers in Muslim–Christian Encounter*. Oxford: Regnum Books, 1987.

—— *Islam: A Christian Perspective*. Exeter: Paternoster Press, 1983.

Neill, S. *Crises of Belief*. London: Hodder & Stoughton, 1984.

Niazi, K. *Mirror of Trinity*. Lahore: Sh. Muhammad Ashraf, 1991.

Noss, J. *Man's Religions*. 6th ed. New York: Macmillan, 1980.

Parrinder, G. *Jesus in the Qur'ān*. Oxford: Oneworld, 1995 (first published 1965).

Parshall, P. *Beyond the Mosque: Christians in Muslim Community*. 3rd ed. Grand Rapids: Baker Books, 1992.

—— *Bridges to Islam: A Christian Perspective on Folk Islam*. Grand Rapids: Baker Books, 1983.

—— *The Cross and the Crescent: Understanding the Muslim's Mind and Heart.* Wheaton, Ill.: Tyndale House, 1989.

—— *The Fortress and the Fire: Jesus Christ and the Challenge of Islam.* Bombay: Gospel Literature Service, 1975.

—— *Inside the Community: Understanding Muslims through their Traditions.* Grand Rapids: Baker Books, 1994.

—— *New Paths in Muslim Evangelism: Evangelical Approaches to Contextualization.* Grand Rapids: Baker Books, 1980.

Petersen, K. (ed.) *Religion, Development and African Identity.* Uppsala: Scandinavian Institute of African Studies, 1987.

Pfander, C. G. *The Mīzān-ul-Ḥaqq: Balance of Truth,* revised by the Rev. W. St Clair Tisdall. London: The Religious Tract Society, 1910.

Poston, L. *Islamic Daʿwah in the West: Muslim Missionary Activity and the Dynamics of Conversion to Islam.* New York: Oxford University Press, 1992.

Powell, A. *Muslims and Missionaries in Pre-Mutiny India.* London: Curzon, 1993.

Qadri, A. H. *Dimensions of Christianity.* Islamabad: Daʿwah Academy, 1989.

Rahbar, D. *God of Justice: A Study in the Ethical Doctrine of the Qurʾan.* Leiden: Brill, 1960.

Robinson, N. *Christ in Islam and Christianity.* London: Macmillan, 1991.

St John, P. *Patricia St John Tells Her Own Story.* Carlisle: OM Publishing, 1995.

Schlorff, S. *Discipleship in Islamic Society.* Marseille: Ecole Radio Biblique, 1981.

Schuon, F. *The Essential Writings,* ed. S. Nasr. New York: Vantage Press, 1979.

Shafaat, A. *Islam, Christianity and the State of Israel as Fulfillment of Old Testament Prophecy.* Indianapolis: American Trust Publications, 1989.

Sharpe, E. *Comparative Religion: A History.* 2nd ed. London: Duckworth, 1986.

Sherif, F. *A Guide to the Contents of the Qurʾan.* Garnet: Reading, 1995.

Shorrosh, A. *Islam Revealed: A Christian Arab's View of Islam.* Nashville: Thomas Nelson, 1988.

Siddiqui, A. 'Muslims' Concern in Dialogue: A Study of Christian–Muslim Relations Since 1970'. Ph.D. thesis, University of Birmingham, 1994.

Smith, W. C. *Islam in Modern History.* Princeton: Princeton University Press, 1957.

—— *The Meaning and End of Religion: A New Approach to the Religious Traditions of Mankind.* New York: Mentor, 1964.

—— *On Understanding Islam.* The Hague: Mouton, 1981.

Southern, R. W. *Western Views of Islam in the Middle Ages.* Cambridge, Mass.: Harvard University Press, 1962.

Speelman, G., van Lin, J. and Mulder, D. (eds) *Muslims and Christians in Europe: Breaking New Ground.* Kampen: Uitgeverij Kok, 1993.

Stanley, B. *The Bible and the Flag: Protestant Missions and British Imperialism in the Nineteenth and Twentieth Centuries.* Leicester: Apollos, 1990.

Stanton, H. *The Teachings of the Koran.* London: Central Board of Missions and Society for Promoting Christian Knowledge, 1919.

Sweetman, J. W. *Islam and Christian Theology: A Study of the Interpretation of Theological Ideas in the Two Religions.* 2 vols. London: Lutterworth Press, 1945–67.

Swidler, L. (ed.) *Muslims in Dialogue: The Evolution of a Dialogue.* Lampeter: The Edwin Mellen Press, 1992.

Thomas, D. *Anti-Christian Polemic in Early Islam: Abū 'Īsā al-Warrāq's 'Against the Trinity'.* Cambridge: Cambridge University Press, 1992.

Thomson, A. *Blood on the Cross: Islam in Spain in the Light of Christian Persecution through the Ages.* London: Ta-Ha Publishers, 1989.

Tisdall, W. St Clair. *The Sources of Islam,* trans. and abridged by W. Muir. Edinburgh: T. & T. Clark, 1901.

Usmani, Mohammad Taqi. *What is Christianity?* Karachi: Darul Ishaat, 1987.

Vander Werff, L. *Christian Mission to Muslims: The Record. Anglican and Reformed Approaches in India and the Near East, 1800–1938.* Pasadena: William Carey Library, 1977.

Watt, W. M. *Islam and Christianity Today: A Contribution to Dialogue.* London: Routledge, 1983.

—— *Islamic Fundamentalism and Modernity.* London: Routledge, 1988.

—— *Islamic Revelation in the Modern World.* Edinburgh: Edinburgh University Press, 1969.

—— *Muhammad at Mecca.* Oxford: Clarendon Press, 1953

—— *Muhammad at Medina.* Oxford: Oxford University Press, 1956.

—— *Muhammad's Mecca: History in the Qur'an.* Edinburgh: Edinburgh University Press, 1988.

—— *Muhammad: Prophet and Statesman.* Oxford: Oxford University Press, 1961.

—— *Muslim–Christian Encounters: Perceptions and Misperceptions.* London: Routledge, 1991.

—— *Truth in the Religions: A Social and Psychological Approach.* Edinburgh: Edinburgh University Press, 1963.

Wolfson, H. *The Philosophy of the Kalam.* Cambridge, Mass.: Harvard University Press, 1976.

Woodberry, D. (ed.) *Muslims and Christians on the Emmaus Road.* Monrovia: MARC, 1989.

World Council of Churches. *Guidelines on Dialogue with People of Living Faiths and Ideologies.* Geneva: WCC, 1979.

Yates, T. *Christian Mission in the Twentieth Century.* Cambridge: Cambridge University Press, 1994.

Zaehner, R. C. *At Sundry Times: An Essay in the Comparison of Religions.* London: Faber & Faber, 1958.

Articles

Aasi, G. 'Muslim Contributions to the History of Religions'. *AJISS*, 8, 1991.

Abedin, S. 'Dawa and Dialogue: Believers and Promotion of Mutual Trust', in Davies, M. and Pasha, A. (eds) *Beyond Frontiers: Islam and Contemporary Needs.* London: Mansell, 1989.

Adams, C. 'The History of Religions and the Study of Islam', in Kitagawa, J. et al. *The History of Religions: Essays on the Problem of Understanding.* Chicago: The University of Chicago Press, 1969.

—— 'Islam and Christianity: The Opposition of Similarities', in Savory, R. and Aguis, D. (eds) *Logos Islamikos: Studia Islamica in Honorem Georgii Michaelis Wickens.* Toronto: Pontifical Institute of Mediaeval Studies, 1984.

—— 'Islamic Religious Tradition', in Binder, L. (ed.) *The Study of the Middle East: Research and Scholarship in the Humanities and the Social Sciences.* New York: John Wiley & Sons, 1976.

Anawati, G. 'Polémique, apologie et dialogue islamo-chrétiens'. *Euntes Docete*, 22, 1969.

Arkoun, M. 'Is Islam Threatened by Christianity?', in Küng, H. and Moltmann, J. (eds) *Islam: A Challenge for Christianity.* London: SCM Press, 1994 (special edition of *Concilium*).

—— 'New Perspectives for a Jewish–Christian–Muslim Dialogue', in Swidler (ed.).

Arnaldez, R. 'Dialogue islamo-chrétien et sensibilités religieuses'. *ISCH*, 1, 1975.

Askari, H. 'Christian Mission to Islam: A Muslim Response'. *JIMMA*, 2, July 1986.

—— 'The Dialogical Relationship between Christianity and Islam', in Swidler (ed.).

—— 'Within and Beyond the Experience of Religious Diversity', in Hick and Askari (eds).

Ayoub, M. 'Islam and Christianity beween Tolerance and Acceptance'. *ICMR*, 2, 1991.

—— 'The Islamic Context of Muslim–Christian Relations', in Gervers, M. and Bikhazi, R. J. (eds) *Conversion and Continuity: Indigenous Christian Communities in Islamic lands – Eighth to Eighteenth Centuries.* Toronto: Pontifical Institute of Medieval Studies, 1990.

—— 'Muslim Views of Christianity: Some Modern Examples'. *ISCH*, 10, 1984.

—— 'Roots of Muslim–Christian Conflict'. *MW*, 79, 1989.

—— 'The Word of God and the Voices of Humanity', in Hick and Askari (eds).

Basetti-Sani, G. 'Christian Symbolism and Christological Typology in the Qur'an'. *BHMIIS*, July–September 1981.

Bennett, C. 'The Legacy of Lewis Bevan Jones'. *IBMR*, July 1993.

Bijlefeld, W. 'Christian–Muslim Studies, Islamic Studies, and the Future of Christian–Muslim Encounter', in Haddad and Haddad (eds).

—— 'Controversies around the Qur'anic Ibrāhīm Narrative and its "Orientalist" Interpretations'. *MW*, 72, 1982.

—— 'The Danger of "Christianizing" our Partners in the Dialogue'. *MW*, 57, 1967.

—— 'Islamic Studies within the Perspective of the History of Religions'. *MW*, 62, 1972.

—— 'A Prophet and More than a Prophet?'. *MW*, 59, 1969.

Borrmans, M. 'The Muslim–Christian Dialogue of the Last Ten Years'. *Pro Mundi Vita Bulletin*, 74, September–October 1978.

Brewster, D. 'Dialogue: Relevancy to Evangelism', in McCurry (ed.).

Brinner, W. 'Prophets and Prophecy in the Islamic and Jewish Traditions', in Brinner, W. and Ricks, S. (eds) *Studies in Islamic and Judaic Traditions*, vol. 2. Atlanta: Scholars Press, 1989.

Caspar, R. 'Parole de dieu et langage humain en christianisme et en Islam.' *ISCH*, 6, 1980.

——'Pour une vision chrétienne du coran'. *ISCH*, 8, 1982.

—— 'Une rencontre avec l'Islam. Evolution personelle et vision actuelle'. *Spiritus*, 32, 122, 1991.

Chapman, C. 'Biblication Foundations of Praying for Muslims', in Woodberry (ed.).

—— 'The God Who Reveals', in Woodberry (ed.).

—— 'Going Soft on Islam? Reflections on Some Evangelical Responses to Islam'. *Vox Evangelica*, 1989.

—— 'Rethinking the Gospel for Muslims', in Woodberry (ed.).

—— 'Thinking Biblically about Islam'. *Themelios*, April 1978.

Charfi, A. 'Polémiques islamo-chrétiennes a l'epoque mediévale', in Waardenburg, J. (ed.) *Scholarly Approaches to Religion: Interreligious Perceptions and Islam*. Bern: Peter Lang, 1995.

Cragg, K. 'Being Christian and Being Muslim: A Personal Debate'. *Religion*, 10, 1980.

—— 'Christian–Muslim Dialogue'. *Anglican Theological Review*, 57, 1975.

—— 'Islam and Incarnation', in Hick, J. (ed.) *Truth and Dialogue: The Relationship between World Religions*. London: Sheldon, 1974.

—— 'Tadabbur al-Qur'ān: Reading and Meaning', in Green, A. (ed.) *In Quest of an Islamic Humanism: Arabic and Islamic Studies in Memory of Mohamed al-Nowaihi*. Cairo: American University in Cairo Press, 1986.

—— 'Temple Gairdner's Legacy'. *IBMR*, October 1981.

Drummond, R. 'Toward A Theological Understanding of Islam', in Swidler (ed.).

D'Souza, A. 'Christian Approaches to the Study of Islam: An Analysis of the Writings of Watt and Cragg', 2 pts. *BHIIS*, 11, 1992.

Duran, K. 'Interreligious Dialogue and the "Islamic Original Sin"', in Swidler (ed.).

—— 'Muslims and Non-Muslims', in Swidler (ed.).

Esposito, J. 'Isma'il R. al-Faruqi: Muslim Scholar-Activist', in Haddad, Y. (ed.) *The Muslims of America*. New York: Oxford University Press, 1991.

Al-Faruqi, I. 'A Comparison of the Islamic and Christian Approaches to Hebrew Scripture'. *Journal of the Bible and Religion*, 31, 1963.

—— 'Divine Transcendence: Its Expression in Christianity and Islam'. *World Faiths*, 107, Spring 1979.

—— 'Islam and Christianity: Diatribe or Dialogue', in Swidler (ed.).

—— 'Islam and Other Faiths', in Gauhar, A. (ed.) *The Challenge of Islam*. London: Islamic Council of Europe, 1978.

—— 'Islamic Ideals in North America', in Abu Laban, B., Waugh, E. and Qureshi, R. (eds) *The Muslim Community in North America*. Edmonton: University of Alberta Press, 1983.

—— 'Meta-Religion: Towards a Critical World Theology'. *AJISS*, 3, 1986.

—— 'The Muslim–Christian Dialogue: A Constructionist View'. *Islam and the Modern Age*, 8, 1977.

—— 'On the Nature of Islamic Da'wah'. *IRM*, 65, 1976.

Ford, F. P. 'The Qur'ān as Sacred Scripture: An Assessment of Contemporary Christian Perspectives'. *MW*, 83, 1993.

Ford, J. 'Isma'il al-Faruqi on Muslim–Christian Dialogue: An Analysis from a Christian Perspective'. *ICMR*, 4, 1993.

Fueck, J. 'The Originality of the Arabian Prophet', in Swartz, M. (ed.) *Studies on Islam*. Oxford: Oxford University Press, 1981.

Ghrab, S. 'Islam and Christianity: From Opposition to Dialogue'. *ISCH*, 13, 1987.

Glaser, I. 'The Concept of Relationship as a Key to the Comparative Understanding of Christianity and Islam'. *Themelios*, January 1986.

——'Towards a Mutual Understanding of Christian and Islamic Concepts of Revelation'. *Themelios*, April 1982.

Goddard, H. 'Each Other's Scripture'. *Newsletter of the Centre for the Study of Islam and Muslim–Christian Relations*, 5, May 1981.

—— 'Modern Pakistani and Indian Muslim Perceptions of Christianity'. *ICMR*, 5, 1994.

Herbert, D. 'Shabbir Akhtar on Muslims, Christians and British Society: An Appraisal and Christian Response'. *ICMR*, 4, 1993.

Hesselgrave, D. 'Evangelicals and Interreligious Dialogue', in Anderson and Stransky (eds).

Hodgson, M. 'A Comparison of Islam and Christianity as Framework for Religious Life'. *Diogenes*, 32, 1960.

Jomier, J. 'L'Évangile selon Barnabe'. *MIDEO*, 6, 1959–61.

—— 'The Kingdom of God in Islam and its Comparison with Christianity'. *Communio*, 13, 1986.

Jones, R. 'Wilfred Cantwell Smith and Kenneth Cragg on Islam as a Way of Salvation'. *IBMR*, July 1992.

Joseph, R. 'Islam: Its Representation in the West'. *The Maghreb Review*, 10, 1985.

Kerr, D. '"He Walked in the Path of the Prophets": Toward Christian Theological Recognition of the Prophethood of Muhammad', in Haddad and Haddad (eds).

—— 'The Problem of Christianity in Muslim Perspective: Implications for Christian Mission'. *IBMR*, October 1981.

Khodr, G. 'Christianity in a Pluralistic World: The Economy of the Holy Spirit'. *Ecumenical Review*, April 1971.

Kronholm, T. 'Dependence and Prophetic Originality in the Koran'. *Orientalia Suecana*, 31–32, 1982–3.

Kraan, J. 'Muslim-Christian Relations and Christian Study Centres'. *Al-Mushir*, 26, 1984.

Küng, H. 'Christianity and World Religions: The Dialogue with Islam as One Model'. *MW*, 77, 1987.

Lin, J. van. 'Mission and Dialogue: God and Jesus Christ', in Speelman, van Lin and Mulder (eds).

Merad, A. 'Christ According to the Qur'an'. *Encounter*, 69, 1980.

—— 'Revelation, Truth and Obedience', in Samartha, S. and Taylor, J. B. (eds) *Christian–Muslim Dialogue: Papers from Broumana, 1972*. Geneva: WCC, 1972.

Moltmann, J. 'Christianity and the World Religions', in Hick, J. and Hebblethwaite, B. (eds) *Christianity and Other Religions*. London: Fount Paperbacks, 1980.

Moubarac, Y. 'La Pensée chrétienne et l'Islam', in Geffré, C. and Moubarac, Y. (eds) *Chrétiens et Musulmans*. Paris: Beauchesne, 1976 (special edition of *Concilium*).

Mulder, D. 'Developments in Dialogue with Muslims: World Council of Churches', in Speelman, van Lin and Mulder (eds).

Nasr, S. H. 'Comments on a Few Theological Issues in the Islamic–Christian Dialogue', in Haddad and Haddad (eds).

—— 'Islam and the Encounter of Religions'. *IQ*, 10, 1966.

—— 'Response to Hans Küng's Paper on Christian–Muslim Dialogue'. *MW*, 77, 1987.

Newbigin, L. 'The Gospel Among the Religions', in Anderson and Stransky (eds).

Padwick, C. 'North African Reverie'. *IRM*, 27, 1938.

Qureshi, J. ' "Alongsidedness – In Good Faith?": An Essay on Kenneth Cragg', in Hussain, A., Olson, R. and Qureshi, J. (eds) *Orientalism,*

Islam, and Islamists. Vermont: Amana Books, 1984.

Rahman, F. 'A Muslim Response: Christian Particularity and the Faith of Islam', in Dawe, D. and Carman. J. (eds) *Christian Faith in a Religiously Plural World*. Maryknoll, NY: Orbis, 1978.

Rasjidi, M. and Barwani, A. 'Christian Mission in the Muslim World: Two Case Studies', in Castro, Ahmad and Kerr (eds).

Rippin, A. 'Literary Analysis of *Qur'ān*, *Tafsīr*, and *Sīra*: The Methodologies of John Wansborough', in Martin, R. C. (ed.) *Approaches to Islam in Religious Studies*. Tucson: University of Arizona Press, 1985.

Robinson, N. 'Massignon, Vatican II and Islam as an Abrahamic Religion'. *ICMR*, 2, 1991.

Rodinson, M. 'The Western Image and Western Studies of Islam', in Schacht, S. and Bosworth, C. E. (eds) *The Legacy of Islam*. 2nd ed. Oxford: Oxford University Press, 1979.

Sanneh, L. 'Christian Experience of Islamic Da'wah', in Castro, Ahmad and Kerr (eds).

—— 'Christian Missions and the Western Guilt Complex'. *The Christian Century*, 8 April 1987.

Sardar, Z. 'The Ethical Connection: Christian–Muslim Relations in the Postmodern Age'. *ICMR*, 2, 1991.

Slomp, J. 'The Gospel in Dispute'. *ISCH*, 4, 1978.

Smith, W. C. 'Is the Qur'ān the Word of God?', in *On Understanding Islam*.

—— 'Muslim–Christian Relations: Questions of a Comparative Religionist'. *JIMMA*, 8, 1987.

—— 'The True Meaning of Scripture: An Empirical Historian's Non-Reductionist Interpretation of the Qur'an'. *International Journal of Middle East Studies*, 11, 1980.

Stott, J. 'Dialogue, Encounter, Even Confrontation', in Anderson and Stransky (eds).

Swidler, L. 'The Evolution of a Dialogue', in Swidler (ed).

Talbi, M. 'A Community of Communities: The Right to be Different and the Ways of Harmony', in Hick and Askari (eds).

—— 'Islam and Dialogue: Some Reflections on a Current Topic'. *Encounter*, 11–12, January–February 1975.

Thomas, D. 'The Miracles of Jesus in Early Muslim Polemic'. *Journal of Semitic Studies*, 39, 1994.

Tibawi, A. L. 'English-Speaking Orientalists', pt.1. *IQ*, 8, 1964.

Vahiduddin, S. 'What Christ Means to Me', in Troll, C. (ed.) *Islam and India: Studies and Commentaries.* Vol. 3: *The Islamic Experience in Contemporary Thought.* Delhi: Chanakya Publications, 1986.

Waardenburg, J. 'Types of Judgment in Islam about Other Religions', in de la Lama, G. (ed.) *Middle East,* vol. 1. Mexico City: Colegia de Mexico, 1982.

—— 'World Religions as Seen in the Light of Islam', in Welch, A. T. and Cachia, P. (eds) *Islam: Past Influence and Present Challenge.* Edinburgh: Edinburgh University Press, 1979.

Waldman, M. 'New Approaches to "Biblical" Materials in the Qur'an'. *MW*, 75, 1985.

Watt, W. M. 'The Christianity Criticized in the Qur'ān'. *MW*, 57, 1967.

Wijoyo, A. 'The Christians as Religious Community according to the Hadīth'. *ISCH*, 8, 1982.

Wilmot, F. 'Dawa: A Practical Approach for the Future', in Davies, M. and Pasha, A. (eds) *Beyond Frontiers: Islam and Contemporary Needs.* London: Mansell, 1989.

Woodberry, D. 'Different Diagnoses of the Human Condition', in Woodberry (ed.).

Zwemer, S. 'The Allah of Islam and the God revealed in Jesus Christ'. *MW*, 36, 1946.

INDEX

Note: For authors who are the main subjects of a chapter, only secondary references in other chapters are listed here.

101441